THE
WRESTLERS'
WRESTLERS

THE WRESTLERS' WRESTLERS

THE MASTERS OF THE CRAFT OF PROFESSIONAL WRESTLING

DAN MURPHY & BRIAN YOUNG

FOREWORD BY "THE SINISTER MINISTER" JAMES MITCHELL

Published by ECW Press
665 Gerrard Street East
Toronto, Ontario, Canada M4M 1Y2
416-694-3348 / info@ecwpress.com

Editor for the Press: Michael Holmes
Cover design: David A. Gee
Cover photos: Daniel Bryan, Kurt Angle, Harley Race, and Bret Hart courtesy WWE; Lou Thesz courtesy Rare Books at University of Notre Dame

LIBRARY AND ARCHIVES CANADA CATALOGUING IN PUBLICATION

Title: The wrestlers' wrestlers : the masters of the craft of professional wrestling / Dan Murphy & Brian Young.

Names: Murphy, Dan (Journalist), author. | Young, Brian, 1974- author.

Identifiers: Canadiana (print) 20200408089 | Canadiana (ebook) 20200408097

ISBN 978-1-77041-553-9 (softcover)
ISBN 978-1-77305-687-6 (ePUB)
ISBN 978-1-77305-688-3 (PDF)
ISBN 978-1-77305-689-0 (Kindle)

Subjects: LCSH: Wrestlers—Anecdotes. | LCSH: Wrestling—History.

Classification: LCC GV1196.A1 M87 2021 | DDC 796.812092/2—dc23

PRINTED AND BOUND IN CANADA

PRINTING: FRIESENS   5 4 3 2 1

TABLE OF CONTENTS

FOREWORD

Politics. Religion. Professional Wrestling. These are three different forms of artistic belief systems, all of which are powered by the charisma and persuasiveness of their practitioners. All three disciplines seek to define good and evil for the masses, based upon that which they feel will satisfy their core audience, while ultimately empowering and enriching themselves. This means that they must pick an enemy against which to rally their chosen troops and faithful, intentionally or not. The result is never less than controversial, much like the picks for *The Wrestlers' Wrestlers*.

As a child, I grew up watching the wrestling presented by the Mid-Atlantic, Georgia, and Florida promotions in the early to late 1970s. When my family traveled or vacationed outside of those areas, I eagerly consumed whatever the local wrestling promotion presented. I was often left scratching my head in bewilderment.

Seeing wrestlers who I'd read about in magazines, often making them my "favorite wrestler" du jour, based upon the exciting, often apocryphal, editorial spin, I was disappointed. They seemed somehow different and less exciting than I imagined. Occasionally, I would see a wrestler that had moved on from my home base and ask myself, "What the hell happened to them?" Alternately, a wrestler I was underwhelmed by on vacation would show up in one of the three wrestling promotions I consumed and be a ball of fire. A new kid to my neighborhood from the Midwest would tell me how shitty the tag team of Ric Flair and Greg Valentine were compared to Crusher and Dick The Bruiser while laying out a convincing argument. The recounting of his truth didn't jibe with my experience, yet it was as passionate as my own opinion. Huh? Hence, my first encounter with cognitive dissonance.

After Vince McMahon Jr. bought the WWWF from his father and went into "Sports Entertainment" mode, he would eventually sign up most of the performers I grew up on and turn them into cartoons. I was outraged! Why must Harley Race be a "King" and wear a crown? Why is Dory Funk Jr. now called "Hoss?" Why does everybody have a goofy nickname and silly vignettes? Why was a tag team I could always count on for heavy bloodshed and violence now acting like goofs hired to perform at a child's birthday party? Why is Bobby Heenan letting Gorilla Monsoon outsmart him every week? Moreover, why did every promotion at the time begin to do the same thing, usually in an embarrassing attempt to follow the trend? The flip side is that there are millions of fans that would be bored out of their skulls looking at their favorite performers doing what used to appeal to my generation.

It would be many years before I realized that every territory had a different style to suit its demographic and many wrestlers had to adapt to get over. They weren't dumbing it down, they were doing what was required to make money at the time. When they came back home they were always working the style that drew money there. An entertainer must entertain. It's a bonus and an honor when his professional colleagues concur with the fans' opinions.

Eventually, I became involved in the wrestling biz, and I had the opportunity to talk to many of my childhood heroes at length. I got their perspectives on my youthful remembrances. They often conceded that something that had "got over" or drew money was garbage from a technical standpoint. Whether I agreed with them or not, they knew whereof they spoke. Their different perspectives made me look at things in an entirely different way, as many of those reading this book may.

It's pretty easy to separate the legit tough guys from the entertainers and the "spot monkeys." Some folks prefer one over the others. Some wrestlers are at least two or all three, and I believe that is the ideal mix in today's environment. Box office is easy to quantify but the emotional connection is up to the individual to decide, so there is always an X factor. This book will give you excellent insight from those who have taken the bumps, put up with the politics, and lived to tell about it.

Deciding upon whom to vote for in politics, worship in your faith, or cheer in pro wrestling is usually a deeply personal, emotional choice. Unlike the former two, your choice of "Wrestlers' Wrestler" won't harm anyone. Let the spirited debates begin!

— "THE SINISTER MINISTER," JAMES MITCHELL

INTRODUCTION

Professional wrestling is a form of entertainment that defies clear classification. To some, it's a lowbrow burlesque, a farce aping a legitimate athletic contest. To others, it's a morality play pitting heroes against villains in a simulated "made for TV" battle; a well-choreographed exhibition of athletic feats, tumbles, falls, and false finishes designed to make a spectator sit on the edge of his seat.

In recent years, some pro wrestlers have even taken to calling their unique vocation a "performance art," a term which still rankles some old-timers and purists who spent their careers (and — in many cases — much of their lives) "keeping kayfabe" or "protecting the business" — and doing anything in their power to maintain an air of credibility around the spectacle. Breaking kayfabe could get a wrestler fined, fired, or blackballed from the industry completely.

For more than a century and a half now, professional wrestling has been revered and ridiculed, had its ups and downs, been both sideshow and center stage, but through it all, it has survived and still gains new fans every generation. Fans of all ages, races, genders, and socioeconomic backgrounds love professional wrestling. Yes, all but the most innocent or naïve fans know that wrestling is a "work," a fight with a scripted outcome. WWE CEO Vince McMahon testified as much himself in 1989 when he told the New Jersey State Senate that pro wrestling was entertainment, not an athletic competition, to get out from under the thumb of the various state athletic commissions. Today, anyone with access to YouTube can find hundreds of "shoot" videos where all of wrestling's inner secrets — the ones that were guarded so passionately during the kayfabe-fearing territory days — are exposed for the world to see. Yet fans are still willing to suspend their disbelief — to buy in on the illusion; to passionately follow storylines and argue their points of view on various social media platforms.

Why?

Wrestling is a lot like magic, in a way. We in the audience know the woman isn't being sawed in half, yet we hold our breath until she steps out of the box in one piece. But good professional wrestling operates on another level as well by making its fans become emotionally involved with not only the show or match but the personalities themselves. To accomplish this, or *get over*, a wrestler has to be part superhero/super villain, part athlete, part actor, part storyteller, and part magician. And a select few have something extra, something that makes them stand out from the pack.

These special few are what we call a "Wrestlers' Wrestler."

Ironically, being a Wrestlers' Wrestler involves more than just pure technical wrestling proficiency. It's more than just being able to take down an opponent and turn their shoulders to the mat. And, as wrestling has evolved from a carnival sideshow attraction to a billion-dollar "sports entertainment" spectacle, the definition of what constitutes a Wrestlers' Wrestler has evolved as well . . . though, perhaps, not as much as one might expect.

So . . . exactly what does it take to be considered a Wrestlers' Wrestler?

A WRESTLERS' WRESTLER:
The Criteria

A "Wrestlers' Wrestler" is a competitor who has earned the respect of his peers in the locker room for his dedication, professionalism, work ethic, and mastery of the craft of professional wrestling.

To compile this book, we turned to the wrestlers themselves. We interviewed more than 50, representing more than a half-century of experience in the business. After all, who can better identify a Wrestlers' Wrestler than the wrestlers themselves? These are the men who have dedicated their lives to the art of professional wrestling. Writers, historians, fans, and others may have their own opinions, but as much as possible, we went straight to the experts and asked a series of wrestlers who they most admired and considered to be true Wrestlers' Wrestlers. Some writers and historians were willing to add their expert perspective as well.

We also relied heavily on the written words and primary sources left from wrestlers who have passed, such as Lou Thesz's seminal book, *Hooker*. Thesz may have pulled his punches in the ring, but he certainly held nothing back in his autobiography.

This book is an opportunity for the wrestlers themselves to define the term, to tell their stories and to discuss who they feel are the wrestlers who deserve recognition. This book is not intended to be solely for the fans and historians, but it is also for *the boys*. It is our attempt to preserve an oral history straight from the sources; a unique insight to this business, told by those who lived and continue to live it. It is an attempt to recognize the masters of *the craft of wrestling* from a wrestler's perspective, while maintaining the objectivity of an outsider.

Naturally, if you ask multiple wrestlers their opinion on a given wrestler, you're going to get a wide range of responses. After all, old grudges die hard. And, as it is with actors, musicians, and artists, taste is subjective.

The responses we received were varied. Some wrestlers identified a true Wrestlers' Wrestler as the one who was able to draw the biggest crowds and make the most money. They were the ones who brought the fans into the buildings, night after night. If that was the sole criterion, Hulk Hogan, "Stone Cold" Steve Austin, the Rock, and Bruno Sammartino might be our Mount Rushmore.

Others talked about the "carpenters," the undercard craftsmen whose job was to make their opponents look like a million bucks. And others named wrestlers who had the skill, the athleticism, and the technical ability, but simply never got the proper "push" because they weren't in the right place at the right time. After all, you can't build a good house without good carpenters.

"That phrase 'a Wrestlers' Wrestler,' I think, stems from the term 'a comics' comic,'" said Colt Cabana, a former NWA heavyweight champion who has dabbled in stand-up comedy. "The comics' comic may not be the best comic as far as a money-making tour, but all the other comics will be in the back of the room watching him because they *have to* watch him. He's that good. A Wrestlers' Wrestler, the wrestlers in the back will always want to watch that person's matches because they really appreciate the nuances of their wrestling."

"A Wrestlers' Wrestler is someone who is able to engage the crowd and can blend with any other wrestler and their style," offered Sinn Bodhi, who wrestled as Kizarny in WWE. "A Wrestlers' Wrestler can be put in the ring with just about anyone and make a good match. It's someone who is able to direction-change.

"Say you and I both go into a match planning on working the arm, but then you sprain your ankle when you hop over the rope into the ring," Bodhi continued. "Well, if you just hurt your leg, it wouldn't make any sense for me to work your arm. We have to be able to change direction based on what happens. We're going to switch things up. I'm going to have the ref check on you to make sure you're okay, and then I'll whisper to you, 'It's a leg match now.' I'll ground you and take care of you, maybe work the leg or do something different if your leg hurts. You have to be able to be a great ad-libber. That's what makes a Wrestlers' Wrestler."

"You have to be flexible about the way you approach the ring," said Baron Von Raschke, who made his pro debut in 1966 after a successful amateur wrestling career, showing that the importance of being able to call it on the fly in wrestling is nothing new. "I never knew exactly how I would react until the crowd reacted. So I reacted to the crowd — what they did made me do something to make them react more the way I wanted them to or less the way I wanted them to. What my opponent did may or may not help or hurt that, but I tried to incorporate all these little factors; it's a lot of crowd psychology, and doing the best job you can to get the story across. That was my job."

Historian Steve Yohe touched on the concept indirectly in a footnote to an article he wrote on Ed "Strangler" Lewis. Though he didn't use the term Wrestlers' Wrestler, his description fits nicely:

"There is a booking rule in pro wrestling that says the talented wrestlers can afford to do jobs and stay over," Yohe wrote. "The performer types with little talent can't do many jobs without losing what the fans were willing to pay for. So you find guys in the sport like Danno O'Mahoney, Primo Carnera, Hulk Hogan (well I don't know if that is fair, Hogan was a smart worker and had something, but some fans perceive him as having no talent), French Angel, Antonino Rocca, Undertaker, etc., not doing jobs. As you couldn't really kill the popularity of a Chris Benoit, Hiroshi Hase, or Rey Mysterio in the 1990s by making them do jobs." The latter wrestlers — those who have the ability to remain over by virtue of their consistent workrate — are a step closer to Wrestlers' Wrestlers.

There are some wrestlers who bristle at being called a Wrestlers' Wrestler, however.

"It's a backhanded remark, in my opinion," said Chris Jericho. "It means somebody that's really good that never made it to the main-event level. It's almost like being called 'a hell of a hand' or 'a journeyman.'"

NXT color commentator and former Ring of Honor champion Nigel McGuinness also said the term "a Wrestlers' Wrestler" made him feel uneasy.

"When people refer to someone as a Wrestlers' Wrestler — certainly when you refer to someone as a carpenter — it almost feels like a negative thing," McGuinness said. "For me, there are some guys where

I might think, 'Yeah, they're good carpenters,' but I would never say it because I feel that they'd say, 'Oh, that means that I don't have the charisma to draw money or I don't have that sort of attitude in the locker room.'"

However, for most, the term is heavy praise, especially coming from their peers.

"I personally find it to be the ultimate compliment," Cabana said. "For me, if the art that I do is appreciated by the ones who have studied it the most and they get it, to me that means the world. If the ones who are training on it and doing it like me, then — in my head — that means the fans that I want to get it will get it. I find it a huge compliment."

In this book, we have compiled the results of our interviews and research. This is not a comprehensive list of every great Wrestlers' Wrestler ever to lace up a pair of boots. If it was, this book would likely be 2,000 pages long, and we'd still be leaving some out.

Some inclusions, and exclusions, nonetheless, are bound to be controversial.

There are some wrestlers who have achieved success, but they were not held in particularly high regard by their peers.

Some fans and historians — and a growing number of wrestlers who came after him and were influenced by him — consider Shawn Michaels to be one of the greatest wrestlers of all time, because for a time, he was the best in-ring performer in WWE, if not the business as a whole. Michaels was involved in 11 matches voted as Match of the Year by readers of *Pro Wrestling Illustrated* between 1993 and 2010. But his backstage antics, refusals to do jobs, and unprofessional behavior (such as the notorious "Curtain Call" kayfabe-breaking incident at Madison Square Garden in 1996 and his mocking overselling of Hulk Hogan's offense at SummerSlam 2005) blemished his image with some wrestlers.

Ric Flair, a proven main-eventer for more than two decades, has critics who say his matches all follow the same script. Chops, bodyslam off the top rope, corner flip, "Flair flop," figure-four, go-home — if you've seen one match, you've seen them all, they say.

"The Golden Greek" Jim Londos was a huge marquee attraction during the 1930s and 1940s. Thesz — one of the most respected men in wrestling — called him "a thief" who had run a side racket of placing bets on his own fixed matches early in his career and swindling bettors out of money.

Bruiser Brody, a top star of the 1970s and 1980s in both the U.S. territories and Japan, was, in the words of Bobby Heenan, "very selfish . . . he would screw up matches purposely and try to destroy business." While respected by many of his peers for standing up to promoters, he was known to no-sell for opponents, walk out of territories, and hold up promoters for more money if he felt he was being shortchanged. To some, that made Brody something of a folk hero; to others, he was a loose cannon.

Even within the wrestling fraternity itself, the label can be challenging. From George Hackenschmidt to Kenny Omega, wrestlers will attract their fair share of admirers and critics, even among their peers. Doubtlessly, there will be readers to decry some of the wrestlers profiled in this book, and readers who will throw a conniption that their favorite wrestler isn't included. Unfortunately, that's the nature of the beast.

Our goal is to profile some of the wrestlers who were widely admired by their peers during their individual eras. In essence, many of the people profiled in these pages are your favorite wrestlers' favorite wrestlers.

Given the historic rise of women's pro wrestling over the past several years, some readers might be surprised that only a handful of women are featured in this book. That does not reflect a bias against women's wrestling by any means (after all, Dan Murphy co-wrote *Sisterhood of the Squared Circle: The History and Rise of Women's Wrestling* with Pat Laprade).

There are a few reasons why there aren't many women included. For one thing, women were mostly presented as novelty attractions in the U.S. and Canada throughout the 20th century. Mildred Burke and The Fabulous Moolah — the two top females from the 1930s through the 1970s — controlled their own titles and largely wrestled women they had a hand in training, often performing essentially the same match around the circuit. While popular in their day, these matches were never regarded as classics. Few wrestlers today cite either woman as an influence or someone they attempt to emulate. In all of the interviews we conducted for this book, neither Burke nor Moolah came up as an example of a Wrestlers' Wrestler.

Of course, there were some very respected women wrestlers who competed during this era, such as Judy Martin, Ella Waldek, Vivian Vachon, and Elvira Snodgrass to name just a few, but their influence did not extend beyond their immediate contemporaries and therefore did not rise to the standard for this book.

In the modern and post–"Women's Revolution" era, the biggest impediment for women wrestlers to be recognized as Wrestlers' Wrestlers seems to be experience; experience in terms of length of career as well as experience beyond the tightly scripted WWE style. Charlotte Flair, one of WWE's most decorated females and a headliner of *WrestleMania* 35, had only been wrestling for eight years as of this writing (and only five years on the main roster). Regarded by some as WWE's top all-around female, she never competed outside of the WWE system. On occasions when matches don't go exactly as planned, she often looks lost; she lacks the fluidity and versatility to improvise or change direction, which is the true hallmark of a Wrestlers' Wrestler. Perhaps that will come with more experience and seasoning.

Ronda Rousey only wrestled for one year before stepping away from the ring to focus on family. WWE Hall-of-Famers Trish Stratus and Lita only wrestled for six and seven years, respectively, before retiring (though both returned to WWE for some matches in 2018 and 2019). Most of the wrestlers featured in the following pages spent two decades or more perfecting their craft. To date, relatively few women have been afforded that opportunity.

The women who we have included competed in multiple promotions, were versatile in different styles of wrestling, and have left a legacy that sees their work studied and imitated today. They were also mentioned by name by some of the wrestlers interviewed. If you're looking for more on women's wrestling, please check out *Sisterhood of the Squared Circle* (Really, you'll love it! – Dan).

Here is how we define "A Wrestlers' Wrestler" for the purpose of this book.

Believability: A true Wrestlers' Wrestler values believability against all else. His matches look like legitimate wrestling contests or fights. Holds and strikes are stiff enough to look real to the fans in the front row without injuring his opponent. A true Wrestlers' Wrestler presents himself as real and provides legitimacy to wrestling itself, and can serve as a solid ambassador of professional wrestling with the general public.

Versatility: The all-time greats can wrestle anywhere on the card — from the opening match to the main event. They can wrestle as a heel or a babyface, go for five minutes or 30 minutes. They understand that a wrestling card should have highs and lulls, and are versatile enough to change their game to fit to where they are slotted on the card.

Adaptability: There's an old saying in wrestling that a great wrestler can "work with a broom" and deliver a good match. Adaptability refers to a wrestler's ability to work with any opponent — from grizzled veteran to wet-behind-the-ears greenhorn — and to deliver a solid match every time out. In wrestling, it is widely considered to be the ultimate compliment.

Respect: This refers to respect for "the business" of wrestling and its history as well as respect for one's opponent. Wrestlers who treat an opponent without respect, or look at the wrestling business as a stepping-stone to Hollywood or as a flight of fancy, generally are not considered to be Wrestlers' Wrestlers.

Dedication: This is closely related to respect. The wrestlers we feature in this book endeavored to master the craft of professional wrestling. They took the time to learn how to properly apply the holds, but also to transition between holds. They put in extra time and often served as mentors to their peers. They took wrestling seriously and it shows.

Aura/Presence: Terry Funk — a Wrestlers' Wrestler by any criterion — defined a Wrestlers' Wrestler as "a wrestler who continually creates an atmosphere where you have a maximum amount of people pay to see him. The guy that produces sell-out after sell-out." Be it by his physical size, his personality, or his in-ring demeanor, this wrestler connects with the audience in such a way that they are willing to pay to cheer for him, or pay to see him get his head kicked in. Call it charisma or star quality; when he's in the ring, fans are paying attention.

Safety: Accidents happen in wrestling, as they do in any other workplace, but a true Wrestlers' Wrestler doesn't take unnecessary liberties with his opponent. He may give out "a receipt" here and there (hitting a bit harder than needed after an opponent has hit him or made a dangerous mistake in the match), but these are often teaching moments designed to make an opponent slow down or get control of himself before a situation becomes dangerous.

While this book is not a chronological history, we tried to organize profiles in something of a chronological order. We have also included some introductory sections and breakout pieces designed to provide context and additional insight from the wrestlers interviewed for this project. Wrestling has evolved considerably from the early 1900s to today, and while the qualities of a Wrestlers' Wrestler have not fundamentally changed during that time, they have progressed with the times, which is why grouping biographies in chronological blocks seems appropriate.

Champions and legends of the past and present. Insiders taking us inside. The highs and lows, the glory and the pain, the glitz and the grime, and perhaps most importantly, the truth in their own words. This project is a labor of love, but also a tribute to those who have given so much of themselves for our entertainment.

Note: All quotes included in this book come from interviews conducted by the authors for this project unless otherwise noted. An appendix of wrestlers and historians interviewed for this book can be found on page 358.

PART 1:
The Founding Fathers

While the history of what we now call professional wrestling has its origins in the carnival circuit (where traveling carnivals would stage exhibition matches or have a resident grappler take on challengers from the crowd, either local tough guys or plants who were in on the act) and in prize fights in the dingy back rooms of saloons and boxing gymnasiums, the first true pro wrestling star of the 20th century was the Estonian strongman Georg (George) Hackenschmidt. Hackenschmidt was an all-around athlete — a gymnast, cyclist, strongman, and wrestler. Starting as a Greco-Roman champion, he was to become the first "catch-as-catch-can" wrestling star, touring England, playing to sold-out crowds in theaters and music halls. Hackenschmidt was managed by the legendary showman C.B. Cochran, who not only managed and promoted "The Russian Lion" in England, but also managed a little-known American magician/escape artist named Harry Houdini.

Cochran had a gift for showbiz. He made stars. It is said that it was Cochran who convinced Hackenschmidt to "lighten up" on his opponents, allowing them to last several minutes with the champ who was, in reality, able to defeat most opponents in a very short period of time. These were not "fixed" matches, but they could very well be where the mixing of wrestling as both sport and entertainment began. Hackenschmidt (and Cochran) "worked" the crowd to convince them that the match was a closer contest than it truly was.

In a given night, Hackenschmidt might defeat up to five opponents, delighting the music hall patrons and drawing big houses everywhere he went. Fluent in seven languages with a physique that looked like it was chiseled out a block of granite, Hackenschmidt made the ladies swoon and made the men green with envy. "If I wasn't the president of the United States, I would like to be George Hackenschmidt," President Theodore Roosevelt once declared. Hackenschmidt was an athlete and an entertainer, the template for what pro wrestling would become.

A 1904 match between Hackenschmidt and "The Terrible Turk" in London caused traffic back-ups that snarled traffic for miles, resulting in gridlock from the Olympia exhibition centre to Piccadilly Circus.

"The Russian Lion" racked up wins worldwide. He defeated American heavyweight champion Tom Jenkins in a Greco-Roman contest at Royal Albert Hall in London. He defeated Scottish heavyweight champion Alexander Munro in Glasgow's Ibrox Park in 1905 in front of a reported crowd of between 16,000 and 20,000 spectators. After a tour of Australia, he journeyed to the U.S. for a rematch against Jenkins at Madison Square Garden, this time beating Jenkins in two straight falls in a catch-as-catch-can contest, bolstering his claim as wrestling's true "world champion."

In 1908, Hackenschmidt faced Frank Gotch, an Iowa native who had previously scored a win over Jenkins to be recognized as the top American grappler. On April 3, 1908, Gotch defeated Hackenschmidt in Chicago and was recognized as "world champion," though there was no true sanctioning body to recognize the claim. The rematch was held three years later in Comiskey Park, Chicago, drawing 25,000 spectators and a record-setting gate of $87,000 (the equivalent of $2.3 million today). Gotch won the rematch in two straight falls, locking in his vaunted toehold on Hackenschmidt and threatening to break his foot. Hack rolled to his back to be counted down.

Though it wasn't widely known at the time, "The Russian Lion" came into the rematch with an injured right knee. But given all of the tickets sold and the international hype dubbing the bout "the fight of the century," Hackenschmidt wrestled despite the injury and went down easily to his American opponent.

Gotch retired as champion in 1913 (the first of several retirements), but even though he had vanquished Hack, he still had his critics. He was regarded by some (including Lou Thesz) as a bully, someone who would gouge eyes, pull hair, or even break bones if he had the opportunity to do so. But Gotch and Hackenschmidt showed that pro wrestling — and a great pro wrestling rivalry — could draw big money at the box office.

Professional wrestling experienced its so-called first "Golden Age" during the 1940s and 1950s, bolstered by the growing popularity of television. Names like Killer Kowalski, Gene Stanlee, Verne Gagne, Antonino Rocca, Freddie Blassie, Dick Hutton, Pat O'Connor, Édouard Carpentier, Gorgeous George, and Lou Thesz became as well known as baseball stars like Stan Musial, Ted Williams, and Mickey Mantle or boxing champions like Sugar Ray Robinson, Willie Pep, and Archie Moore.

And it wasn't just the boys. Women like Mildred Burke, Penny Banner, and Mae Weston became stars as well. Yes, pro wrestling was more progressive than most professions, including sports, at this time.

The success of wrestling's "Golden Age" was largely due to the work put in by a group of Wrestlers' Wrestlers, and the example they set for their contemporaries and the generations that followed.

ED "STRANGLER" LEWIS

There is no shortage of myths and tall tales when it comes to Ed "Strangler" Lewis, but it's still impossible to overstate his importance to professional wrestling in the 20th century.

"Ed Lewis was the authentic item as a wrestler," wrote Lou Thesz in *Hooker*. "If it came to actual wrestling, and sometimes it did in his era, no one was even close. He rescued pro wrestling at a time when it was floundering, and for that reason alone, he deserves to be respected and remembered by every wrestler and promoter who came after him. It's entirely plausible to me that, without him, there might not have been any professional wrestling in this country after 1920, certainly not on the scale it has enjoyed for the past 70 years."

Thesz, a six-time world champion and the cornerstone of the National Wrestling Alliance for three decades, saw Lewis as a father figure and has called Lewis the greatest wrestler of all time. As far as being a Wrestlers' Wrestler, Lewis was a respected shooter (an expert wrestler who could compete legitimately at an elite level), mentor, and coach, was the most famous wrestler of the 1920s, and he helped usher in the modern era of storylines, signature moves, and "highspots" such as bodyslams and suplexes.

According to the mythology surrounding him (most of which was created and spread by Lewis himself, as well as his manager, business partner, and hype-man Billy Sandow), "Strangler" wrestled more than 6,200 matches over his 43-year career and had won all but 32. Though his exact win-loss record is unknown due to incomplete records and a lack of widespread coverage of wrestling at the time, while he was active, he wasn't *that* active, and he had certainly done more than 32 jobs.

Nevertheless, those figures persist in some places today. It has also been claimed that Lewis earned $16 million over the course of his wrestling career. Though the exact dollar amounts are impossible to know, he was certainly among the highest-paid professional athletes of the 1920s, up there with Babe Ruth, Jack Dempsey, and Red Grange.

Born Robert Friedrich on June 30, 1891, he grew up in Nekoosa, Wisconsin, the son of German immigrants (weighing 15 pounds at birth, if the hype is to be believed). He took up wrestling at the age of 14, putting on an exhibition wrestling match to help his high school baseball team raise money for a road trip to Pittsville, about 20 miles away. Friedrich took a liking to wrestling. By 1910, Minneapolis promoter Billy Potts booked him in a three-on-one handicap match where he and two other wrestlers faced Stanislaus Zbyszko. Zbyszko later called Lewis the strongest wrestler he had ever seen.

A year later, he wrestled Fred Beell of Wisconsin (who popularized the Beell throw hip toss). Though Lewis lost the match, he impressed Beell enough for Beell to take him in as a protégé. In January 1913, during a tour of Kentucky, he adopted the ring name of Ed "Strangler" Lewis, taking the name in honor of 1880s star Evan "Strangler" Lewis. He signed Jerry Walls as his manager, who scored him bookings in Kentucky, Georgia, and Illinois.

Lewis met Sandow in Lexington, Kentucky, in February 1914. Sandow, a wrestler who dabbled in promoting, answered a challenge Lewis had made, offering any taker $1 per minute they could last against him, and $25 if they could make it 15 minutes. Sandow lasted 10 minutes. But, more importantly, he saw money in "The Nekoosa Strangler." He signed Lewis away from Walls and pushed him as the top star in his stable of wrestlers.

On July 4, 1916, Lewis faced the recognized world champion Joe Stecher at the Fairgrounds in Omaha, Nebraska. The match lasted five and a half hours in the summertime heat before being declared a draw and attracted an estimated 20,000 viewers. "Folks began to run automobiles up to the ring so that they could throw their headlights on the men, that they might see each other (as it grew dark)," Sandow later recounted. "To show the stuff that the Strangler's made of, let me add that Lewis took a shower, had a light supper and danced until 4:30 the next morning."

On May 2, 1917, he defeated John Olin in Chicago to win a version of the "world title." On December 13, 1920, he defeated Stecher in a relatively "short" 1:41:56, capturing another version of the "world title." He held that championship for five months before dropping it to Stanislaus Zbyszko in New York, regaining the title on March 3, 1922.

Behind the scenes, Sandow had recruited shooter Joseph "Toots" Mondt. Sandow, Lewis, and Mondt — later dubbed "The Gold Dust Trio" — controlled the world title through the 1920s. Lewis was the champ, Sandow was the brains, and Mondt was the enforcer, keeping all the wrestlers in line and looking to protect the trio from being "double-crossed" by a wrestler looking to go rogue and shoot on the champ. Mondt also went over finishes, developing exciting endings for matches designed to hook fans and capture their interest for a rematch.

These three pro wrestlers decided to change the state of the game. They came up with radical new ideas such as putting a time limit on matches and inventing flashy new holds and moves. They also had a stable of wrestlers that would travel around together putting on their show. Probably most importantly, they created "characters" and rivalries, storylines that would continue on, getting the public invested in this new form of wrestling.

While Lewis was, no doubt, a superb shooter, what made him special as a professional wrestler was his signature side headlock and head-and-arm throw, which fit in with his "Strangler" nickname. Though he was a knowledgeable grappler, Lewis was a pioneer in developing "pro wrestling psychology" and sticking to what would much later come to be known as a signature move. Lewis would wrap his left arm around an opponent's head, applying pressure to a standing or grounded headlock. On the mat in a pinning position, he would settle his bulk on his opponent's chest, compressing the lungs and making it difficult to breathe, while pulling their neck upwards into a right angle, making it difficult to inhale.

"The 'Strangler' term stuck to me because early in my wrestling career, I originated a headlock, being convinced that the human brain would yield to pressure, and that if such pressure was consistently applied, it would constitute a knockout just as soporific as a solid punch to the jaw by a hard-hitting boxer," Lewis said in a kayfabe-heavy interview with

Wrestling World in 1962. "I devised a wooden facsimile of a human head. It was split down the center, the two halves connected by powerful steel springs. To increase the power of my grip, I carried this gadget with me, and worked on it for hours, until I had developed a grip that could crack a skull, and would certainly stun the recipient. But it was not a stranglehold. Never in the course of my long career was I disqualified for seeking to strangle an opponent, by putting pressure on the throat. The pressure was on the head, through the jaw. It took a bit longer than a hard-hitting boxer's blow to the jaw, to effect a knockout, but it had the same result. Pressure cut off the blood supply to the brain."

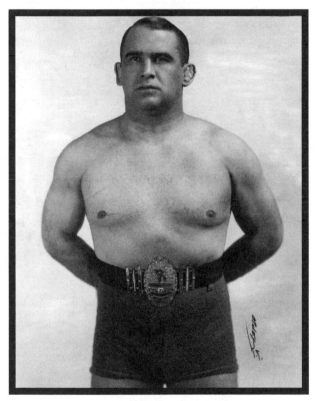

Ed "Strangler" Lewis.

Psychology-wise, opponents would be on guard for the headlock, and Lewis would surprise them with right-handed forearm shots, or take them to the mat with a double-leg takedown, catching them unawares. Lewis's style made wrestling accessible for mainstream audiences. Even if an observer couldn't grasp the intricacies of moves and countermoves, they could understand the cat-and-mouse game employed by the "Strangler." He was popularizing a new style of wrestling, one he defended in a 1936 interview with the *Winnipeg Free Press*.

"The public has shown they like it. Gate receipts have demonstrated it beyond our wildest prediction," Lewis said. "You may not 'go' for this modern wrestling. Neither do I, but the public wants it and I'm only merchandising my wares."

Lewis would hold the recognized world title on four occasions between 1920 and 1935, accounting for a combined total of more than 3,000 days as champion. On September 20, 1934, a title fight between Lewis and Jim Londos drew 35,275 spectators to Wrigley Field for a record-setting gate of $96,302 (nearly $2 million in today's dollars).

In his memoirs, Thesz recalled meeting Lewis in Des Moines, Iowa, in 1935. He was star-struck.

"Ed had been my greatest hero since I was a kid, so I was tongue-tied when I was introduced to him during a break in his workout," Thesz wrote. "I dropped by the Coliseum every day during the next two weeks when I was in town, just to watch the workouts, and what I saw amazed me. Ed would line up all six of the shooters and take them one after another without a break, a fresh man every five minutes, and then he would run through them again. It was an amazing display of power and stamina, one made all the more incredible by the fact that Ed looked as fresh at the end as he did at the beginning."

In 1935, Lewis moved into semi-retirement, though he would return to the ring in 1942. But, entering his 50s and with his eyesight failing him (he would ultimately go blind from trachoma), he retired from wrestling for good in 1948. He trained several wrestlers, including Thesz, Joe Savoldi, and Danny Hodge, and was named the goodwill ambassador of the National Wrestling Alliance.

He died on August 8, 1966, at the age of 75.

"WHIPPER" BILLY WATSON

Some athletes build their legacy by what they accomplish on the field. Others are remembered for what they have done in their community. A select few are remembered for both.

"Whipper" Billy Watson was one of that select few.

When Greg Oliver sat down to write *The Pro Wrestling Hall of Fame: The Canadians*, Watson was an easy pick as the number-one Canadian wrestler of all time. He was "easily the biggest name in Canadian pro wrestling history," he wrote. Watson's perennial arch-rival, Gene Kiniski, was number six in the top 20 ranking.

William Potts was born on June 25, 1915, in East York, Ontario. An athletic child, he competed in multiple sports before learning wrestling from Phil Lawson, a trainer at the local YMCA. Under Lawson's tutelage, Potts developed into a formidable wrestler and he began competing on amateur wrestling cards in the Toronto area.

In 1936, Potts joined a cadre of amateur wrestlers booked for pro style events in England, along with the grapplers' manager, Harry Joyce, who pulled the trip together. In an effort to promote the newcomer, the London promoter re-christened Potts as "Whipper" Bill Watson, the "inventor" of "the whip" (a variation of the Irish Whip, which was popularized by Danno O'Mahony) overhead throw. He was billed as the "light heavy-weight champion of Canada."

Watson learned the ins and outs of the English pro style — including shooting — on this tour of England and Ireland. He returned to Ontario in 1940, as war was breaking out in Europe, and took bookings for Toronto promoter Frank Tunney. Though Watson had fared well in the United Kingdom, Tunney kept him in undercard bouts at Maple

Leaf Gardens. Eventually, "The Whip" was able to work his way up the card, becoming both Tunney's top draw and business partner in Maple Leaf Wrestling.

A consummate babyface, Watson carried himself with dignity and professionalism, touring throughout Canada, the U.S., and the United Kingdom. He specialized in the art of selling, particularly against bruising, physical heels. Watson understood the psychology of wrestling and was able to connect with fans by taking a beating and rallying back for more, embodying a good old-fashioned Canadian underdog. Even as a main-event talent, Watson was willing to put others over because his connection with the fans was so solid that a loss here and there wouldn't affect his popularity or drawing ability at all, while a win over "The Whip" could make his opponent's career (or at least solidify them as a viable threat for a rematch).

On February 21, 1947, Watson defeated "Wild" Bill Longson to win the NWA world title at the Kiel Auditorium in St. Louis. He only held the title for two months before he lost the belt to Lou Thesz. Years later, when Thesz decided he needed a break from the rigorous schedule of a world champion and was suffering from an injured ankle (Thesz would say it was "broken," but he was wrestling on it just three weeks later), he agreed to drop the belt to Watson, whom he deemed to be a solid steward of the championship. Watson defeated Thesz on March 15, 1956, beating him by count-out in a match officiated by boxer Jack Dempsey.

Watson dropped the belt back to Thesz on November 9, 1956, in St. Louis in another count-out finish. But by then, "The Whip" was a made man in Canada. A two-time world champion, he was every bit as famous as Gordie Howe and Maurice "Rocket" Richard.

While Watson was a civic hero, it was his devotion to charity that made him a national treasure. He worked extensively for the Ontario Society for Crippled Children, and was a major fundraiser for Easter Seals. He was active in fundraising for several hospitals and the Multiple Sclerosis Society, and served on the Ontario government's advisory council on physical disabilities, among other organizations. He was made a Member of the Order of Canada in 1974, the second-highest honor for merit recognized by the Canadian government. He was personally involved with raising millions of dollars for various charitable organizations. He even threw his hat into the political ring, running for a seat in the House of Commons as a Progressive Conservative in 1965.

Watson wrestled until late 1971, when his career came to a premature end after he suffered severe leg injuries after being struck by a car. In addition to his two NWA world title runs, Watson held a host of regional titles throughout his career, including the British Empire heavyweight title (12 times), and more than 20 tag team titles with partners including Bruno Sammartino, Johnny Valentine, Lord Athol Layton, Ilio DiPaolo, and Billy Red Lyons.

"Frank Tunney used to book me on his Toronto shows, and 'Whipper' Billy Watson would be coming out of retirement," said Baron Von Raschke. "He would go out and do his thing. He was a legend. He didn't do much by then, but he was still over. He was past his prime but he still drew the houses."

Watson died of a heart attack at his winter home in Florida on February 4, 1990. He was 74.

GENE KINISKI

"I had a product to sell and it was Kiniski. And I sure as hell did a good job."

—Gene Kiniski (from *The Pro Wrestling Hall of Fame: The Canadians*)

He called himself "Canada's Greatest Athlete" and he had the raw power and toughness to back up that boast. Born Eugene Kiniski on November 23, 1928, in Edmonton, Alberta, Kiniski would go on to have success on the gridiron and have a hall-of-fame career in the squared circle

One of six children, was blessed with natural size, tipping the scales at 195 pounds at the age of 15, and eventually developing into a six-foot-four, 275-pound monster of a man. He played football and wrestled in high school and trained in boxing and wrestling at the local YMCA. He was recruited by the Edmonton Eskimos of the Western Interprovincial Football Union (a precursor to the Canadian Football League). In 1950, he received a scholarship to the University of Arizona, where he played on the defensive line.

While attending the University of Arizona, Kiniski met "Lightning" Rod Fenton, a fellow Edmonton native who was wrestling in the area. With Kiniski's size, athleticism, and love of amateur wrestling from his days on the mats at the YMCA, Fenton thought he was a natural for the ring and he put him in touch with Dory Funk and Tony Morelli to train him for the pro game so he could wrestle in the off-season. He wrestled his first match on February 13, 1952, with a win over Curly Hughes.

In 1952, he returned to Alberta to play for the Eskimos, but a serious knee injury put a premature end to his burgeoning football career. Once he recovered from the injury, he made wrestling his full focus. By 1954, he was already earning world title matches against Lou Thesz.

It wasn't until more than a decade later that "Big Thunder" would take the title. On January 7, 1966, Kiniski defeated Thesz in St. Louis to become the NWA world champion. He would hold that championship for three years, losing it to Dory Funk Jr. — the son of the man who trained him — in Tampa, Florida.

Among the highlights of his run as NWA world champion was a wild 65-minute draw against Giant Baba on August 14, 167, drawing 25,000 fans to Osaka Stadium.

Kiniski helped define the role of a heel world champion, a model the NWA would follow for most of the 1970s and 1980s while Harley Race and Ric Flair held the championship. With his brash, bigger-than-life personality, Kiniski was one of wrestling's top draws throughout the United States, Canada, and Japan. He also maintained high standards of professionalism, dressing in neat suits and staying in hotels befitting a champion. When he was on the road, he made a point of looking over the local newspaper so he knew the hot topics in town and could reference them as talking points in promos and in interviews with the media.

Kiniski also held the AWA world title for one month in the summer of 1961, winning the belt from Verne Gagne and dropping it back to Gagne in a rematch.

Kiniski's career would span four decades. He served as the special guest referee for the main event of *Starrcade* 1983, officiating the world title bout between Harley Race and Ric Flair. He retired from wrestling in 1992.

Kiniski died on April 14, 2010, after a lengthy battle with cancer. He was 81.

GEORGE GORDIENKO

If Lou Thesz had his way, George Gordienko would have beaten him for the NWA world title in March 1956. Unfortunately, the United States federal government stood in the way.

Thesz met Gordienko — a native of Winnipeg, Manitoba — while working for Stu Hart's Stampede promotion in Calgary. "We once worked a sixty-minute draw, and I couldn't run him out of gas, which almost never happened," Thesz later recalled in an anecdote in his memoirs, *Hooker*.

Gordienko was born on January 7, 1928. He took up wrestling at the age of 15. Already an accomplished and powerful football player, he excelled in wrestling and began weight training to further improve his strength and conditioning. "I had been training with weights for a couple of years," he recalled in an autobiographical piece written for the Cauliflower Alley Club in 2000. "Our equipment was homemade and crude compared to the competition sets, but that may have been advantageous since we (he and his friend Albert Olsen, who had introduced George to wrestling) were principally concerned with feats of strength more than bodybuilding."

Gordienko trained at the local YMCA alongside Gordon Nelson, Harold Nelson, Steve Kozak, and Jimmy Trifunov, a former Olympic wrestler (he won the bronze medal in the bantamweight division in the 1928 Games) who would coach the Canadian Olympic wrestling team in 1952, 1956, and 1960.

"One night when I was training at the Y, Wally Karbo and Joe Pazandak made a visit," Gordienko wrote. "Joe worked out with me and didn't take me off my feet for six minutes, when Wally called out that Joe should conserve his energy for his coming bout. Not bad for an 18-year-old. I was very strong but lacked knowledge."

That knowledge came through Minnesota wrestling promoter Tony Stecher. Encouraged by Pazandak and Karbo ("I think Joe decided that I would make a good training mate," Gordienko said), Stecher invited Gordienko down to Minneapolis to train. Gordienko accepted and made his pro debut in 1946.

"Gordienko was really the best in America in those days," wrote Billy Robinson in his book *Physical Chess: My Life in Catch-as-Catch-Can Wrestling.* "Of all the guys I've wrestled around the world, he was probably the naturally strongest that I've ever met."

Verne Gagne recruited Gordienko as a training partner to prepare for the 1948 Olympics, Robinson wrote. "Verne said, 'Okay, go down. I'll get behind you. Try to escape.' And Gordienko went *bam*! He exploded and escaped. So then Gagne got down and Gordienko said, 'Okay. Now I'll escape. You hold me down,' and Gordienko held him down until Verne quit. Verne no longer wanted to spar with him."

But Gordienko didn't make the trip to the States just for wrestling. He enrolled in the University of Minnesota where he studied pre-med. He fell in love with a Minnesota girl named Ruth. They were married in 1948, had a son, and moved back to Winnipeg. However, Ruth and George soon parted ways, and Ruth testified that her ex-husband was a member of the Communist party and that they had attended

George Gordienko.

COURTESY OF THE PFEFER ARCHIVES

Communist meetings of the Marxist Socialist Club at the University's Coffman Memorial Union Hall. Ruth and her son moved back to the U.S. Gordienko was barred from returning.

When Thesz decided he needed time off after suffering a broken ankle in 1953, he lobbied to drop the world title to Gordienko, who he felt was already one of the best young wrestlers in the world and a future star. He had defeated Gordienko in May in Edmonton and decided he would be a worthy champion. But the State Department wouldn't budge. Gordienko could not return to the U.S.

"It's a shame that we couldn't get him into the country," Thesz wrote. "That was during the McCarthy era, though, and it wasn't going to happen." Thesz instead dropped the belt to "Whipper" Billy Watson. Despite wrestling until 1976, Gordienko would never hold a recognized world championship.

Gordienko took a sabbatical from wrestling for a time, downplaying the accusations of Communism. "While I was young and had a lifetime ahead of me, I decided to make a break," he wrote. "In hindsight, I did the right thing because now I am doing 'my thing' which to me is so satisfying and interesting. It is life itself. I think some people were critical of my departure and rumors flew."

Though a career in the U.S. never came to fruition, he had success internationally, winning the British Commonwealth heavyweight title, the NWA Pacific Coast (Vancouver) heavyweight title, and the New Zealand version of the British Commonwealth title. He was named the top wrestler in the United Kingdom in 1963 and 1970 and competed in Europe, India, Iran, Iraq, Libya, Japan, Africa, and the Caribbean.

Gordienko went on to have success as a painter. His background as a wrestler earned him an audience with Pablo Picasso in Paris. "There were a couple of boys there who were into paintings and had personal showings," he wrote. "They knew Picasso, since he watched wrestling on television and was said to be an avid fan. He would not be disturbed when the bouts were on. Eventually, and to my very good fortune, while I was in the company of the lads who painted we encountered Picasso and had coffee together. What a polite, well-mannered person. He even insisted on paying. This was truly a high spot in my life."

Gordienko died from melanoma in 2002. He was 74.

DICK HUTTON

It was the fall of 1957 and NWA world champion Lou Thesz was ready to take a break.

Having just wrestled a series of bouts against Japanese icon Rikidozan (including six time-hour draws) throughout Japan, Thesz put in a request for some time off, or at least without having to keep a world champion's schedule. The NWA championship committee wanted Thesz to drop the belt to "Nature Boy" Buddy Rogers, but Thesz outright refused to put Rogers over, threatening to shoot on Rogers and stretch him in the middle of the ring if the match was made. Instead, he suggested he drop the title to a former Olympic wrestler by the name of Dick Hutton.

Born on October 4, 1923, in Amarillo, Texas, Hutton grew up in Tulsa, Oklahoma, becoming a two-time state finalist in wrestling. He enrolled in Oklahoma A&M (Oklahoma State) but after only six months there, he postponed his studies for a deployment with the U.S. Army and was stationed in Italy during the last two years of World War II.

He returned to school after the war and was a four-time All-American in wrestling. He won the NCAA wrestling championships in 1947, 1948, and 1950. His 1949 quest for the NCAA championship was ruined when he lost to Verne Gagne in the tournament finals in controversial fashion, where the referee took away takedown points awarded to Hutton, saying time had expired before he completed the move, and awarded the match to Gagne. The controversy prompted the NCAA to add two judges (in addition to the referee) for championship matches the following year.

Hutton competed in the 1948 Olympic Games in London, England, finishing fifth in the men's freestyle heavyweight division (Gagne was an alternate). He had no interest in going pro until he got wind of the money he could make.

"I was looking at a newspaper and saw 'Verne Gagne, wrestler, makes $160,000.' I said to myself, 'Gosh, I can do that,'" Hutton said in an interview with the *Wrestling Perspective* newsletter.

Hutton trained under Ed Lewis and made his pro debut in 1952, earning decidedly less than Gagne — a $7 pay-out for his first match. He started out in Texas but made a name for himself in the Columbus territory. There, he adopted a gimmick where he issued an open challenge to any member of the audience. He began to offer $1 per minute for any fans who could stay in the ring with him and $1,000 to any fan that could manage to beat him — a prize he never had to pay out. He had two runs as Ohio heavyweight champion. Years later, he would offer $1,000 to any wrestler who could beat him in under 20 minutes.

Thesz was impressed with Hutton's Olympic credentials and hand-picked him to be the world champion. "I became a Dick Hutton fan the moment I saw him, and I loved it when I was booked with the guy because we'd actually wrestle each other during our matches, just for fun," Thesz wrote. "Hutton was a special situation, though, because he may have been the best mat wrestler of all time. I've seen a lot of wrestlers, amateurs and pros alike, who were fast on their feet and quick on takedowns, but once they hit the deck they were lost. Hutton was completely at home on the mat and it was an incredible thing to see because he was built like a chunk of reinforced concrete. He looked like he would be stiff and slow, but the guy was so fast and mobile that he could almost float — no matter what kind of move you made, he would have a counter for it."

On November 14, 1957, Hutton defeated Thesz in Toronto, Ontario, to become world champion. Hutton countered a flying scissor hold with an abdominal stretch, earning a submission victory in the one-fall bout. During his 14-month reign, Hutton successfully defended the world title against the likes of Thesz, Gene Kiniski, Bill Miller, "Whipper" Billy Watson, and Don Leo Jonathan before dropping it to Pat O'Connor in January 1959. Despite his impeccable credentials and the endorsement of Thesz, Hutton never truly connected with the fans. Just five years after he dropped the world title, his pro wrestling career would be finished.

Hutton had a run in California in 1960, wrestling in dungarees as "Cowboy" Dick Hutton, adopting more of a roughhouse style. He held the NWA Canadian tag title with Hard Boiled Haggerty, the NWA North American tag title with Dory Funk Sr., and the WWA TV tag title with Sam Steamboat, but he never had a serious singles run after his world championship reign.

When asked, Thesz would regularly call Hutton the toughest man he ever wrestled.

He retired from wrestling in 1964, due to heart troubles and various other injuries. He died on November 24, 2003, at the age of 80. He has received recognition by the National Wrestling Hall of Fame, the NCAA Hall of Fame, the Oklahoma State University Hall of Fame, and the Cauliflower Alley Club.

"There are very few men like him left," then–CAC vice president Karl Lauer said at the time of Hutton's passing. "Danny Hodge, Verne Gagne, Lou Thesz, and just a small handful of men were of that same caliber. Everybody cared for and respected Dick Hutton. He was a great man and a class act."

PAT O'CONNOR

Thesz may have refused to lie down for Buddy Rogers, but "The New Zealand Strong Boy" Pat O'Connor didn't mind putting over "The Nature Boy." And neither did his pocket book. The June 30, 1961, NWA world title clash between O'Connor and Rogers set a new attendance record and did monster business, drawing 38,622 fans to Chicago's Comiskey Park and bringing in a reported gate of $148,000. That would stand as wrestling's biggest house for a quarter of a century.

Billed as "The Match of the Century," O'Connor/Rogers set the tone for what professional wrestling would become in the second part of the 20th century, with the world championship going from a legitimate amateur wrestling champion to a pure showman with negligible wrestling skills. It was — more than 30 years before Vince McMahon Jr. coined the phrase — the triumph of "sports entertainment" over technical wrestling.

Rogers wearing the world title may have sickened Thesz and other wrestling purists, but there was no denying the fact that Rogers was a draw. And in this title match, the fair-and-square, play-by-the-rules O'Connor was the ideal foil.

Patrick O'Connor was born on August 22, 1924, in Raetihi, New Zealand. He attended Massey University, where he wrestled, played rugby, and ran track. He worked as a farmer and blacksmith and served six months in the New Zealand Royal Air Force during World War II, but he never lost his passion for wrestling. He represented New Zealand in the 1948 Pan-American Games in London and the 1950 British Empire Games in Auckland where he won a silver medal. He won the New Zealand heavyweight title in 1949 and 1950. He trained for the pro game under Len "Butch" Levy and made his debut in 1950.

American promoters had caught sight of O'Connor in international amateur competition, and promoter Tony Stecher invited him to come to the "Twin Cities" of Minneapolis and St. Paul.

"Pat was a true main-eventer from the time he came from New Zealand," promoter and historian Larry Matysik told the *St. Louis Post-Dispatch* in 1990. "Pat wasn't really a big man, but he was a real athlete with a very smooth and fluid style. He was a great crowd pleaser, especially in his matches with Lou Thesz, Fritz Von Erich, Gene Kiniski, and some others."

Matysik also credited O'Connor with innovating the reverse rolling cradle (known as the "O'Connor roll"), though O'Connor was also noted for his spinning toehold and sleeper hold.

On January 9, 1959, O'Connor beat Hutton with the spinning toe hold to win the NWA world title at the Kiel Auditorium in St. Louis. Over the course of his two-and-a-half-year title reign, O'Connor had more than 130 successful title defenses, collecting wins over such luminaries as Thesz, "Whipper" Billy Watson, Johnny Valentine, Gene Kiniski and reigning junior heavyweight champion Danny Hodge in a rare champion-versus-champion bout.

O'Connor was the NWA champion in 1960 when Verne Gagne and Wally Karbo decided to take their Minneapolis Boxing and Wrestling Club out from the NWA banner. Karbo issued a challenge to O'Connor to defend his title against Gagne, the top contender of their new American Wrestling Alliance (later to become the American Wrestling Association). After 90 days, the AWA declared that since O'Connor had failed to defend his world title against Gagne (naturally, since Gagne and Karbo had pulled out of the NWA), the AWA would recognize Gagne as the legitimate champion. This storyline gave some credibility to the AWA version of the title without requiring O'Connor to put Gagne over. O'Connor eventually did the honors for Gagne in 1963, after he had dropped the NWA strap. He also held the AWA tag title with Wilbur Snyder in 1967, as well as several regional titles, but never again captured a world title (though he did challenge for the AWA title several times).

O'Connor retired from wrestling in 1982, though he did participate in a special "legends battle royal" on November 11, 1987, at a WWF house show in East Rutherford, New Jersey, which would be his final match.

He worked as a promoter in Kansas City and St. Louis for a time. He died of cancer on August 16, 1990. He was 65.

O'Connor also had an indirect role in the development of the World Wide Wrestling Federation, now known as WWE. Once Rogers beat O'Connor for the title, the majority of his title defenses took place in the Northeast for Vince McMahon Sr. Rogers was a big draw for McMahon, and when the NWA championship committee voted to take the belt off Rogers, McMahon responded by splintering away from the NWA and creating the WWWF with Rogers as his first champion. O'Connor was the last NWA champion of the pre-WWE wrestling world.

JOHNNY VALENTINE

A quote frequently attributed to Johnny Valentine (and repeated by many others over the years) perfectly encapsulates his approach to wrestling: "I can't make you believe professional wrestling is real. But I sure as hell can make you believe I am."

That was Valentine's mission statement, and a promise he delivered on each time he stepped into the ring.

Born John Wisniski in Maple Valley, Washington, on September 22, 1928, "The Champ" would earn a reputation as a stiff worker and a genuine tough guy. He wanted his matches to be as believable as possible and encouraged his opponents to lay it in against him, and he would give the same back. He was — in the words of Lou Thesz — "one of the toughest men ever to pull on a pair of tights."

Valentine started out a pro boxer when he was discovered by the local wrestling promoter, who persuaded him to try his hand at the mat game. "He had almost no wrestling ability, but he didn't need any, because he rose to the top on toughness and pure guts," Thesz wrote in *Hooker*. "Once you got past the hookers and the serious shooters, he was probably the one man in pro wrestling that you least wanted mess with. The fans could sense his toughness, too, and they always turned out in droves to see him."

Valentine made his wrestling debut in 1947. At six-foot-three and 250 pounds, he was a natural heavyweight and imposing specimen, and he relished getting physical. He got in with the Zbyszko brothers — Stanislaus and Wladek — who were promoting wrestling events in Argentina, but in 1948, journeyman wrestler and aspiring talent scout Nick Elitch stole him away from the Zbyszkos. A year earlier, Elitch had stumbled upon

Antonino Rocca while touring South America. Rocca had gone on to become a major star in the States, winding up wrestling for Toots Mondt in New York. Elitch was looking to find gold a second time, and he convinced Valentine to take him on as manager.

The business deal between Elitch and Valentine proved to be brief, but it helped Valentine get a foothold in the U.S. and opened some important doors. In 1950, Valentine captured the NWA (Florida) Southern heavyweight title, the first of a multitude of championships throughout the territories. Over the course of his 28-year career, Valentine won championships in every major territory in the U.S. and Canada. He is considered by many to be one of the greatest wrestlers to have never held a world championship (though he did hold the National Wrestling Federation title in 1972, a time it was considered, by some, to be a world title). In his 2013 book, *The 50 Greatest Professional Wrestlers of All Time: The Definitive Shoot*, venerable wrestling historian Larry Matysik ranked Valentine 16th on his list, ahead of such luminaries as Jack Brisco, Andre the Giant, Bret Hart, and the Undertaker — world champions all. "Any study of the greatest 50 that does not include Valentine is a fraud, plain and simple," he wrote.

Johnny Valentine cinches up an armbar on Johnny Powers.

PHOTO COURTESY OF GEORGE NAPOLITANO

He also had a series of matches against Antonio Inoki in Japan. Though he was an established star and draw, Valentine was willing to put Inoki over, helping give Inoki credibility with fans in his home country.

"I had so many matches with J.V. I finally went to (Jim) Crockett to ask if I had heat with him. I was getting the heck beat out of me every day and I loved it," Jerry Brisco said in an interview with Mike Mooneyham.

Valentine had a storied rivalry with Wahoo McDaniel that has been credited with helping revive the Mid-Atlantic territory during the early 1970s. Valentine's bouts were marked with blistering chops and wince-inducing punches — "strong style" long before the term was coined.

Valentine was also known for his slow, methodical style. He stalked opponents and wore them down with holds, but could explode with elbow smashes, punches, and strikes at the right moment. "You just listened to (Johnny) and you couldn't go wrong," Ken Patera said in a 2012 interview with *Pro Wrestling Illustrated*. "You learn more in five or six matches working with him than you would working a year with someone else. He was a master of psychology."

Valentine's life changed forever on October 4, 1975. Valentine was a passenger onboard a twin-engine Cessna 310, along with Tim "Mr. Wrestling" Woods, Bob Bruggers, David Crockett, and Ric Flair. The wrestlers were flying to Wilmington, North Carolina, when the plane ran out of fuel and came falling to earth, dropping 4,000 feet and crashing into a grove of trees. The pilot died of his injuries after being in a coma. Valentine, Flair, and Bruggers suffered broken backs, but Valentine — seated in front next to the pilot — suffered permanent damage to his spinal column. He would need crutches to walk for the rest of his life. His wrestling career was over. He tried his hand at managing for a while, including a stint managing Dale Hey (under the name Dale Valentine) in the Houston territory.

In 2000, Valentine suffered a fall at his home, which resulted in several injuries and complications, including a fractured back, pneumonia, and collapsed lungs. After a valiant fight, he died on April 24, 2001, at the age of 72.

The Valentine name was carried on by his son, John, better known as Greg "The Hammer" Valentine, who was enshrined in the WWE Hall of Fame in 2004.

SPUTNIK MONROE

At the pool halls of Memphis they still talk of the night
That Sputnik Monroe refused to fight
Until all of the people, be they black or white,
Could sit together, side by side.
There's a basic language every promoter speaks
Based on bills in hands and asses in seats.
The promoters gave in and they drew record crowds,
The first desegregated sporting event in the south.

—Otis Gibbs, from the song "Sputnik Monroe"

Sputnik Monroe wasn't a technical virtuoso. He wasn't a body beautiful — in fact, he looked like a run-of-the-mill barroom bully; not a guy you'd like to mess with, but not someone you'd ever peg as a professional athlete. Unlike most of the other wrestlers in this section, he was never a world champion and never a national main-eventer (though he set box office records in the Memphis territory). But Sputnik Monroe left a legacy that changed not only pro wrestling but all professional sports.

"Obviously I've never met him, nor would I be the person to speak on his behalf, but I will say that it's very hard to speak up in wrestling for fear of so many things, mainly losing your job or position within a company," said Colt Cabana, who featured Monroe on his *Pro Wrestling Fringe* podcast in 2019. "For Sputnik to do what he did undeniably makes him a bigger person than most. Does that make him a Wrestlers' Wrestler? Maybe. As a wrestler, though, I have the utmost respect for him and all that are like him. A person like Sputnik would always be welcome in my locker room."

Born Roscoe Monroe Merrick on December 18, 1928, he grew up in Dodge City, Kansas. His father died in a plane crash a month before Roscoe was born, and he was raised by his mother and his grandparents. His mother eventually married a baker by the name Virgil Brumbaugh who later officially adopted Roscoe as his own.

As a teenager, Roscoe took an interest in boxing and wrestling. He also spent a lot of time at his stepfather's bakery, which had several Black employees. Roscoe formed friendships with some of these Black workers at a time when Jim Crow laws ruled the South and lynchings were still all too common in the United States.

After a three-year stint in the navy, he took up wrestling at local carnivals. He got his pro wrestling training under Jack Nazworthy and moved on to the pro circuit. He was a journeyman, competing under such names as Rock Monroe, Pretty Boy Roque, and Elvis Rock Monroe. To increase his visibility, he took to bleaching a patch of his hair blond right in the middle of his scalp, giving him a skunk-like streak in his jet-black hair. He was 235 pounds of "twisted steel and sex appeal." He described his wrestling style as "scientifically rough."

A chance encounter in 1958 would prove to be not only a turning point in Monroe's career but a pivotal moment in the cultural zeitgeist. Monroe was driving to a wrestling card in Mobile, Alabama, where he encountered a Black man who was hitchhiking his way into town. Eager for company on the drive, or sympathetic to the hitchhiker's plight, Monroe picked him up. The two struck up a conversation and the hitchhiker came along to the arena to see Monroe wrestle. Fans queued up outside the arena saw Monroe arrive in the company of a Black man, a scandalous action in the cultural landscape of the time.

Ever the heel, Monroe must have gotten a kick out of the reaction. He wrapped his arm around the Black man, then planted a big kiss on his cheek, further infuriating the white fans, but earning him considerable respect from the African-American fan base. One woman was apparently so infuriated by Monroe's indecent antics that she spat the most insulting epithet she could come up with at him — "You're nothing but a damn Sputnik!" It was a reference to the Soviet satellite of that name that had recently been successfully launched; her way of calling him a Communist.

Monroe immediately took it as his ring name — Sputnik Monroe — wearing it as a badge of honor. His affection to the Black hitchhiker wasn't a gimmick, either. Unlike most other white Southerners of the time, he had grown up around Black people and didn't believe in segregation. When he started in the Memphis territory in January 1959, he took to hanging out the Black gin joints and nightclubs of Beale Street. He became a working-class hero of the Black community, passing out tickets and flyers for the wrestling shows. He began dressing flamboyantly, complete with a purple cape and a diamond-headed walking stick. He called himself "The Diamond Ring and Cadillac Man" and Black fans ate it up. White fans wanted his skunky scalp.

On August 17, 1959, Monroe faced local boy (and Shelby County sheriff's deputy) Billy Wicks, drawing 13,749 fans to Russwood Park baseball stadium, a Memphis attendance record that would last nearly 40 years. Boxing champion Rocky Marciano served as the special "enforcer" referee. The match was ruled a no-contest.

Monroe's antics weren't sitting well with the local authorities either. On January 14, 1960, he was arrested on the charge of "mopery" and accused of "drinking in negro cafes with negroes." He hired Russell B. Sugarmon Jr., a Black attorney, to represent him in court, paid his $25 fine, and went right back out to the juke joints with his people.

Under the Jim Crow laws of the time, Black audience members were segregated at the Ellis Auditorium. White attendees had the ringside seats and lower bowl, while their Black counterparts were sent upstairs. More and more Black fans were showing up at the auditorium to see Sputnik wrestle, but they were being turned away when the balcony filled up. Monroe took exception. His fan base was being prohibited entry. He went to promoters Nick Gulas and Roy Welch and told them he refused to wrestle unless fans of all races would be allowed to sit anywhere in the Ellis Auditorium. Seeing how big a draw Monroe was becoming, the promoters acquiesced. It was a major blow against segregation and it proved to be so profitable that other promotions — and other sports — began to integrate as well.

*Sputnik Monroe (left)
with his "protégé" and
tag team partner,
Rocket Monroe.*

Monroe formed a noteworthy tag team with Norvell Austin, winning tag titles in Florida and Tennessee. He retired in 1988 and became a car salesman. He died on November 3, 2006, at the age of 77. He was inducted into the WWE Hall of Fame as a legacy member in 2018.

"He was an innovator in a variety of fields, from the psychology of professional wrestling to equal rights for all races and creeds," Billy Wicks wrote, in a statement read by Jerry "The King" Lawler on a Memphis wrestling television broadcast announcing Monroe's death. "His contributions to both these fields are still in use today and most don't even know it. Sputnik managed to fit 120 years of life into only 78 years."

KARL GOTCH

If Rikidozan was the father of pro wrestling in Japan, Karl Gotch was the eccentric uncle you might be tempted to leave off the invitation list for the next family party.

A self-described "hard-headed Kraut," Gotch was opinionated, outspoken, and stubborn; a maverick who played by his own set of rules and didn't give a damn whose feathers got ruffled along the way. Kinder critics have called him "arrogant." Less kind critics have gone on record calling him "an asshole" . . . and worse. But it's hard to ignore the impact Gotch had on wrestling (particularly in Japan) and the influence he left on the sport. Simply look at the prevalence of the German suplex today for one example of Gotch's legacy.

Born Charles Istaz on August 3, 1924, in Antwerp, Belgium, he started Greco-Roman wrestling as a boy and learned how to fight on the docks. He represented Belgium in the 1948 Olympics in both freestyle and Greco-Roman competition, though he failed to medal. Following the Olympics, he moved to England, drawn by the magnetic pull of Billy Riley's notorious "Snake Pit" in Wigan. There, he learned the finer points of hooking and built a reputation as a top shooter.

He started his pro career under the ring name Karl Krauser in 1955 and wrestled throughout Europe on the carnival circuit. He moved to the United States in 1959, having been invited by Édouard Carpentier, whom he had met while wrestling in France. Columbus promoter Al Haft was impressed with Gotch's athleticism and began teaching him the art of the promo and grooming him for TV, changing his ring name to Gotch in honor of former world champion Frank Gotch.

His Olympic credentials caught the eye of Verne Gagne and he enjoyed a good push in the AWA in 1961, though he never won a title belt there (he did, however, hold the Ohio version of the American Wrestling *Alliance* title, a belt he later lost to Lou Thesz).

Gotch was a physical fitness fanatic who followed an arduous calisthenics program of Hindu squats and bridges coupled with a copious amount of running. He took joy in leaving other wrestlers sucking wind and was able to outwork and outwrestle most opponents, but despite all his training and expertise, Gotch simply wasn't getting over with fans or getting big pushes with the top U.S. territories.

"He was a good wrestler, he was a shooter. But he was making five, six, seven moves at a time, including the amateur. The people didn't understand what he was doing," Dominic DeNucci, who was having a main-event run in Roy Shire's territory while Gotch's matches against Ray Stevens failed to draw, told SLAM! Wrestling. "He said to me one time at the Embassy Hotel in San Francisco, 'I don't understand.' I said, 'What do you mean you don't understand?' He said, 'You can't amateur wrestle like me.' I said, 'No, I cannot. I wrestled amateur, but I don't know all that you know. But in this business, I don't have to know everything. You have to know how to defend yourself.' So he said yeah. But I could see in his face that he was not happy because I sold out and he drew $24,000."

As an elite wrestler, Gotch could never quite reconcile himself with the showmanship aspect of professional wrestling, and he didn't bother to hide the lack of respect he felt for wrestlers who he felt didn't live up to his demanding standards. One of those was the reigning NWA champion, "Nature Boy" Buddy Rogers. When Gotch got wind that Rogers wouldn't wrestle him because he was afraid that Gotch might double-cross him and shoot on him in the ring, Gotch and "Big" Bill Miller cornered Rogers in the locker room. Gotch challenged him to a fight right then and there as Miller held the door and prevented Rogers from escaping. Rogers was able to escape with some lacerations and a broken hand and filed assault charges against Gotch and Miller.

The incident caused Gotch to be labeled as a loose cannon by many promoters and he found himself blacklisted by several promotions, though

Haft continued to use him. After a disappointing stint in San Francisco, he won the Worldwide Wrestling Associates tag title with Mike DiBiase. He moved on to Florida, where he helped train a young Hiro Matsuda, and then on to the World Wide Wrestling Federation, where he won the tag team title with Rene Goulet.

In 1972, Gotch was contacted by Antonio Inoki. Inoki loved Gotch's credentials and wanted him as an opponent and trainer for his students for his newly created New Japan Pro-Wrestling. Gotch accepted the offer and on March 6, 1972, in the main event of New Japan's first card, Gotch defeated Inoki. But Inoki got his win back when he scored the pinfall over Gotch in a tag bout pitting Inoki and Seiji Sakaguchi against the dream team of Gotch and Lou Thesz, giving Inoki instantaneous credibility and putting New Japan firmly on the wrestling map.

Gotch beat Inoki to win the NJPW Real World heavyweight title on October 10, 1972, and he took over training duties at the New Japan dojo, where he trained Tatsumi Fujinami, Yoshiaki Fujiwara, Akira Maeda, Satoru Sayama (the original Tiger Mask), and many others. He was given the nickname Kamisama — "The God of Professional Wrestling."

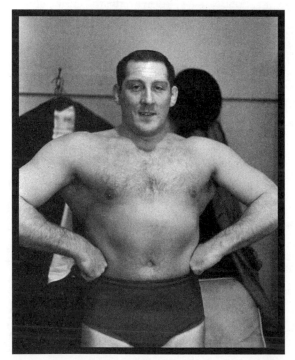

Karl Gotch, the originator of the German suplex, was always ready for a fight.

PHOTO COURTESY *PRO WRESTLING ILLUSTRATED*

His signature move, the atomic suplex — a move he performed multiple times on Andre the Giant — has come to be known as the German suplex in his honor, though Gotch's high-arching bridge finish is rarely done today.

Gotch retired in 1982 and settled down in Tampa, Florida, where he largely avoided wrestling and the press. He did, however, grant an interview to the *Wrestling Observer Newsletter* in 1990. In that interview, he discussed how wrestling had changed through the years and how much he disliked what pro wrestling had become.

"Wrestling is the hardest and most difficult sport in the world. You have to have it all," Gotch said. "They asked me in Japan what you need to be a good wrestler. I said you need it all. You've got to be strong, like a weightlifter, and by that I mean a competitive weightlifter, not a bodybuilder. You've got to be agile like an acrobat. You've got to have the endurance of a middle distance runner, the quickness of a sprinter and the mind of a chess player. You have three positions you have to fight from, standing up, on the knees and from underneath. . . . I mean to be a good show wrestler, you should at least practice wrestling. Now all you have is routines. Before, when you went somewhere, no matter what part of the world you were from, you could wrestle with the guys. Now these guys can't. They're stuck on the same old thing and their matches are always the same. It's like a song and dance routine. The only thing missing is the music."

Gotch died at the age of 82 on July 28, 2007.

DANNY HODGE

In a sport built on ballyhoo, Danny Hodge was the real deal.

A perfect 46–0 as a collegiate star at the University of Oklahoma, where he was never once taken down by an opponent. A three-time NCAA champion. An Olympic silver medalist (in the 1956 Games in Melbourne, Australia). A Golden Gloves boxing champion with an undefeated 17–0 record. The top honor for college wrestlers is named after him — the Dan Hodge Trophy, collegiate wrestling's answer to the Heisman Trophy.

"Danny Hodge may have been the toughest man alive during his era," said Kyle Klingman, a former director of the National Wrestling Hall of Fame Dan Gable Museum, which houses the George Tragos/ Lou Thesz Professional Wrestling Hall of Fame. "Hodge had pure power. He looked superhuman. With his combination of physical strength, legitimate wrestling ability, and boxing, he was MMA before MMA existed. He could have taken anyone in a shoot. He was perfect for pro wrestling."

Born May 13, 1932, in Perry, Oklahoma, Hodge became synonymous with wrestling in the 1950s. The son of an oilfield rigger, Hodge started wrestling at age 13, and won the Oklahoma state 165-pound title in 1951. He became the first wrestler ever to be featured on the cover of *Sports Illustrated* (the April 1, 1957, edition) in a story entitled "The Man to Beat," which came out right before the 1957 NCAA championship tournament, where Hodge won the 177-pound division.

When asked by *SI* reporter Don Parker if the wrestling ring was in his future, Hodge brushed off the suggestion. "Professional wrestling? Not for me. I want to be a teacher," he said.

After graduation, he tried his hand at boxing, winning the 1958 Golden Gloves tournament. He went pro for a year before going back to his wrestling roots, in a way. There was big money that could be made in the world of pro wrestling for a man with Hodge's credentials, and eventually the lure of the squared circle proved to be too much for him to ignore. Hodge trained under Strangler Lewis and Leroy McGuirk and made his professional wrestling debut in October 1959. On July 22, 1960, he defeated Angelo Savoldi in Oklahoma City to win the NWA junior heavyweight title. He would hold that championship seven times between 1960 and 1976 for a combined total of 4,134 days.

Danny Hodge — "he was MMA before MMA existed."

PHOTO COURTESY *PRO WRESTLING ILLUSTRATED*

By 1962, Hodge was earning a reported $80,000 per year, the equivalent of nearly $700,000 by 2020 standards.

Unlike other amateurs who had difficulty adjusting to the showmanship aspect of the pro game, Hodge fit right in as a pro. He would display his impressive strength by crushing an apple in the palm of his hand, snapping the handles on pliers, and ripping thick telephone books in half, earning the sobriquet "Homicide Hodge."

In January 1968, Hodge defeated Lou Thesz in Tokyo to win the Trans World Wrestling Association title, establishing Hodge as a demigod in Japan. "Thesz was management and chose to lose the title created for him out of respect for Hodge being No. 1 in his mind at the time, even though a junior heavyweight," Dave Meltzer wrote.

In 1976, he suffered a broken neck when he fell asleep behind the wheel of Volkswagen station wagon and the car careened off the road, down an embankment, and into a creek in Louisiana. Despite the broken neck, he managed to hold his head in place, escape the rapidly sinking vehicle through a shattered window, and swim his way to safety. A passing truck driver found him by the side of the road and called for help, and he made a full recovery after surgery to fuse part of his pelvic bone to the base of his neck.

The injury forced Hodge to relinquish the NWA junior heavyweight title and retire from the ring, though he was able to make a brief comeback in 1983 before retiring once and for all.

Fellow Oklahoma native Jim Ross became a Hodge fan at the age of 10, watching the NWA junior heavyweight champion on TV each week. "He was a legitimate Oklahoma hero, along with guys like Jim Thorpe and Mickey Mantle. He was right there with them," Ross told veteran wrestling reporter Bill Apter in a 2010 interview, after Ross inducted Hodge into the NWA's Hall of Legends.

Hodge has a place of prominence in every physical wrestling hall of fame there is. He was awarded the Lou Thesz Award for lifetime achievement by the Cauliflower Alley Club in 2007. He died on December 24, 2020 at the age of 88.

BILL MILLER

At six-foot-six and tipping the scales at a steak-and-potatoes dinner short of 300 pounds, "Big" Bill Miller could have been a standout wrestler by virtue of his size alone. Instead, he used his impressive agility, footwork, creativity, and body positioning to redefine exactly what a superheavy-weight could be, and influenced countless wrestlers to follow in his sizeable footsteps.

Born June 5, 1927, William Miller grew up on a farm in Ohio, where he gained an appreciation of animals. He enrolled at Ohio State University and took up veterinary studies. But when he wasn't in the classroom, he was on the athletic field, earning nine letters — three in football, three in wrestling, and three in track (competing in shotput and discus). He was an All-American heavyweight wrestler, a two-time Big Ten champion in the heavyweight division, and placed fourth overall in the 1951 NCAA tournament.

Miller's exploits on the gridiron caught the eye of the Green Bay Packers, who drafted the big tackle in the 26th round of the 1951 draft. But instead of playing pro football, he was persuaded by Columbus, Ohio, promoter Al Haft to try his hand at professional wrestling instead.

After graduating with his veterinary degree (he would later use "Doctor" as part of his ring name once he earned his graduate degree), he made his pro wrestling debut for Haft in 1952. Miller stayed close to home to start so he could focus on his graduate studies and he earned a reputation as a bookworm in the wrestling locker room, sitting apart with a book in hand while other wrestlers played cards or drank beer.

Miller was a legitimate athlete who quickly picked up the showman-ship and entertainment aspect of wrestling. He became good friends and workout partners with respected shooter Karl Gotch, and few opponents were willing to try any funny business with someone with Miller's size and athletic pedigree. In a Kayfabe Commentaries shoot video, Bruno Sammartino recounted a time when Miller shot on him mid-match because Miller felt Sammartino and his tag partner, Tony Parisi, were taking liberties with Miller's partner, Curtis Iaukea. "Bill Miller came in and he gave me a kick. I thought his foot came into my chest and came out of my back, that's how hard he kicked me." That's the kind of power Miller had.

One of Miller's signature spots saw him get his ankle or torso tied up in the ropes, leaving him trapped helplessly (sometimes upside-down) while the babyface unloaded on him and the referee frantically scrambled to free him. It was a spot that always got a fan reaction, particularly because of Miller's size, and a variation of it was also done by Andre the Giant later in his career. It was an ingenious way for a bigger heel to get a laugh at his expense or give a smaller babyface a way to get some fire, and it illustrated Miller's keen psychology towards wrestling.

Miller was also adept at using his massive frame to obstruct the referee's vision for chokes and hairpulls, a savvy touch that never failed to generate heat. Those little things made the big man a model for other wrestlers.

"I would put Dr. Bill Miller in the same category as Lou Thesz and Karl Gotch as guys where the other pros studied their every move," said wrestling historian Steve Johnson.

By the mid-1950s, Miller had become one of the top heels in the country, making stops in Portland, St. Louis, Detroit, the Northeast (and Ontario, Canada), and California.

In 1959, he played off his medical background by donning a mask and wrestling as Doctor X (not to be confused with the Doctor X played by Dick Beyer). He won the Omaha, Nebraska, version of the world title (later unified with the AWA world title) on two occasions in 1959, trading the title with fellow giant Don Leo Jonathan. On August 20, 1960, Doctor X fought Verne Gagne (one of Miller's old collegiate mat rivals) in a Texas death match that went 14 falls until the masked man was unable to continue. Gagne unmasked the mysterious doctor, exposing him as Miller.

On January 9, 1962, Miller got his revenge on Gagne, this time under a mask as Mr. M. He defeated Gagne to win the AWA (Minneapolis) world title. He was forced to vacate the AWA U.S. title he held at the time once he won the world title. Mr. M held that title for seven months before dropping it back to Gagne.

Lou Thesz was a big fan of Miller's work and wrote about a match he had against Miller in in his book, *Hooker*. "I once wrestled a television match there (in Indianapolis) with Dr. Bill Miller, the great Ohio State star who was a tremendous villain wrestler, that even had the boys in the dressing room applauding. The match never appeared on TV, though, because (Dick The) Bruiser had it erased as soon as he saw it. He couldn't stand the idea of anyone looking better than he did. The same thing happened with a TV interview Miller had taped to promote an upcoming main event against Bruiser. Miller was boasting about himself and merely said he couldn't understand how the Indianapolis fans could cheer for a 'five-foot, eight-inch runt like Dick the Bruiser' when they had a real man like himself on the scene. It was a great interview, but Dick erased it because he didn't like having his actual size advertised to the fans."

Miller excelled in both singles and tag team competition, and frequently teamed with his "brother" Ed Miller (Edward Albers) and his real-life little brother, Danny. Bill and Danny held the World Wide Wrestling Federation U.S. tag team title from August 1965 (winning the straps from Gorilla Monsoon and Bill Watts in a clash of superheavyweights) through February 1966, losing them to Johnny Valentine and Antonio Pugliese in Madison Square Garden. Miller also challenged Sammartino for the WWWF world title several times in 1965, including both a one-hour Broadway (the judges ruled Sammartino the winner) and a 48-second squash loss.

Miller, in a roundabout way, was one of the reasons Sammartino was considered to be a world champion at all. A few years earlier, he and Gotch had intimidated Buddy Rogers backstage, prompting Rogers to finally do the job for Thesz, which ultimately prompted Vince McMahon Sr. to split from the NWA and recognize his own world champion, which just ended up being Sammartino.

Miller also completed several tours of Japan throughout his career — including a win over a young Shohei Baba and a clash with Rikidozan (as Dr. X) — and in Australia, where he held the International Wrestling Alliance tag team title with Killer Kowalski.

The last major feud of Miller's career was in 1969, in the San Francisco territory, when he went to war with "Crippler" Ray Stevens over the NWA U.S. (San Francisco version) championship. Miller was able to build remarkable heat against the beloved Stevens, and the former heavyweight boxing champion Rocky Marciano was brought in to serve as guest referee for their June 21, 1969, "death match" at the Cow Palace. Marciano ended up landing a knockout punch on Miller when he was fed up by Dr. Bill's rulebreaking.

Miller had another run under a mask as the Crimson Knight in the St. Louis territory. The Knight rose through the ranks to earn an NWA world title shot against Dory Funk Jr., but lost to Funk and was unmasked.

Miller retired from wrestling in 1976 and set up his own veterinary practice in Ohio. He died of a heart attack on March 24, 1997, at the age of 69.

"Bill Miller was the prototype of what a pro wrestler should be: educated, goal-oriented, fit, and a man of his word, notwithstanding being an amazing athlete," said Jim Ross, longtime announcer and former WWE executive vice president of talent relations. "He was one of the few pro wrestlers that rarely had a bad word said about him."

BREAKING IN: WHERE DO WRESTLERS COME FROM?

How does someone actually become a professional wrestler? And for that matter, where does the desire to become a professional wrestler come from? There are more answers to those questions than you might think. Some aspiring wrestlers became enthralled with the squared circle at a young age. They saw these "real life" superheroes and villains on television and dreamed of one day becoming as big and strong as these larger-than-life figures.

"When I was a kid growing up in Maryland around 1950 or so, I had a paper route, and one of my customers had a TV," remembered Buddy Colt. "I asked if I could come by some night and watch wrestling, and they said sure. That is where I — this skinny little kid — started daydreaming about becoming a wrestler."

But daydreaming about becoming a wrestler and actually following through are two different things. Sometimes real life gets in the way.

"When I was in the Marines, I was stationed in Japan and I took judo lessons, plus I started weightlifting and bodybuilding," Colt said. "I still wasn't even thinking about professional wrestling; even then I thought I was too skinny. Once I was out of the Marine Corps, I continued weightlifting and bodybuilding, and when I was living in Houston, I met one of the wrestlers in a weightlifting room. He said to me 'You know, you'd make a good babyface.' I said, 'What the hell is a babyface?' So he tells me. Then he trains me and works me."

Often, professional wrestlers come to the ring from other sports. Countless amateur wrestlers and former football players and other athletes have taken on the role of professional wrestler once their first sporting vocation ended. For standout collegiate — even Olympic-caliber — wrestlers, the sport offers a very narrow window. Once you've passed your mid-20s, your best years are behind you. In professional wrestling, a mat grappler willing to learn the ropes can take that athleticism and skill and transition to the pro game. Maurice "Mad Dog" Vachon, Karl Gotch, Bob Roop, Hossein Khosrow Ali Vaziri (the Iron Sheik), Mike Rotunda, Brock Lesnar, and Kurt Angle all went on to successful pro wrestling careers. Their amateur wrestling skills gave them credibility. And credibility can get a wrestler over.

"Look at the Varsity Club — 'Dr. Death' Steve Williams, Rick Steiner, Mike Rotunda. They were fabulous," said Kevin Sullivan, who served as the manager of that group in Jim Crockett Promotions in the late 1980s. "They all had different personalities. They were like the Three Stooges but they could wrestle. They could wrestle amateur wrestling and pro wrestling, and they could blend both of those art forms together."

Football has given wrestling more than its fair share of legends. Gus Sonnenberg, Bronko Nagurski, Dwayne "The Rock" Johnson, Jim Duggan, Brian Pillman, Tito Santana, Bill Goldberg, Dusty Rhodes, Wahoo McDaniel, Ernie Ladd, Baron Corbin, Roman Reigns, and Bruiser Brody are just some of the former college or professional football players to find greater success in the ring than they had on the gridiron. That isn't to say that every football player to try their hand at wrestling was successful. There were far more failures than success stories. And not every football-player-turned-wrestler resorted to wrestling because they couldn't cut the mustard playing ball. Wahoo McDaniel (who played for the Houston Oilers, the Denver Broncos, and the Miami Dolphins) wrestled during the off-season and was able to make more money as a professional wrestler than an NFL player.

Others, like Paul Orndorff, simply preferred wrestling to the rigors of the gridiron.

"I loved wrestling, I really did, I gave my life to it, gave my all," Orndorff said. "I could have played for the New Orleans Saints. I was drafted by the Saints, but I choose wrestling. I loved it, I really loved it."

Athletes of all kind have become wrestlers. Ken Patera and Mark Henry were Olympic weightlifters. Tony Atlas and "Superstar" Bill Graham were some of the first bodybuilders to jump into wrestling. Danny Hodge was an Olympic wrestler but was also a Golden Gloves boxing champion. Dan Severn, Ken Shamrock, and Ronda Rousey came into wrestling from the world of mixed martial arts. But having success in one sport didn't necessarily mean an athlete was cut out to be a professional wrestler.

"There were a lot of guys that were one-hit wonders who came from other sports because they didn't get it. They don't put the time into learning and training," said Brian Blair. "They find out it's a lot more difficult than it looks if you want to be a real star."

Simply put, professional wrestling isn't like other sports. It relies on so much more than athleticism. Pro wrestling is about psychology and the ability to tell a story. That's one of the things that sets a "Wrestlers' Wrestler" apart from the pack. Others may be able to execute all the moves and flips perfectly, whereas a true Wrestlers' Wrestler knows *when* to execute the moves and how to keep the fans invested in his (or her) match. It's all about the nuances of the performance. Perhaps the wrestlers that understand that best are the ones who grew up around the business.

"I attended my first match at nine days old," said Ron Fuller, a third-generation wrestler and promoter known professionally as "The Tennessee Stud." "Obviously I don't remember that match, but my grandfather and his two brothers were wrestling in a six-man tag. I got to see a lot of the great shooters in the '50s, when I was like five or six years old. My dad had a wrestling territory and he liked to have those guys, he kept them in his territory because that's what he grew up around, I got to see it and later on in life I actually got to work with a lot of those guys."

Still, having wrestling as "the family business" was no guarantee of success. Second- (and third-) generation wrestlers often had the challenge of following in the footsteps of a successful father, and many (such as David Sammartino and Erik Watts) were never to escape the shadow of their famous fathers.

Fuller certainly felt it was an advantage. "It really helped because you got to see (wrestling) your entire life, and you grew up in it," he said. "You would be totally blown away by seeing wrestlers. You'd seen so many, and you looked at wrestlers a different way when you grew up in a wrestling family. You'd have respect for most all of 'em. They all worked their butts off to get where they got.

"My grandfather told me a lot of stories. He did a lot of shooting in his early career," Fuller said. "He built his wrestling company in Tennessee by shooting. He went into towns where they were having wrestling matches and basically shut them down. He'd go to the dressing room and kick the door open and say 'My name's Roy Welch and there's not a son of a bitch here who can wrestle. I don't ever want to see you call yourselves wrestlers again.' And if he had anybody that would give him shit, he took care of it right there in the dressing room. Then he would go to the other dressing room (heels and babyfaces kept separate locker rooms) and do the same thing. Then he'd find the promoter, he'd get the promoter by the throat and say 'This is my town from here on, and if you ever want to promote wrestling here again, don't do it because I'm comin' to getcha.' And he built one of the largest territories in the history of wrestling, 12 states, just a monstrous damn territory, by going in and strong-arming his way into owning it."

Becoming a professional wrestler, no matter the method, has never been easy. Most who dream about it and try never get close. Of those that do actually make it, very few go on to extended successful careers. And, of these few, only a handful can be called a true Wrestlers' Wrestler.

"A Wrestlers' Wrestler is someone who can go out there with anyone, on any night, whether they met before or not, and can make it not only look effortless but feel effortless when it comes to their opponent," said Al Snow. "They do the right thing, hit the right highs, get the right reaction. There has always been a saying that anyone can be a wrestler. Get someone a pair of boots and trunks and call them a wrestler. But to be a great *worker*, that's a skill. Not only to be a great performer, but be able to use somebody to work, and they work together, to generate drama, to tell a story and sell the outcome. They make the people believe the lie we're selling. We have a lot of incredible athletes, a lot of great performers, but a true great, the best, can convince an audience, and they are involved in it."

PART 2:
Bumpers, Shooters, and Psychologists

As wrestling progressed into the 1970s and 1980s, the effects television was having on the sport were impossible to ignore. Wrestlers accustomed to big, exaggerated movements that could be seen by fans in the cheap seats were having to alter their approach to play to the cameras at ringside. Having matches featured on television also meant wrestlers had to change things up, as opposed to working the same match around the horn as they had done in the 1950s and 1960s.

Television also rewarded "TV stars," not just cauliflower-eared grapplers. Credit Gorgeous George, Buddy Rogers, Haystacks Calhoun, or any or the scores of the gimmick wrestlers of the early days of television (such as "The French Angel" Maurice Tillet and the various "Germans" and "foreign menace" heels that crowded the ring at the time), but television audiences wanted some razzle-dazzle along with their rasslin'.

Wrestlers needed to become entertainers. Realism — while vitally important in the early days — was less important than it had been a generation earlier. Wrestlers needed to have a stage presence. They needed to be able to talk, to cut promos. They needed to be well-rounded athletes who could connect with fans in the balcony and fans on the BarcaLounger.

To set themselves apart from the pack, some grapplers doubled down on their pure technical skills, introducing British catch-as-catch-can style holds and locks. Others borrowed from the fast-paced acrobatic action of Lucha Libre in Mexico. Still others perfected the art of the bump, taking wild and exciting falls just as the match reached its crescendo and bringing the fans to their feet.

The hands and utility players of the 1970s and 1980s helped the territories survive and set the groundwork for televised wrestling as we know it today.

RAY STEVENS

Though he stood just five-foot-seven, "The Crippler" was a larger-than-life figure, both inside the ring and out.

"Through the '60s, '70s, and '80s, Ray was, as far as I was concerned, the most premier wrestling talent in the profession. Even better than me," Nick Bockwinkel told SLAM! Wrestling's Greg Oliver in a 2004 interview. "Now a lot of people get perplexed by that because I was the individual AWA Champion four times, let alone tag team champion three times with him. And if he was better than me, why wasn't he world champion? It's because Ray was the biggest kid in the world. He loved to play with toys. He accomplished what he did, so to speak, running at 53 throttle. I concentrated very hard, and in my concentration I guess I made up enough of the difference that I achieved the individual championship."

Ray Stevens lived a life of wine, women, and song. He was known to lament that all the time he spent in the ring cut into his drinking time. According to a popular aphorism heard in locker rooms during the 1960s and 1970s, "God takes care of those who don't take care of themselves, little children, small animals, and Ray Stevens."

With his tumultuous marriages, his barroom brawls, and his hard-drinking, carefree lifestyle, Stevens was — in the words of Northern California television announcer Walt Harris — "a little boy who never grew up."

Born Carl Raymond Stevens on September 5, 1935, in Point Pleasant, West Virginia, Stevens broke into the wrestling game in 1950 at the age of 15. He discovered wrestling growing up in Columbus, Ohio, and began hanging out at the Toe Hold Club wrestling training center. Despite

Ray "The Crippler" Stevens: one of the best bump-takers ever to grace the ring.

PHOTO BY GEORGE NAPOLITANO

being a short and heavyset teenager, Stevens was dead set on becoming a wrestler, and in time wrestlers Donn Lewin and Jim Henry began teaching him the basics. In his rookie year, he was already working a program with Gorgeous George. He was working main event matches by the age of 17.

Stevens shined as a tag team competitor, teaming with Roy Shire (as his "little brother," Ray Shire) and with Don Fargo. Stevens developed into a 235-pound fireplug of a competitor, a hard-nosed scrapper and one of the best bump-takers the business had ever seen.

"I hate to say this because Ric is a very dear friend of mine, but Ric Flair is a poor man's Ray Stevens," said Kevin Sullivan. "Stevens innovated the highspots. Before him, it was mostly ground attacks. You know the upside-down bump that Flair takes? He used to take that and before he went over the top, he'd be bleeding!" Stevens would blade himself mid-air so the blood would be free-flowing by the time he climbed back into the ring from the floor.

A heel for most of his career, Stevens broke through to the next level when he moved on to Big Time Wrestling in San Francisco in 1961.

In one of the most unforgettable angles of the era, Stevens ignited a red-hot feud with Pepper Gomez in 1962. In a display of his rock-hard abdominal muscles, Gomez had issued an open challenge, inviting wrestlers to jump off a ladder and stomp on his midsection to show he could withstand the attack with ease. Stevens accepted the challenge and — after a few jumps failed to affect Gomez — he climbed to the top of the ladder and dropped his "Bombs Away" knee drop instead of jumping feet-first.

The underhanded attack caused Gomez to spit up blood and put him out of action for weeks.

"When Gomez returned for his grudge match, it broke a record set by Elvis Presley for the largest crowd ever to attend an event at the Cow Palace in San Francisco — in excess of 17,000 fans — roughly 2,000 fans more than the building's capacity at the time, with thousands more turned away and a $65,000 house, which stood as a Northern California record for nearly 20 years," wrote Bryan Alvarez in the May 13, 1996, *Wrestling Observer Newsletter*.

That feud with Gomez — and the heat Stevens generated with fans in San Francisco — made "The Blond Bomber" perhaps the top draw in wrestling in 1961–62, regularly drawing turn-away crowds at the Cow Palace. He went on to have big-money feuds with Cowboy Bob Ellis, Bill Watts, Bobo Brazil, and Dick the Bruiser, among others. He also scored a count-out win over WWWF world champion Bruno Sammartino in 1967.

Stevens moved to the American Wrestling Association in 1971. There, he did an angle where he "broke the leg" of Dr. X (Dick Beyer), which caused the "Bombs Away" knee drop to be banned and led to Stevens earning the nickname "The Crippler." He won the AWA tag team title on four occasions — three with Nick Bockwinkel and one with Pat Patterson. He had a brief run in the WWF in the early 1980s, where he was managed by Freddie Blassie, but by that time, he was well past his prime. The decades of fast living had taken their toll. After a few matches in the AWA in the early 1990s, he quietly retired from the ring in 1992.

While he was widely known for his big bumps and deceptive grace and agility, Stevens was also very good at doing "the little things."

"He was so fluid and his punches looked so real. That's the thing today. I look at the punches that these guys are throwing. It looks like they can't break an egg," Sullivan said. "He was just a solid, solid wrestler. Ray Stevens may have been the greatest worker of all time."

In 1995, in recognition of Stevens's remarkable career in Northern California, Mayor Frank Jordan (San Francisco) and Mayor Joe Serna Jr. (Sacramento) proclaimed April 5 "Ray Stevens Day."

He died in his sleep on May 3, 1996. He was 60 years old.

"Stevens, I think, going through the 20th century, was the all-around best worker of any of them in the profession. "When I ask my cohorts about that, when I say, 'Who was the best?' — time and time again, it's Stevens," Bockwinkel said.

JOHNNY SAINT

Johnny Saint was known as "The Man of a Thousand Holds," but he probably knew 1,001 counters and even more escapes.

John Miller was born on June 29, 1941, in Failsworth, a small town in Greater Manchester, England. He took up boxing as a teenager until a chance meeting with Billy Robinson introduced him to the world of professional wrestling. He trained under Robinson and Scottish wrestling veteran George Kidd and made his wrestling debut in 1958, adopting the name ring name Johnny Saint.

A slender man at a billed five-foot-eight and about 154 pounds (or 11 stone), Saint blossomed into a technical virtuoso and one of the United Kingdom's top lightweight competitors. While he excelled at takedowns, dropkicks, and flying shoulder tackles, Saint also seemingly had a counter for any hold. His flashy reversals and escapes would delight the fans and leave foes flummoxed.

In one of his patented reversals, Saint would escape a test of strength-style lockup by lifting his left knee against his opponent's near wrist, turn into a hammerlock, leapfrog his opponent from behind, evade an angry charge by crawling through his opponent's legs, and then connect with a precision dropkick as soon as the opponent turned to face him.

If Saint was caught in an overhand wristlock, he would square his body up to his opponent, drop to the mat (creating space), and slide his right leg in between his opponent's outstretched arms, using the leg as a lever to break the grasp, then spring to his feet, catching his opponent's left wrist for a fluid transition into a standing wristlock.

All of these moves were done quickly, smoothly, and executed to look as "real" as any move in any more legitimate athletic contest.

Saint's innovative work went on to influence a generation of technicians. Daniel Bryan offered his assessment of Saint in a 2018 video released by WWE upon the announcement that Saint would serve as the general manager of NXT United Kingdom.

"Johnny Saint, amongst my generation of wrestlers — these were guys who grew up watching tapes, trying to learn as much as they could from tapes, because there weren't a lot of veterans around to learn from," Bryan said. "And when you talk about technical wizardry — and I'm someone who really appreciates technical wrestling — there is nobody better than Johnny Saint."

Saint was a fan favorite on England's World of Sport throughout the 1960s, 1970s, and 1980s. He won the British "world lightweight title" 10 times from 1976 through his retirement in 1996.

"Johnny Saint definitely was a Wrestlers' Wrestler. Back then, it was hard to be a top guy unless you were a Wrestlers' Wrestler," said Nigel McGuinness. "It's funny — you talk about 'spot monkeys' (today). It's really funny because most of those — if not all of those guys, and not just from World of Sport but you watch the old stuff in the territory days — they all had their spots. Yes, there was more punching and kicking because that's what the expectation for a wrestling match was back then. It was very different. And people weren't watching matches on DVD back and back again. You didn't have to change your match every time. They were able to have their spots. And a lot of the British guys — Johnny Saint was one of those guys as well — you watch two or three of his matches and you'll see a lot of the same stuff that he does. That's kind of his stuff. But it would work perfectly back then. And it probably would still today!"

Saint came out of retirement a handful of times, as the style he pioneered came into vogue with a new generation of technical grapplers. In 2008, he was invited to CHIKARA, where he faced CHIKARA founder Mike Quackenbush.

"Johnny Saint inserts elegant and clever moments into an artform that is usually smashmouth and violent in its presentation," Quackenbush said. "He supplies a contrast within the context of a single match that most wrestling lacks."

In 2009, Saint participated in CHIKARA's signature King of Trios six-man tournament, teaming with Quackenbush and Jorge "Skayde" Rivera as "The Masters of a Thousand Holds." They were eliminated from the tournament by the team of Bryan Danielson (Daniel Bryan), Claudio Castagnoli (Cesaro), and Dave Taylor.

"What made him a Wrestler's Wrestler is when he'd get gritty with his wrestling," Bryan said in a 2018 article on WWE.com. "I wrestled him when he was 60-something years old and was still absolutely phenomenal in the ring. He was so good at what he did, technique-wise."

In 2016, Saint was hired by WWE as a trainer at the Performance Center. In 2018, he was named general manager of NXT United Kingdom, receiving an on-screen authority figure role. A new generation is now benefitting from his knowledge and experience . . . this time, in person instead of through VHS tapes traded by the wrestlers.

BILLY ROBINSON

A true "Wrestlers' Wrestler" commands the respect of his peers . . . but that doesn't always mean he's the most popular guy backstage.

Case in point — Billy Robinson, the British shooter and "catch-as-catch-can" style master who literally wrote the book entitled *Physical Chess: My Life in Catch-as-Catch-Can Wrestling*.

Several wrestlers have gone on the record saying they hated facing the Englishman in the ring — making him unusual among the wrestlers in this book. He had a bad habit of stretching opponents he didn't respect.

"He wanted everyone in the world to think that wrestling was real because of his background," Dan Kroffat told SLAM! Wrestling. "He was a bully. He was an antagonistic sort of guy, he bullied guys, he stretched guys. He was really not a likeable guy."

"A really gentle gentleman outside the ring, is Billy. But he could be a bit vicious inside it," wrote "Mr. TV" Jackie Pallo in his 1985 autobiography, *You Grunt, I'll Groan*.

But Robinson was admired within the circle of shooters, and could do no wrong in the eyes of Verne Gagne, Lou Thesz, and Antonio Inoki, all of whom respected his submission technique. And if a wrestler stood up to his strongarm tactics in the ring, they were likely to win Robinson's grudging respect.

William Alfred "Billy" Robinson was born on September 18, 1938, in Manchester, England. He was born into a family of legitimate tough guys; his great-grandfather, uncle, and father were all boxers. But an eye injury suffered at age 11 prevented Billy from obtaining his boxing license, so he took up wrestling. By age 14, he was already tipping the scales at a powerful 180 pounds. He found work about 30 miles east of

Manchester at a wholesale fruit market in Wigan. He couldn't resist the draw of the notorious Wigan "Snake Pit" run by Billy Riley.

The Snake Pit developed out of the Lancashire sporting tradition of "catch wrestling." Unlike most other wrestling forms, there was no standard starting grip in catch (such as collar-and-elbow), so grapplers could use a variety of techniques. Bouts would end with a pinfall or a submission, and matches could last for hours until one man was declared the victor.

To excel in catch wrestling, a grappler had to be well-versed in every new fighting art that emerged, and the Snake Pit trained in all styles, gaining a reputation as a grueling school that quickly separated the men from the boys.

"My dad said, 'Look, if you're going to learn to wrestle, learn the best style that there is, the best form of fighting there is which is catch-as-catch-can wrestling. And the greatest gym in the world is in Wigan, run by a man called Billy Riley,'" Robinson later wrote.

After winning the British National Wrestling championship on the amateur mats in 1957 and the European Open Wrestling championship in 1958, he transitioned into the squared circle, eventually developing a unique hybrid style that combined hooks with flashy (though still technically precise) cradles and reversals, standing monkey flips, and somersaulting escapes; flamboyant flourishes that might have raised a few eyebrows in the Snake Pit but drew applause inside the squared circle.

Robinson was wrestling in Hawaii when Lord James Blears put him in touch with Verne Gagne and suggested that the English shooter could be a good fit in Minneapolis. Gagne concurred and brought Robinson into the American Wrestling Association, where he became one of Gagne's favorite opponents.

Robinson enjoyed his best run in the AWA through the 1970s, and wrestled a one-hour time-limit draw against then-WWF champion Bob Backlund in 1982, but he never got a world championship push from an American promotion. (He did hold the AWA British Empire championship three times until it was abandoned.) And there was a good reason he didn't.

"The people liked Billy, but I don't think that he would have drawn as a champion," said Greg Gagne in a 2019 Kayfabe Commentaries interview with Jim Cornette. "His personality on TV . . . it came across more arrogant, like the British do sometimes."

"Eddie Graham made a comment. We heard it from Kevin Sullivan that he was watching a Billy Robinson and Tony Charles match in Florida with Eddie Graham," Cornette recalled. "And Kevin said, 'Wow, this is the greatest wrestling I've ever seen.' And Eddie said, 'Yeah, it's good on the card but it's a shame it won't draw you any money on top.'"

Another reason Robinson never won the AWA crown may have been because Verne Gagne never fully trusted him. After all, if he put the belt on Robinson and Robinson decided he didn't want to cooperate, who could Gagne get to possibly take the belt off Robinson by force?

Robinson had his share of dust-ups outside the ring. His brawls with Dick the Bruiser and "High Chief" Peter Maivia have become the stuff of legend.

While technically proficient, and considered by many to be one of the top tough guys of the era, Robinson was lacking in both charisma and adaptability. When he was paired with another wrestler who couldn't keep up with his grappling, his matches were mediocre at best. But when he was paired up with a Thesz, Gagne, Inoki, or Nick Bockwinkel, Robinson truly shined and was one of the best pure wrestlers of his era.

Robinson's credentials earned him the respect and admiration of Inoki, and in 1975, the two squared off in a contest billed as "The Match Between the World's Top Two Technicians." The match went to a 60-minute draw and cemented Robinson's status as a grappling legend in Japan.

Robinson continued to compete until the mid-1980s, but by that time, his style had grown passé. He also looked out of a place in a business attracting more and more bodybuilders, though he always had a place in the AWA, which prized technique over physique.

His final match was a 10-minute exhibition against Bockwinkel for the fledgling UWF-I pro wrestling/shoot-style hybrid promotion in Yokohama, Japan, in May 1992. After retiring from the ring, he took up coaching and released a series of instructional videos, as well as his autobiography.

"I learned so very much from Billy, not just in holds or moves, but in philosophies towards wrestling," former UFC heavyweight champion

Billy Robinson, one of wrestling's all-time greatest technicians.

and Robinson protégé Josh Barnett posted online following Robinson's passing. "He taught me what I consider one of the most important aspects to becoming great at anything; 'You have to learn how to learn.'"

Robinson remained active as a coach into his 70s, even getting down on the mats with wrestlers young enough to have been his grandchildren, despite hip replacements, knee replacements, and neck surgery.

He died on March 3, 2014, at the age of 75.

YOSHIAKI FUJIWARA

Antonio Inoki always presented himself as an elite shoot fighter. He was, after all, the man who went toe-to-toe with Muhammad Ali — or, more accurately, *foot-to-shin*, as Inoki spent that entire 1976 crab-walking to avoid Ali's reach and throwing kicks at Ali's legs. Still, Inoki was a student of Karl Gotch, and was the man who popularized strong-style wrestling.

And, throughout the 1970s, Yoshiaki Fujiwara was his bodyguard. As tough as Inoki was, Fujiwara was tougher.

"The word *kagemusha* means 'double,'" said historian and writer Fumi Saito, co-host of the *Pacific Rim* podcast. "Way back in the ancient Samurai period, your Shogun usually had a *kagemusha* who looked like him to protect himself from being assassinated. Inoki took Fujiwara under his wing to be his *kagemusha*, his double. They always dressed alike. He was Inoki's training partner, he carried Inoki's bag for 12 years. He was the best shoot wrestler in the New Japan dojo."

Born April 27, 1949, Fujiwara studied judo and Muay Thai kick-boxing before enrolling in the New Japan Pro-Wrestling dojo in 1972. He trained under Gotch and Inoki and quickly took to the submission grappling they taught. Gotch called him his star pupil. He was the first graduate of the New Japan dojo and established himself as the dojo's resident enforcer. "Any karate fighter who came to the dojo, Fujiwara would break his arm" to protect the business, Saito said. "When Inoki went to Brazil, Pakistan, the Philippines, South Korea, when you go on an international tour like that, you never know what's going to happen. Fujiwara was always standing right next to Inoki and he'd take a bullet for him if he had to."

In 1975, Fujiwara won the Karl Gotch Cup tournament, a precursor to what would become the Young Lion Cup. But despite his technical skills, he remained on the undercard and was not featured on New Japan television until the early 1980s. Inoki was the flashy, handsome star. Fujiwara was content to stay in the background, content in the knowledge that he could submit virtually any opponent or enemy at any time.

Fujiwara took pride in having the "hardest head in wrestling" and, during a feud with the equally hard-headed "Bad News" Allen Coage (who had trained at the New Japan dojo), Fujiwara would repeatedly slam his head full force into the steel corner post to show off.

In 1984, Fujiwara was placed into a high-profile angle when he laid out New Japan's top villain, Riki Choshu. Fujiwara became one of New Japan's most popular stars, but after that program, he jumped to the newly established Universal Wrestling Federation, which was promoting a more realistic mixed-martial-arts-based style. The UWF fizzled out after a couple years, and Fujiwara returned to New Japan, chasing Inoki's IWGP title. In 1986, he and Inoki teamed to win the NJPW Cup tournament.

In 1989, Fujiwara again left New Japan and tried to get a new version of the UWF (Newborn UWF) up off the ground. When that flopped, he created Pro Wrestling Fujiwara-Gumi, a shoot-style, gangland-type promotion and stable. He brokered talent exchanges with several promotions and ran a major show at the Tokyo Dome in 1992. The company disintegrated a couple years later when most of the roster jumped ship to start the BattlARTS promotion and Fujiwara returned home to New Japan.

In recent years, he has had success as an actor in Japanese movies and on television. He is frequently called Kumicho, a title similar to "godfather" in the Mafia, as a sign of respect. He was a major influence in the early MMA movement in Japan and trained Minoru Suzuki and Masakatsu Funaki, who went on to found the Pancrase promotion. He wrote a book and released instructional DVDs based on the lessons he learned from Gotch, passing on that knowledge to subsequent generations of grapplers. He even tested his shoot fighting skills by wrestling an unmuzzled bear outdoors; the bear got the better of that match-up. He innovated the Fujiwara armbar, which was named in his honor and remains a popular and effective finisher. As a testament to his stamina and conditioning, he was still wrestling occasionally at the age of 70.

"Fujiwara and Karl Gotch are very similar because they're not shiny, superstar types," Saito said. "But they are the best and the boys all know it. They all know their own ability and Fujiwara always sat there smiling because he knew he was the best."

DICK MURDOCH

Much like Ray Stevens, Dick Murdoch was widely regarded to be one of the best workers of his era, but his hell-raising habits and double-fisted beer drinking kept him away from world title consideration.

"Dick Murdoch would go at 50 percent on some nights. He would go 70 percent some nights. But at 95 and 100 (percent), there was no one who could touch him. Period," said Dusty Rhodes, Murdoch's former tag team partner, in an interview on Steve Austin's podcast.

"One of the best workers in the world when he wanted to be," Jim Cornette said of Murdoch in a 2017 podcast episode.

Hoyt Richard Murdoch was born August 16, 1946, in Waxahachie, Texas. His stepfather, Frankie Hill Murdoch, had held the NWA Southwestern junior heavyweight title and had feuded with Dory Funk Sr. in the Amarillo territory.

Dick grew up in Amarillo and took up wrestling in high school. In 1965, he made his pro wrestling debut in the Gulf Coast territory under the name Ron Carson, billed as the brother of Don Carson. Before long, he dropped the Carson surname and began competing as Dick Murdoch. In 1968, he fell in with Dusty Rhodes, and the Texas Outlaws were born. The Outlaws were a pair of beer-drinking good ol' boys, and they found success in the Kansas City, Detroit, Toronto, Ohio, and Florida territories until Rhodes split to Michigan to try his hand as a singles competitor.

By March 1969, Murdoch was already earning world title bouts against NWA champion Dory Funk Jr., going around the horn with Funk that spring. In April 1971, Murdoch beat Dory's little brother Terry Funk to win the NWA Florida Southern heavyweight title. Though he never had an athlete's physique, Murdoch had the right blend of raw-boned power, technical know-how, and surprising stamina that made him an upper-midcard player — and a credible world title challenger — for the NWA throughout the 1970s.

"Dick Murdoch truly, at the time, was one of the best punchers in the business," Kevin Sullivan said. "He taught me to tie a soup can up with a string and to hit that soup can until it didn't move. After some practice, I could throw people into the ropes and then go off the ropes and hit 'em square in the jaw and not touch 'em. In today's age, I'm seeing more fore-arms and I'm glad to see it. If you don't punch (well) it looks horrible. With an elbow to the head, you can kind of cover up, no matter what. It's going to have connection. But a punch to the head looks really silly."

Murdoch's abilities were also greatly appreciated in Japan and he completed several tours of Japan throughout the 1970s and 1980s, wrestling in both All Japan Pro Wrestling and New Japan. In May 1978, he wrestled Harley Race to a 60-minute draw in Chiba, a bout that cemented his reputation as a world championship–caliber competitor in Japan.

Murdoch had a run as a babyface in Mid-South Wrestling in the early 1980s and jumped to the WWF in 1984 and won a WWF tag team title with Adrian Adonis. After Murdoch and Adonis dropped the belts to the U.S. Express (Barry Windham and Mike Rotunda), Murdoch returned to Mid-South and then on to Jim Crockett Promotions in 1986. As a baby-face, "Captain Redneck" became the top contender to Ric Flair's world title, facing Flair several times that year. But as the 1980s came to a close, Murdoch's best years were behind him. He continued making tours of New Japan (facing Antonio Inoki for the IWGP heavyweight title in 1987) and earned some shots at Steve Williams's Universal Wrestling Federation title that year, but his days as a main-eventer were coming to a close.

After a stint in Puerto Rico's World Wrestling Council, Murdoch returned to Jim Crockett Promotions and was placed in a tag team called the Hardline Collection Agency with fellow grizzled vet Dick Slater. The Hardliners had a series of stiff matches with the Steiner Brothers in 1991 but were unable to win the NWA tag team title.

Murdoch's final high-profile appearance was a surprise spot at the 1995 WWF Royal Rumble in Tampa.

He died of a heart attack on June 15, 1996. He was 49.

BUDDY ROBERTS

Michael Hayes was the promo man. Terry Gordy was the powerhouse. Buddy Roberts? In a lot of ways, he was the straw that stirred the Jack Daniel's.

"Buddy was the guy it took a little longer to appreciate," Mick Foley wrote in a 2013 blog post, following Roberts's death. "I'm not sure if I appreciated him at first. I was in the Garden in New York City the night (the Freebirds) made their sole appearance. . . . Out came this legendary team I'd been reading about for years in *PWI*, and to tell you the truth, I wasn't that impressed — mainly by Buddy. I was less than a year away from entering the wrestling business myself, and looking at Buddy, I thought I had a realistic shot at him. But that was actually part of his charm. Half the audience on any given night in the Sportatorium probably thought they had a reasonable shot against him — yet there he was, on a weekly basis, creating mayhem, delivering cheap shots, dishing out punishment to the heroic Von Erichs.

"When I did get into the business, in the spring of 1985, and slowly came to learn the inner working of the business — or at least the inner workings of the workers in the business, I came to marvel at Buddy Roberts. He was the guy who took the beating. He was the guy who dropped the fall, but somehow maintained his heat. He would do anything to make his matches exciting — including the rumored dropping of the first elbow off the ring apron. He could make anyone and anything around him look better. If someone around him was bad, he could make them look good. If they were good, he could make them look great. And if something was great — like The Fabulous Freebirds — he could help turn greatness to legend."

Dale Hey was born in Oklahoma on June 16, 1947, and grew up in Vancouver, British Columbia. He broke into wrestling in 1965, training under Ivan Koloff, and debuted under the name of Dale Valentine, the "brother" of Johnny Valentine.

Hey got his first major break in 1970, when promoter Bill Watts paired him up with Jerry Brown as the Hollywood Blonds. Watts changed Hey's name to Buddy Roberts, and the Blonds were off and running. Along with manager Oliver Humperdink (who joined the Blonds in Montreal in 1972), the team went on to win multiple titles throughout the 1970s, including the NWA Americas title (on four occasions), the Mid-Atlantic tag title, the NWA Florida tag title (twice), and the AWA Southern tag title.

But Roberts hit the big time after the Blonds split up, when Bill Watts joined Roberts up with Hayes and Gordy in 1979. Hayes had the charisma, but was green as grass. Gordy had the athleticism, but was still a wet-behind-his-ears teenager. Buddy Jack (so-named because of his legendary affinity for Jack Daniel's whiskey) was the wily veteran who took the young 'birds under his wing.

The Freebirds became one of the hottest heel acts in the business following the events of December 25, 1982, when Gordy slammed the door of a steel cage into Kerry Von Erich's cranium, robbing him of an NWA world title victory over Ric Flair. The subsequent Von Erichs/ Freebirds feud was wrestling's greatest rivalry of the era and one of the most successful of all time.

"Buddy was the technician of the Freebirds. He could work with anyone and any style," said James Beard, the referee for many of the Freebirds' matches in World Class Championship Wrestling. "And he could lose over and over and never lose his heat. That factor was extremely valuable to the Freebirds team because it saved Michael and Terry from having to do jobs until the time was right and gave them a perfect foil to give fans satisfaction without affecting the perception of the team. Buddy was often the instigator the fans hated most.

"Great heels always came across as believing they were right in doing the things they'd do, even if, in reality, no logical person would do those things and believe that it was okay," Beard said. "He was the guy who would always let his actions and his mouth get him in trouble and because of the brother-like relationship among the Freebirds, the other two could excuse their actions by defending the honor of their brother, even as obviously wrong he may have been. It was a perfect system for getting heat as a three-man team. Buddy was the key to making that work over and over again."

In his most memorable angle, Roberts "lost his hair" after his head was slathered with the infamous "Freebird hair cream," supposedly a super-powerful depilatory. Roberts took to wearing a ridiculous wig, held in place by boxing headgear, to hide the shame of his "baldness."

The comedy angle was a testament to Roberts's versatility as a performer. When the moment called for it, he could be the grizzled veteran tough guy, the conniving and cowardly heel, or the clown. He could pull off any role.

The Freebirds briefly joined the WWF in 1984 (hence the appearance at Madison Square Garden) but left the for the AWA and on to the Universal Wrestling Federation. Roberts had a singles run as the UWF TV champion in 1986 and retired from wrestling in 1988. He briefly managed the Samoan Swat Team in World Class before leaving wrestling for good once WCCW ceased operations.

Roberts died of pneumonia on November 26, 2012, following a lengthy battle with throat cancer. He was 65 years old. He was post-humously inducted into the WWE Hall of Fame as a member of the Fabulous Freebirds in 2016.

ADRIAN STREET

Like an iron fist in a velvet glove.

It's an apt description of "Exotic" Adrian Street, the coal miner's son and Welsh tough guy who became wrestling's glammiest gender bender during the 1970s and 1980s.

Street stood only five-foot-seven (well, a few inches higher if you measured him to the top of his pigtails), but beneath the makeup, the prancing, and all the frills and glitter was one of the toughest pound-for-pound wrestlers of his era.

Born December 5, 1940, in Brynmawr, Brecknockshire, in South Wales, he followed in his father's coal-cracking footsteps, working in the dank, frigid mines, swinging a pickaxe six days a week. He quickly decided that mining — a life of backbreaking labor where workplace disputes were settled with bare-knuckle fights — wasn't the life he wanted to live.

He dropped out of school and headed to London to find fame and fortune. A bodybuilding enthusiast since he was 11 years old, Street found work as a model for muscle magazines and a low-level prize-fighter, earning a pound per fight for a touring carnival. He literally fought to survive.

As he worked out in the gyms of London, Street met some area wrestlers and began training under Chic Osmond and Mike Demitre. He wrestled his first match in August 1957 under the name Kid Jonathan; he was 16 years old.

As a young man, Street had a front row view as post-war London entered the "Swinging Sixties." The city became an epicenter of fashion, art, and youth culture, and Street embraced it in full.

In 1962, he reinvented his look. He grew out his hair and died it platinum-blond and began wearing a blue velvet gown with silver lamé and adopted what we might call today a more "sexually ambiguous" persona. "Exotic" Adrian Street elicited an immediate reaction from fans. He was taking Gorgeous George's gimmick and dialing it up to 11. He became a wrestling glam-rock star before anyone ever heard of glam rock. He continued to add to his unique look with makeup, glitter, rhinestones, and the flashiest costumery he could find (or make himself).

In 1969, he met Linda Gunthorpe Hawker, who would become his valet, "Miss Linda." His pairing with Miss Linda gave a new dimension to his persona — fans couldn't tell if he was gay or straight . . . all they knew was he was one freaky dude.

In 1981, Street took his act to Calgary, where the prancing Welshman must have seemed like he came from a different planet than the farmhands and cowboys of Alberta.

"About a year and a half after I brought Dynamite over, Ted Bentley called me up and said he had a couple other guys he wanted to send over; it was Davey Boy, who I had met in England, the other was Adrian Street," said Bruce Hart, who was coordinating talent exchanges for Stampede Wrestling. "I had wrestled in England and had heard of Adrian. He was, well, kind of flamboyant. He was kind of a mix between Gorgeous George and Boy George.

"When he arrived, I had never seen him before and he was so small, height-wise, but you could tell he was a true professional," Hart said. "English wrestlers, in general, they did very little on the mic, so for all intents and purposes they had to be technically sound. When Adrian arrived in Calgary, he was already established. He was very stabilizing with the young guys and he fit right in with the veterans we had. On road trips, Adrian, and guys like the Cuban Assassin and Ron Starr, they were tirelessly imparting the little things. It's the little things that make the big things in this business. And those had a profound impact on people like Bret, and Davey Boy, and Dynamite, and Benoit, too. They were able to pick up on some of those subtleties that are essential and a lot of people, at first glance, comprehend."

Street went on tours of Mexico and California, and had an extended run in the American Southeast. "Cowboy" Johnny Mantell worked a brief program with Street in Mid-South Wrestling, but a disagreement with the booker ended the feud prematurely and sent Mantell off to World Class Championship Wrestling.

"Bill Watts wanted me and Adrian to work this little angle in Mid-South, so we started working around the loop," Mantell said. "I loved working with him. Our playbook was wide open, as we both wanted people to believe. . . . (Working with) Adrian was a night off."

Street was also willing to do what he could to make his opponent look good. One wrestler who benefitted from his willingness to cooperate was "Handsome" Jimmy Valiant.

"Jimmy was a great showman and extremely popular with the fans, but if he'd been hung for being a wrestler, he would have died innocent," Street wrote in *Violence is Golden*, one of his series of self-published autobiographies. "Before our very first contest he came up to me in the dressing room and told me, 'Hey Brother, we're rasslin' each other tonight. You're a great wrassler, but I don't know how to get into those holds. I don't know how to get out of them. So if you get me locked up in any of those holds of yours, I'll be there until you let me loose.' I was surprised by his honesty. 'Don't worry, Jimmy,' I told him. 'We'll get by — I'll show you a few things that will actually make you look as though you know what you're doing.'"

In the ring, Street would play his gimmick to the hilt, drawing remarkable heat from the "less-than-woke" fans of the era. Entering the ring to the song "Imagine What I Could Do to You" (which he wrote and recorded himself) Street would strut, twirl his boa, thrust his hips, and blow kisses to the crowd. Miss Linda would take her time helping him remove his robe, wristbands, and other accoutrements, and then he would skip around the ring before locking up with his opponent. Sometimes he would even surprise his foe with a big sloppy kiss on the lips. But once that bit of showmanship was done, Street would batter opponents with forearms, kicks, and chops (with Miss Linda interfering whenever possible). When the babyface made the inevitable comeback, Street begged off and bumped like a master, making every opponent look like the world's strongest man.

Even though he was pushing boundaries, Street was steadfast in protecting the business. In 1971, he was matched up against television personality Jimmy Savile. Street balked at the idea of facing a celebrity non-wrestler. When the match happened, Street pulled a shoot, savagely attacking the DJ and TV personality.

"I kicked his legs from underneath him so he hit the deck, then I picked him up by his hair, held him upside down and dropped him on his skull," Street told WalesOnline in 2013.

Street held the NWA Southeastern title five times and inspired a generation of wrestlers (Adrian Adonis and Goldust) and musicians (Marc Bolan and David Bowie are said to have been influenced by Street's fashion).

He retired in 2014 and ran the Skull Krushers Wrestling School in Florida, then designed custom wrestling ring gear. Wherever he was on the card, Street always shone brightly, and he never failed to get a rise out of the fans.

"Guys like Adrian, there aren't enough of them in our business today," Hart said. "There are a few still kicking around, Dave Finlay, William Regal. I hope they are valued by the young guys."

RIP ROGERS

For 23 years, "The Hustler" was one of wrestling's most underrated and well-traveled journeymen. From the heartland of Seymour, Indiana, to the wrestling rings of Europe, Japan, and Puerto Rico, Rip Rogers made the towns, did the jobs, and always made an impression.

Rogers was born Mark Sciarra in Seymour, Indiana, on February 7, 1954. He became a wrestling fan at a young age and was a card-carrying member of the Jimmy Valiant fan club. After graduating from Indiana Central College, where he played football and baseball, he decided to try his hand at wrestling. He worked a few matches on the local circuit before Paul Christy put in a good world for him with Angelo Poffo, who ran the International Championship Wrestling outfit out of Lexington, Kentucky. There, he worked closely with Poffo and his sons, Randy and Lanny.

"Every principle I got I pretty much learned from your family," he told Lanny Poffo in a 2017 episode of the podcast *The Genius Cast*. "I was always a laid-back guy. I learned intensity from Randy."

Still new to wrestling, having virtually walked into the business off the street, he kept quiet and soaked up knowledge wherever he could, earning a Ph.D. in wrestling knowledge out on the road. He won the ICW tag team titles with Pez Whatley and Gary Royal, defending the belts under the "Freebird Rule" (allowing any two members of a three-man team to defend the title at their discretion). He had a short run in Nick Gulas's promotion in Nashville as the Disco Kid, then wound up in Mississippi, where the Great Mephisto christened him Rip Rogers.

"The Hustler" nickname came a bit later.

"Buddy Rose and I were at a newsstand, looking at some of the magazines," Rogers said. "He sees *Playboy* magazine and he says, 'That's it. I'm going to call myself "Playboy" Buddy Rose.' So I became 'Hustler' Rip Rogers. And that's that."

Rogers also took up bodybuilding and adopted an intense workout regimen of his own design.

"I was nuts. I would do 300 reps (for) every body part every day, with light weights with minimal rest. Sometimes sets of 100. A normal guy can't do that," Rogers said. "Guys would try to train with me, and I'd say, 'You can't do that.' And they'd barf right there. And I'd say, 'I've done this for a while.'"

(Author's note: I can verify Roger's dedication to training. In 2019, during the Cauliflower Alley Club reunion in Las Vegas, I went in for an early-morning workout at the fitness center at the Gold Coast Hotel and Casino. Rogers was there, lifting and doing cardio, while wrestlers half his age were still sleeping off the previous night's hijinks. —Dan Murphy)

Rogers worked the Pacific Northwest with Rose and Ed "Colonel DeBeers" Wiskoski, with forays farther north into Vancouver and Western Canada.

"I traveled with Rip in Atlantic Canada, but I never worked with him because we were both heels," said wrestler and trainer Ron Hutchison. "He was just as entertaining outside the ring as he was inside, just a funny, funny guy. And frugal. Very frugal. If you wanted to learn how to survive on the road and come home with money in your pocket, all you had to do was follow Rip's lead."

Rogers was a rolling stone that gathered no moss in the 1980s, bouncing around between Jim Crockett Promotions, the Continental Wrestling Association, the Central States territory, Florida, the Gulf Coast, and Stampede up in Calgary. He also made his first tour of Japan, wrestling for All Japan Pro Wrestling against the likes of Tiger Mask, Genichiro Tenryu, the Great Kabuki, and John "Earthquake" Tenta in 1988. He won the World Wrestling Council Caribbean title in Puerto Rico in 1989 and made brief appearances in World Championship Wrestling, the Global Wrestling Federation (where he participated in the light heavyweight, TV, and tag team (with Scott "Raven" Anthony) title tournaments, Smoky Mountain Wrestling, Germany's Catch Wrestling Association, and the WWF.

With his hot-pink tights, flashy jackets, and platinum-blond hair, Rogers had the look to stand out from the pack everywhere he went. He was confident in the ring, and vocal, always playing to the camera, jaw-jacking the crowd. But his begging off and selling made him a perfect "job guy" to make the local talent look their best.

"I learned to take your normal bumps and oversell them," Rogers said.

By 1997, Rogers had put down roots in Ohio Valley Wrestling, where he captured the OVW heavyweight title on three occasions. However, Rogers's wrestling career came to an end in 2000, when he was hit by a car, sustaining career-ending injuries.

He remained with OVW as a trainer, passing on his mastery of ring psychology, fundamentals, and showmanship to the likes of John Cena, Randy Orton, and Batista.

"Rip was wily," said Sinn Bodhi, who trained under "The Hustler" in the WWE developmental system. "He wanted the details to be on point. He wanted you to understand the moment. Who cares about the moves? You can do a suplex here, or a suicide dive, or an abdominal stretch, or whatever move. The important thing is *the moment* — know when to be angry, when to beg off, when to be scared, when to dig deep and rally back. That's the key to the fire. That's the key to the heat. That's what makes wrestling *wrestling*. If I'm doing a move to you and you're doing a move to me, and then it's my turn, and we're both fine, that's not wrestling. It's Ping-Pong. Then the moves don't matter and the fans wander off to go buy pizza. The wrestlers have to understand the moments, and Rip was a stickler for that."

DAVE FINLAY

"Wrestling is my passion. It's my life. It's how I survive."

Wrestling runs deep in the Finlay family. David "Fit" Finlay's father was a pro wrestler, promoter, and Olympic wrestling coach. His grandfather was a wrestler. And his son, David, is a wrestler, currently competing for New Japan Pro-Wrestling.

Finlay was born on January 31, 1958, in Belfast, Northern Ireland. One day, at the age of 14, young David was pressed into service and asked to perform when another wrestler failed to show up for a card.

"My dad was running a little show, it was in a little tiny, tiny village in Northern Ireland," Finlay told *Pro Wrestling Illustrated* in a 2011 interview. "There might have been maybe 20 houses in the village at that time. There was a rugby club and they put up this big tent for our event, a fundraiser. My dad and I and a couple others were putting the ring up in the afternoon. I was just having fun. I loved being around wrestling and that's what I'd done all my boyhood years, being around him and helping him put up the ring. Nighttime came around and someone didn't show up, and he's looking around the locker room when he looks at me. 'You. You're gonna have to wrestle. You're gonna have to go.' So, of course, I'm 14 years old, I had to put my dad's boots on, all of his wrestling gear, and it's all way too big for me, of course. Of course, I'd had people teaching me, but that was my very first match in front of anybody, so I was thrown into the deep end and that was the start of it. It snowballed from there."

Finlay began to wrestle full-time throughout Ireland, and also helped his father coach his amateur wrestling teams. He also trained in — and taught — judo. "(Wrestling) has always been there," he said. "Pass it along, give a few hints. Anyone I've crossed paths with who has asked me for advice, I'm happy to give it. Sometimes, I give it unasked; some people need to be redirected."

After a few years in Ireland, Finlay moved to England, where he won the British heavy middleweight championship in 1982, his first title. More titles followed in rapid succession, including the British light heavyweight title, the British heavy middleweight title, and the British heavyweight title. He had rivalries with a young Steven (William) Regal, Steve Wright, Mark "Rollerball" Rocco, Marty Jones, and Danny Collins. He completed tours of Japan (where he was able to face Terry Funk and Bob Orton Jr.) and toured Europe with the Catch Wrestling Association for a decade until he finally got an opportunity to compete in the U.S. In 1995, he joined World Championship Wrestling as "The Belfast Bruiser." It didn't take long for him to rekindle his rivalry with Regal. However, it was hard for Finlay to gain traction in the talent-heavy WCW.

"WCW really didn't know what to do with my style," he said. "It was like, 'What is this guy, he's so aggressive.' Ric Flair didn't want to get in the ring with me because he thought I was tearing people's heads off, and that's the image that I portrayed, that I *was* going to rip your head off. And it looked like that."

Fit Finlay wearing the WCW TV title in 1998.

PHOTO BY GEORGE NAPOLITANO

Ironically, for a wrestler with superior technical and mat wrestling abilities, Finlay was stuck in WCW's hardcore division, where he sustained a gruesome injury when he was slammed through a Formica-topped table, an injury which almost cost him his leg and kept him sidelined for five months. After WCW closed in 2001, Finlay was brought in to WWE as an agent. He was instrumental in helping WWE build its women's division, helping the company move away from exploitive "bra and panties" matches and into competitive contests that set the groundwork for the "women's revolution" in the 2010s. "Fit Finlay has done more for women's wrestling than most women have," said Sarah Logan.

But his competitive fire hadn't burned out.

"All I was doing was training people and taking care of everybody and doing what producers do. I'd been sitting on the sidelines watching, and I just got itchy feet again," he said. "Vince and I came to an agreement that I would have another go in the ring, and that's basically what it was. I got itchy feet. I got sick of sitting outside watching people doing this when I think I can do it as good, or possibly even better, than most of them."

So, at age 47, Finlay started with WWE, billed as "a man who loves to fight." With his stiff, mat-based style, innovative offense (including the spot where he entangles an opponent in the ring apron and batters them while they're helpless), he got over in WWE, where he enjoyed solid feuds with Chris Benoit and Bobby Lashley.

Naturally, being Irish wasn't enough of a gimmick in WWE, so "The Belfast Bruiser" was paired with his own "leprechaun," Hornswoggle. Somehow, Finlay managed to make it work and went on to win the U.S. title from Lashley in 2006. Finlay turned babyface in 2008 when he protected Hornswoggle from Vince McMahon when Hornswoggle was revealed as McMahon's "illegitimate son." Finlay later "admitted" that Hornswoggle was his son and that they had been in cahoots with a harebrained plan to humiliate the McMahon family.

"Using Hornswoggle as heel I felt was a great thing, but I knew it wasn't going to last. People were going to start cheering me because they liked the little guy, they liked the stuff we did. It was obvious that it wouldn't be long until I was a babyface," he said. "I enjoyed it. I had never been a babyface in my life. I had never had people cheering for me or clapping for me; in fact, I was offended if they did. It was a bit of a transition to be in that situation, but I embraced it and we went with it. I had fun and I enjoyed it. It probably didn't do much for the character of Finlay that I had built over 30 years, but we had a lot of fun, and every little ha-ha spot that Hornswoggle did was all my idea. I ran with it and made the most of it. I'd rather be pulling people's heads off and throwing them away, though."

In 2010, Finlay began a transition from the ring to the office, resuming his duties as a backstage agent. He was released by WWE in 2011 after he greenlit an angle where the Miz interrupted the national anthem on a house show — and angle designed to get heat that worked too well — but he was brought back into the fold in 2012, after a short farewell run on the independents.

"My philosophy throughout my career was that no matter where I went, no matter who wanted me in whatever country or whatever promotion, I basically kept my same style throughout my career," Finlay said. "You have to adapt somewhat, you have to fit in a little bit, but I think I stayed true to my style and my upbringing and my European background. . . . You've got to stay true to who you are."

BOB ORTON JR.

It's rare in the world of athletics that someone achieves their greatest fame and success once they are past their athletic prime, but this was indeed the case with Bob Orton Jr.

Most wrestling fans under the age of 40 remember "Cowboy" Bob Orton, also known as "Ace," the bodyguard of Roddy Piper in the Hulkamania-era of the WWF's dominance of the wrestling world. Orton was the brooding figure standing behind Piper in "Piper's Pit," with his ever-present arm cast from a break that never seemed to heal.

But before his days as a role player, Bob Orton Jr. was one of the most underrated Wrestlers' Wrestlers of all time.

"You want to know who was really good? Bob Orton Jr.," said Paul Orndorff, who wrestled against and alongside "Cowboy" Bob during the mid-1980s. "I worked with him in my early days, then again with Vince. Man, I loved working with him. He was tough. He was really good."

Pro wrestling flows through the bloodline of the Orton family. "The Big O" Bob Orton Sr. was a star in the NWA Florida territory, winning the tag team title with Eddie Graham. The elder Orton didn't want his sons to follow him into the ring, but the lure of the ring nevertheless reached his two sons, Bob Jr and Barry. Bob Jr. eventually became an even bigger success than his father.

Dropping out of college and trained by legendary Hiro Matsuda, Bob Orton Jr. entered the territory where his father was already a star. Calling himself "Young Mr. Wrestling" and sometimes appearing as the Invader, a masked wrestler, Orton from the start showed that he was not a carbon copy of his old man. Junior was more a pure athlete who could execute more scientific wrestling moves, but also get heat with psychology.

Orton Jr., like his father, became a great tag team competitor, not only with his father, with whom he won the NWA Florida tag team title, but more famously with Bob Roop. "Bobby was a genius in the ring. We traveled just me and him, we'd talk about our match all the way to a town. We'd drink beer on the way back, but we would also, still talk about the match we just had," Roop said.

The team of Orton and Roop won multiple tag team titles together and were trusted by promoters and bookers because of their professionalism, in-ring ability, and brain for the business. Roop explained, "The booker would have a full card of matches to come up with and he could come up and say, after just a few matches with us, 'You know what you got to do, right?' And we could say, 'Do you want a count-out? A DQ? What?' And if he'd say, 'I want you to get (the other team) over,' fine, we could do that, too. He was good with letting us do our own thing because he knew we could get someone over and still keep our heat."

After success in Florida, Georgia, Mid-South, and other NWA territories, Orton went to the growing WWF in 1981 and even challenged champion Bob Backlund for the heavyweight title on two occasions (winning by count out, a non-title-changing way to beat the champ) in their first match.

In 1983, Orton returned to the NWA, where he took part in an angle where newly crowned champ, Harley Race, put a bounty on the head of former champ Ric Flair. Orton had been a babyface at the time, and a friend of Flair, until the night he and Dick Slater attacked Flair, re-establishing him as a vicious heel.

When that storyline concluded, Orton returned to the WWF, and it was during this run that he would gain his lasting fame. As Cowboy Bob Orton, Piper's bodyguard, Orton played a major role in the first *WrestleMania* as the cornerman for Piper and Paul Orndorff. It was Ace's attempted interference (accidentally hitting Orndorff with his ubiquitous cast) that cost his team the match. This incident set up a feud between Orton and Orndorff.

"We had some good matches then," Orndorff said. "Orton was good. He was better than Hogan, for real. Don't get me wrong, we were all good. We had to be then. But Bob, yeah, he was just good, you know? And he didn't mind doing the job, no questions. I look at

Underrated and innovative, "Cowboy" Bob Orton Jr. was ahead of his time.

PHOTO BY GEORGE NAPOLITANO

pictures and stuff from then. I'm looking at them now, in fact. I miss those days. It was fun."

In addition to being an underrated wrestler, Orton was also quite inventive in the ring. He is credited with popularizing the "super-plex" suplex off the top rope, a move he used as his primary finisher in the WWF. He and tag team partner Dick Slater also innovated several double-team moves that were later adopted by teams like the Midnight Express.

Orton's career continued both in and out of the WWF, including appearances in WCW, New Japan, and the independents. He wrestled as recently as 2015.

Today, Orton is best known as the father of third-generation star Randy Orton, one of WWE's top stars of the past 20 years.

"If you ever go back and watch any of Bob Orton's matches, he invents so much stuff on the fly," said wrestler and student of the game "Brutal" Bob Evans. "He actually did a very primitive version of the

RKO in 1986 against 'Leaping' Lanny Poffo in a house show match in Landover, Maryland. Just on the fly. Just grabbed him in a chancery and dropped because it seemed like the right thing to do. I thought it was funny because that's the move his son is so identified with. He would do stuff like that all the time.

"One time, him and Pedro Morales — they were in Boston one night and in New York the next night and they had two completely different matches," Evans said. "One was technical and one was just a fight. I have a lot of admiration for him. I'm not anywhere as good as him but I always tried to pattern the way I work after him. He's a guy who can invent stuff on the fly and kind of go with the punches, and knows what to do all the time."

TERRY TAYLOR

In 1985, Terry Taylor was the reigning NWA North American heavy-weight champion, the top dog in the Mid-South territory, and the heir apparent to Ric Flair's world championship.

Three years later, he was a rooster. A Little Red Rooster, to be exact.

Taylor was an elite wrestler who got saddled with one of the most infamously lousy gimmicks in wrestling history, and his career never quite recovered. But before we get to "Poultry in Motion," let's look back to when Taylor was one of wrestling's hottest young up-and-coming stars.

Paul Taylor as born August 12, 1955, in Greenville, South Carolina. He played football at Guilford College. He wrestled his first match in 1979, debuting on television before he even learned how to bump.

"It was such a close-knit fraternity that you had to have a connection or were related to somebody," Taylor told SLAM! Wrestling in 2014. "And I had a friend who I knew in college who broke into the business, and he was in a match one night in West Palm Beach, and he took me back to the locker room with him and introduced me to all my heroes. I mean, I was a huge wrestling fan . . . They were all very nice to me and I guess they thought I was a wrestler. Then Steve (Travis) said, 'Why don't you come to TV on Wednesday in Tampa?' And I did. That's when (promoter) Eddie Graham tapped me on the shoulder and said, 'Have you got your stuff, kid?' I'd never had a match and didn't have any lessons, so I bought a pair of boots and tights and my first match was on TV against Bugsy McGraw."

Taylor turned out to be a natural for the ring game. He was voted Rookie of the Year by readers of *Pro Wrestling Illustrated* in 1980. He won the NWA National Television title that same year. Taylor had charisma and a flashy athleticism, rocking opponents with precision dropkicks and his signature flying forearm. Taylor was the classic "white meat babyface," a handsome young wrestler with flowing blond hair and a big toothy smile that made female fans swoon. Often facing larger, plodding opponents, Taylor would sell most of the match before scoring the "upset victory" with a roll-up out of nowhere.

"Every match I had, somebody helped me along. Somebody gave me advice and helped me improve," Taylor said when he accepted the prestigious Iron Mike Mazurki Award from the Cauliflower Alley Club in 2014. In introducing Taylor, Jim Ross — the emcee at that awards banquet — referred to Taylor as "one of the greatest psychologists in wrestling history."

After runs as NWA Southeastern champion and NWA Central States TV champion, Taylor began wrestling for the Continental Wrestling Association, where he held the AWA Southern tag team title with Steve Keirn and had a pair of runs as AWA Southern heavyweight champion. He moved on to Mid-South Wrestling in 1984 and feuded with Krusher Kruschev over the Mid-South TV title. In the spring of 1985, Taylor wrestled a series of 30-minute matches against NWA champion Ric Flair, including a draw in Shreveport, Louisiana, and in the main event of Mid-South Wrestling's "Superdome Extravaganza" at the New Orleans Superdome.

Taylor seemed to be on the cusp of winning the NWA world title, but a world title push never materialized. He remained with Mid-South as Bill Watts splintered off from the NWA and formed the Universal Wrestling Federation. Taylor turned heel in shocking fashion, turning on his tag team partner, "Gentleman" Chris Adams. He dropped the UWF TV title to NWA TV champion Nikita Koloff in a title unification match at *Starrcade* 1987, then continued his feud against Adams in World Class Championship Wrestling. But when the WWF came calling, Taylor was ready to make the move. At least, he thought he was.

"Terry and I started around the same time," said Koko B. Ware (Taylor started wrestling in 1979, and Ware began wrestling in 1978). "He really caught on to this business so fast. He's got a great mind for wrestling. That's why he's been able to work for the office so long. He had a nice baby face on him, and the girls liked that. He didn't do things

Terry Taylor is all smiles as he poses with the NWA National championship belt.

PHOTO BY GEORGE NAPOLITANO

like I did or Ric Flair did — he didn't dance on the apron or do the flip on the ropes like Flair, the showmanship kind of things. He just wanted to be plain Terry Taylor and go out and wrestle. There's nothing wrong with that. He just couldn't find the right gimmick to suit him."

Taylor wrestled a series of undercard matches, eventually settling into a team with Sam Houston. After a televised loss to the hapless team of the Conquistadors, Taylor turned on Houston, a pale imitation of his turn on Chris Adams. Now a heel, Taylor was partnered with manager Bobby Heenan. Heenan appeared on "The Brother Love Show" and introduced the "newest member of the Heenan Family" in less-than-glowing terms.

"He's limited when it comes to wrestling," Heenan said. "He's limited when it comes to size. He's limited with a won-and-loss record. . . . As limited as you are by being short, by being not that muscular, by not having a great, great gift at the sport of wrestling, there is one thing, one added factor, one ingredient that will make you a superstar. And that is me." It was a burial from which Taylor would never fully recover.

Heenan would go on to re-christen Taylor "The Little Red Rooster," and Taylor would take to dying a red stripe of "feathers" on top of his head and adopting a rooster strut and other silly mannerisms. Even after he gave Heenan his comeuppance in a 31-second squash at *WrestleMania* V, the fans never took to the plucky (pun fully intended) Red Rooster.

"I didn't understand it," Taylor admitted to SLAM! Wrestling. "I had gone from being a heel who had turned on Chris Adams, to bleeding every night and getting heat that was very believable, to a territory of Akeems and Hillbillies and Macho Men and Hulks. And Vince said to me, 'We need to give you a character that makes you unique and I've got the one for you.' And I just didn't get it. That was one of those things in life where, if I would have done what was best for my employer, instead of what I thought was best for me, I might have still been The Red Rooster and gotten a 10-to-15-year run out of it. But I was immature and I didn't get it. They were good to me, I mean, they gave me opportunities. Heck, they gave me Bobby Heenan, and I worked with Curt (Hennig). What's better than that? I didn't see it at the time and a year later I quit."

In 1990, Taylor returned to Jim Crockett Promotions, but his credibility as a viable title contender was shredded. He became a member of the heel York Foundation and won the short-lived WCW six-man tag title (with Richard Morton and Thomas Rich), then competed as "The Taylor Made Man," winning the U.S. tag title with Greg Valentine. Though he was mired in the midcard, Taylor was still voted "Most Underrated Wrestler of the Year" for 1991 and 1992 by readers of the *Wrestling Observer Newsletter*.

By 1996, Taylor had begun the transition to a backstage role. He went on to work as a writer, agent, and interviewer in both the WWF and WCW. He became head of talent relations for Total Nonstop Action in 2003 and returned to the WWE as a coach at the Performance Center in 2012.

"Terry is my true mentor. He worked with me for over a year, and that's where I learned to do this craft properly," said "Textbook" Tyson Dux, who had a series of independent bouts against Taylor in 2001–02 for Border City Wrestling. "His sense of timing and overall psychology is untouchable. His true art was finding the *in-between*; between making it look real and believable while keeping it moving and exciting. It's almost impossible to duplicate. When I went down to coach at the Performance Center for a week, he was there teaching, and I brought more of his stuff back home with me."

LUNA VACHON

"In a world full of butterflies, it takes balls to be a caterpillar."

—Luna Vachon

To many Americans, The Butcher's Daughter is a chain of vegetarian restaurants in California and New York. But to the wrestling world, the real Butcher's Daughter was Luna Vachon, stepdaughter of Paul "The Butcher" Vachon.

Vachon married Rebecca van Pierce in 1966 and adopted her three-and-a-half-year-old daughter, Gertrude. After the couple divorced, "The Butcher" raised Gertrude as his own daughter, exposing the impressionable youngster to the world of professional wrestling. It didn't take long before she was hooked and became determined to follow in the footsteps of her stepfather, his brother (Maurice "Mad Dog" Vachon), and his sister (Vivian Vachon).

"My family discouraged me at first," she said in a 2007 interview with WWE.com. "My Aunt Vivian was a wrestler, so they knew the kind of toll wrestling could take on a woman's body. I didn't let that stop me, though. It was in my blood, and all I wanted to do was become a wrestler."

Vivian began training her niece at the age of 16 before sending her to the Fabulous Moolah to continue preparation. Moolah had controlled women's wrestling since the 1950s and had helped train Vivian. If a woman wanted to crack into the wrestling business, their best bet was to go through Moolah. Moolah determined that Vachon was "too skinny" to be a heel, so she christened her Angelle Vachon and made her a babyface.

In 1985, she debuted in Florida Championship Wrestling, playing the role of a reporter named Trudy Herd. In a wild angle, Kevin Sullivan interrupted Herd as she was presenting an award to Kendall Windham and slapped her twice.

"I slapped her and when we got back to the dressing room, she told me, 'Is that all you got, pussy? I'm a Vachon!" Sullivan said in an interview with Hannibal TV. "Luna was tough as nails."

As a result of his actions, Sullivan was suspended for two weeks in the storyline. But when he returned, fans were shocked when Trudy begged to become part of Sullivan's Army of Darkness, explaining his slaps made her "feel something she had never felt before." The intrepid reporter became one of Sullivan's slave-girl acolytes. Her hair was shaved into a Mohawk and Luna Vachon was born.

Why Luna? "At the beginning they wanted to call me Moaning Mona, but Nancy Sullivan, Kevin's wife at the time, said that I didn't look like the moaning type. So she proposed Luna, short for lunatic. It was actually Nancy who shaved my hair. Nancy was one of the rare female friends I ever had."

The newly-christened Luna was wild, tough, and unpredictable. She developed a harsh, throaty promo style that sounded like she spent her spare time gargling shards of glass and chain-smoking unfiltered cigarettes, which landed her a gig providing background vocals for the thrash band Nasty Savage. Instead of being a glamorous woman wrestler, Luna took pride in becoming a monster, unlike anyone else.

Her punk-rock look and wild demeanor landed her bookings throughout the Southern U.S. and the AWA, but also internationally. She would tour Japan 17 times during her career, and also compete in Australia, Singapore, Europe, Puerto Rico, and Dubai.

In 1993, she joined the WWF, debuting at *WrestleMania* 9 as the new valet for Shawn Michaels. Michaels's former valet, Sherri Martel, was in the corner of his opponent, Tatanka. After the match, Luna attacked Sherri, setting up a feud that ran several months. She then feuded with Alundra Blayze over the reinstated women's championship before leaving the WWF in 1994.

Nancy Sullivan helped Luna get into ECW where she was brought in as part of the program between Tommy Dreamer and Raven. Though "intergender" matches were rare at the time, Luna had several physical clashes with Raven's sidekick, Stevie Richards, including a bloody steel cage match at Heat Wave 1995, which Luna won.

After a stint in the United States Wrestling Association where she feuded with Miss Texas, Luna joined WCW in 1997 where she resumed her rivalry with Madusa (the former Alundra Blayze) over the WCW women's title. Later that year, she jumped back to the WWF where she was paired with the equally bizarre Goldust. Before long, she was placed in a program with Sable.

"If you want to know how good Luna was, look at those matches. She made Sable look like a million bucks," said LuFisto.

"Sable wasn't a wrestler until I made her one," Luna told WWE.com. "A real wrestler can wrestle a mop and make it look like the mop is kicking their ass, and that's what happened that night. She beat me, and when we got to the back there was champagne and confetti and everyone wanted to celebrate with Sable. I kept walking until Owen Hart came up to me and told me I had just put on the match of my life. It meant a lot to have someone like him say that to me."

It has been reported (and repeated by Luna herself) that she had been penciled in to win the WWF women's title on more than one occasion, but it never happened. Perhaps it was Luna's look, or her independent spirit, or her unpredictability (a result of her real-life bi-polar disorder). Whatever it was, the WWF never entrusted her with the championship belt. She was released from the WWF in 2000.

She continued to wrestle on the independents before retiring due to back and neck injuries in December 2007. In 2009, she was honored by the Cauliflower Alley Club, receiving a Ladies Wrestling Award. She died from an overdose of painkillers in August 2010 at the age of 48.

"Luna was a definite inspiration for me — she had a wild look and was a genuinely tough female wrestler," Lita wrote in her autobiography.

"Luna taught me to take every crazy bump that was out there, mostly by giving it to me," said Malia Hosaka, one of Luna's frequent opponents on the independents. "But she knew what she was doing. She protected me. She would say, 'We're going in the stands' and I would just follow her. I trusted her. She taught me, no matter where you go, how to protect yourself in taking the bumps and giving the fans your all."

BOB ROOP

In the world of professional wrestling, there are some people who are absolutely polarizing figures. Never has there been a better example of this than Robert Michael Roop.

Born in Blacksburg, Virginia, on July 22, 1942, Bob Roop began wrestling in the eighth grade and was a varsity heavyweight by his freshman year. He became the Michigan state champion in his senior year with an amazing 27–0–0 record.

After a year and a half at Michigan State University, he left school to join the U.S. Army and received paratrooper training. While in the service, Roop became a member of the armed forces wrestling team along with one other heavyweight, a young serviceman named Jim Rasher, born James Raschke, and later known the world over as Baron Von Raschke.

After three years in the army, Roop went back to school to Southern Illinois University, where he continued wrestling. He compiled an impressive 66–18 record between 1965 and 1969, earning four Amateur Athletic Union All-American rankings and earning a spot on the 1968 United States Olympic team (Mexico City games) losing early to eventual gold medal winner Aleksandr Medved.

"Bob Roop got inducted into the (George Tragos/Lou Thesz) Wrestling Hall of Fame the same year as Bret Hart (in 2006)," said Kyle Klingman, a former director of the National Wrestling Hall of Fame Dan Gable Museum. "Hart didn't think he belonged in the same class as Roop because Roop was an Olympian. Roop had competed at the highest level and Bret hadn't. Of course, Bret had sold out buildings of 20,000 people and more, and Roop never did that. I've found that pro wrestlers respect amateur wrestlers even more than other amateur wrestlers do."

After graduation, Roop was drawn to the promise of fame and fortune that professional wrestling could bring and went to work for Eddie Graham in Championship Wrestling from Florida. It was a natural fit, according to Ron Fuller.

"Most of the time (Graham's) crews were the Bob Roop type, with that amateur background and that shooting style, guys who could stretch you if needed," Fuller said.

Roop adopted the persona of a cocky heel and would ceaselessly brag about his amateur background and wrestling prowess, a gimmick that earned him several shots at the NWA world title. Probably his most remembered angle was in 1976, when — in a match against Eddie Graham — Roop suffered what was billed as career-threatening injury due to Graham's figure-four leglock. Soon afterwards, a masked wrestler known as the Gladiator arrived in Florida. He was built like Roop and used even Roop's signature moves. During a match on TV, Eddie and Mike Graham ran into the ring and unmasked the Gladiator, proving it was indeed the hated Bob Roop under the hood.

Roop worked several other territories throughout the 1970s, including Mid-South and Amarillo, and did several tours of Japan, Korea, the United Kingdom, Australia, and many other places around the world. His ability to adapt to many styles and "get over" with all kinds of crowds made him a draw everywhere he went.

"He was a hell of a wrestler, one tough son of a bitch," said Terry Funk, who feuded with Roop over the NWA Florida heavyweight title in 1975.

His work ethic, talent, and brains earned him the respect of Harley Race. Race remained a lifelong friend and taught Roop the business side of wrestling, including how to book and how to make sure you got what you earned.

"Harley was the real thing, he was tough," Roop said. "I learned so much of the business and how to handle myself from Harley, except that fast driving. I liked to go the speed limit, but not Harley. That's one thing we disagreed on."

In the 1980s he joined Angelo Poffo's outlaw promotion International Championship Wrestling along with wrestlers such as Ron Garvin,

Bob Orton Jr., Boris Malenko, Ron Wright, and Buddy Landel, where they worked alongside Poffo's sons, Lanny Poffo and Randy Savage. Roop went on to be a booker and trainer in Florida, becoming an early teacher for future stars such as Lex Luger. In 1988, he suffered a career-ending injury in a car accident and left the business for good, moving back to Michigan.

During his career, Roop gained a reputation as a shooter who would stretch and intentionally hurt young wrestlers trying out with Eddie Graham. Videos of some of these incidents still exist. In some circles, Roop built a reputation as a "disturber." He would organize some of the boys and try to take over territories, most notably Roy Shire's promotion in San Francisco and Ron Fuller's Knoxville promotion. In 1979, Roop, along with Ron Garvin, Boris Malenko, Bob Orton Jr., and Ron Wright, attempted a takeover of Knoxville, claiming that Fuller was underreporting attendance and the boys weren't making their fair due.

The attempted coup of Knoxville failed, but Roop's cadre of malcontents had a "Plan B" — a video they figured would ruin the territory for good by breaking kayfabe and exposing the business. This video is an open expose on the wrestling business, describing it as a fake and dirty industry. The five men each take turns explaining how they have never been in a legitimate professional match. It's a damning video that amazingly remained largely unseen for 30 years in the pre-internet era.

In an interview with Hannibal TV, Ron Fuller said, "You know, I have forgiven all those guys, except Roop. I have never seen Roop since. I don't know, I really think that a lot of that war was Roop. A lot of those guys, all of those guys in fact, had worked for me for years and (I) never had a problem with any of them. Bob Roop came in in February, I put him in as a booker and this crap all starts three to four months later, and I believe he's the guy that instigated all of it. I don't have good feelings about him, but I don't like to carry grudges and I don't think the Good Lord wants us to not forgive people."

Roop wrote a pro wrestling novel entitled *Death Match*, published in 2002.

ROAD WARRIORS AND DEATH TOURS: MAKING TOWNS

Professional wrestling, by its very nature, is a traveling show. Much like the circuses of old, once the show is over it's time to pack up and move on to the next town. Leave the crowd entertained, excited, and wanting more so that when the show comes back, none of them will dare miss it.

In some cases, wrestling shows were more like old vaudeville theaters. The show would go on, yet the talent would rotate. In order to keep the fans coming, promoters had to constantly provide not only established stars in their area, but also new faces to keep audiences interested. Some wrestlers would go from city to city and territory to territory to stay fresh and relevant in the minds and hearts of the fans. A good angle or storyline could generate enough interest that it could travel the full loop of the territory and could still draw even when it returned to the same cities again and again.

There were exceptions, of course. Jerry Lawler, for example, could have gone his whole career without setting foot outside of Memphis and still managed to draw main-event houses for decades without burning out the crowd. But, for most wrestlers, the key to success was travel and getting in front of as many different fans as possible.

Traveling between territories — "making towns" — was part of the job description. A successful wrestler would have a main home base but would frequently go to another territory in exchange for other talent to keep things fresh. At its peak, the National Wrestling Alliance consisted of 48 different territories under its banner. Formed in 1948 by a group of six wrestling promoters (Paul "Pinkie" George out of Des Moines, Iowa; Sam Muchnick from St. Louis, Missouri; Al Haft of Columbus, Ohio; Harry Light representing Detroit, Michigan; Tony Stecher out of Minneapolis, Minnesota; and Orville Brown out of Kansas City, Missouri), the NWA banded together to form one giant wrestling organization covering the United States and Japan (later to include Australia, New Zealand, Canada, and South Korea, among other areas).

Each territory would have its own promoter and booker to run its business, but they were all under the control, and protection, of the NWA board of directors. This prevented anyone else coming into an area and taking business away. It was also a way for the regional territories to trade talent back and forth, bringing new names to fans across the regions. This also allowed for there to be one universally recognized "world" champion after a series of embarrassing multiple title claimants and splinter groups throughout the 1920s, 1930s, and 1940s. The champion would travel territory to territory, and go to as many towns as he could in that territory, as not only an ambassador for the NWA but also a guaranteed money-maker wherever he would appear.

Lou Thesz set the standard after he was named world champion in November 1949, receiving the title when champion Orville Brown was forced to retire following a car accident. Thesz was already widely known and respected by wrestling fans and writers across the country, so the fact that he was now considered the "true" champ gave the NWA instant credibility. Everywhere Thesz went, the fans would flock. And any regional wrestler that could "put up a good fight" against Thesz saw their stock rise dramatically.

That being said, there was a risk to being a traveling champ. "When you were NWA champion back in the day, you had to be able to hold your tights up," said Terry Funk, who held the NWA world title from December 10, 1975, through February 6, 1977. "I mean, you would have to go territory to territory and you better be able to take care of yourself, because you never knew where or when someone was gonna try you, cause there are a bunch of nuts in our business, along with a lot of great people. Hell, the nuts were great too. Bunch of hard son-of-a-guns."

Funk was based out of Amarillo, Texas, a territory called Western States Sports that was owned by his father, Dory Funk Sr., starting in 1955. The territory would later be taken over by Terry and his brother, Dory Jr. In addition to being part of their own territory, the Funk brothers worked around the horn.

"The territory days, great territories at the time, were Florida and Texas, both north and south, the Von Erichs and the Funks," Funk said. "But heck, all the territories were great. There were great performers in every territory — great entertainers and athletes, they were in every territory. I miss it, I miss those days."

And while each territory differed in its own ways — St. Louis favored technical excellence, the Northeast enjoyed larger-than-life personalities and ethnic attractions, the Southeast hungered for a good old-fashioned fistfight — one thing was true in every promotion. A wrestler on the road had to be able to hold his own, just in case things didn't go as planned," Funk said.

"Florida was a great bunch of guys, the Briscos, a bunch of wrestlers who could damn sure hold their tights up, they were tough. And Eddie Graham, that's what he wanted down there and that's what he got. Tough guys in Florida, tough guys in Amarillo, tough guys in Atlanta, tough guys all around. It was more important to be a tough guy who could wrestle than being an entertainer at that time," Funk said.

"The Tennessee Stud" Ron Fuller cut his wrestling teeth going from territory to territory before owning and running Southern Championship Wrestling along with his brother Robert, making it one of the largest territories, covering several southern states. Fuller explained that, even though each place was different, you were better off making the territory adapt to you instead of the other way around. But you could also learn lessons on the road.

"You didn't change your style, no matter what territory you went into," Fuller said. "Didn't matter if they were doing a lot of wrestling or a lot of fighting, you built your personality in the ring over years when you got started in the business. For instance, in 1973 I worked almost every show in St. Louis for about two years, and in St. Louis you got to work with the absolute best in the world because Muchnick, being the head of the NWA, almost every card you went to in St. Louis you hardly ever saw the same wrestlers, I was one of the only guys I saw there on a regular basis. Sam was handpicking who he wanted from all over the country. All he had to do was call a promoter and say, 'I want Ron Fuller to come in.' That helped me greatly. I got to work with all kinds of guys from all over and, you pick up stuff. You see them do something, something happens in the ring that they call a spot, and it's a really good spot, you have a tendency to take it back home with you, you want do it again. That's how you got better as a wrestler, depending on how many people you got to work with and how much you could take from those other guys that fit your style."

Florida, in particular, held a special place in Fuller's heart, and he picked up a lot of knowledge there.

"Fans there were being fed a lot of *wrestling*," Fuller said. "Jack Brisco was there because Eddie Graham loved wrestling, he loved to have his guys wrestle a lot, and when he got his hands on Jack Brisco, he said this is the direction I want to go, and he pushed him to be world Champ. And he emphasized that Jack Brisco was not a brawler, he was a pure wrestler, and as he was the top guy in 1970 when I got there, you'd want to emulate Jack. You wanted to wrestle Jack's style. When he went into the ring, there wasn't a lot of blood. Except in his (Eddie Graham's) own matches, he would work with the Great Malenko in a chain match and there would be plenty of blood, but that would be the only blood that night. Graham liked that pure wrestling style, and Florida fans came to love pure wrestling more than most places I went."

The appreciation of the "sweet science" of wrestling even found an audience in the Northeast, where size and gimmicks typically were more valued than technical artistry or reversals, Fuller said.

"In the 1970s, Vince McMahon Sr. liked big guys, guys like Gorilla Monsoon, guys who didn't move very fast and didn't do a lot of wrestling, and there were a couple stations up there that wanted to get another wrestling program," Fuller said. "Vince didn't want to have competition, but he was very close to Eddie Graham, who had worked for him for many years, and was tag team champion for him. And he said, 'Eddie, send me your Florida show.' He put that show on in New York City, and I'm not sure if he did it in other cities as well, but he did in New York and put it on a competing station. He didn't want someone else to give him competition, so he promoted the competition, that way he had control of it."

It wasn't just the traveling *between* territories that could take its toll on wrestling's road warriors. The amount of traveling *within* one territory could be grueling on its own. Former NCAA wrestling champion Bob Roop explained what it was like to travel the loop in the Amarillo territory on a typical weekend run in the 1970s.

"You could go for a Saturday show in Brownsville, Texas, 300 miles each way, so that's 600 miles (round-trip)," Roop said. "Then you'd get home at say four o'clock in the morning. Then you have to get up at around six o'clock, so you've been in bed two hours. Then you'd drive to Albuquerque (New Mexico) to be there by noon for TV. You would be carrying the tape made the night before in Amarillo with you, but because they didn't have time to tape the interviews in Amarillo, the interviews in Albuquerque had to be done live. So you had to be there at noon, for when they ran the tape, and as the tape was playing and the two-minute gap would come for the interview, the boys would have to do them live. That was fine if you were working in El Paso the next night; you'd get a room and stay over then drive to El Paso the next day. But if you were booked in Abilene, that's another 250 to 300 miles, so you had to hit the road again. Then there was another small town after Abilene about 150 miles away. So in one weekend, you might have to drive about 1,780 miles. And wrestle on top of it."

Canada had its own set of territories and towns that packed the houses. Where traveling across the Southern United States may be hard and tedious, imagine putting those miles in during a Canadian winter.

Vern May, better known to wrestling fans as Vance Nevada, spent the majority of his career touring his native land of Canada. As a matter of fact, he literally wrote the book on it. His 2009 book *Wrestling in the Canadian West* goes into incredible detail on the history of the business in the great white north, including the infamous "Northern Hell Tours" promoted by Tony Condello.

"It's probably the most extreme in terms of being a 'man maker' for aspiring wrestlers," May said of Condello's "death tours," having completed four winter "Hell Tours" of the northern provinces and Inuit territories himself. "The talent all assembles in Winnipeg a full day before you head out. You have a day to get ready for the trip. These towns — except for maybe three or four weeks a year — are only available by air, so the price to buy food in the local stores or restaurants was unreal. So if you don't take your food with you, you're going to come back at the end of the tour with a deficit. So you take three bags, a bag with your clothes, a bag with your gear, and a third bag, usually your biggest bag, with your food, all non-perishable food, food resistant to freezing, cause chances are when you get to the town your bag is frozen. You'll get into town and want to brush your teeth but your toothpaste is frozen."

Provided you can keep warm and keep your food edible, there are still the rigors of the ambitious travel schedule to deal with, May said.

"You start off at five a.m. and travel five hours north on paved roads, before you turn off onto the winter roads carved through the wilderness, only available a month or so a year," he said. "A lot of guys are freaked out by driving over the frozen lakes, but after driving on these bumpy muskegs, you welcome the ice roads because it's actually a smooth ride. Plus it's fun, if you've been on the tour before to sort of mess with the other guys, especially the guys from the States . . . who never saw snow before, let alone a frozen lake. You freak them out by saying, 'Hey did you hear that cracking sound? I think we're going through!' In reality, you want to hear that crackle because it lets you know that the ice is breathing. If you don't hear the crack, that's a signal you may be in big trouble.

"You typically arrive in the first town around three p.m. The promoter goes in to make sure everything is lined up with the Native Council in the community and you 'move into' the schools. These communities are very remote, none have hotels, so the school is your accommodations for the night. You roll in, all hands on deck to unload the ring and bags, perform that night, then after the matches we are usually in the home economics room, preparing our meal, and you hope you are one of the first guys to grab a gym mat so you're not sleeping on the floor. It looks like a refugee camp on the floor of the gymnasium, everyone's sweaty wrestling gear is laid out to dry out before you pack it up for the next day. Then, wake up call is seven a.m., you're on the road by eight, then on to the bush trails and frozen lakes to the next town . . . sometimes, you finish the matches, load right up because you have a 20-hour drive around the lake, and you are up there doing this every night for two to three weeks."

May said the term "death tour" isn't simply a reference to the brutal itinerary. "In the First Nations culture, if somebody in the community dies, the whole town shuts down for a week in mourning, so you might drive 20 hours, show up in a town and are told there was a death in the community and the show has been cancelled. And you are on a per-night pay arrangement, so you lost a payday, you're in the middle of nowhere, probably no network connection, isolated from the outside world. The worst one I remember was in Garden Hill, Manitoba. We arrived and they said, 'We're sorry. Your show's been cancelled because there was a murder in the community, and the two men responsible are still on the run and in hiding.' So we were ushered into the school we were going to be working and locked in, with some locals serving as security making sure we didn't go out and nobody could get in."

Also, it's worth noting that it isn't just traveling the United States and or Canada. For many wrestlers, tours of Japan are a necessity. Japan has been a wrestling hotbed since Rikidozan popularized it in the early 1950s. Japanese fans are very passionate, not only about their own home-grown talent, but for Western wrestlers as well. But for many outsiders, the long flight, language barrier, and different style of wrestling can present a serious case of culture shock.

"The first couple of tours (of Japan) I went for six weeks, eight weeks, and that was too long, you start cracking," said former AWA world champion Larry Zbyszko. "But it was a real interesting experience, especially the first couple times I went, because it was so different, the culture is so different. When you would walk to the ring, the women would try to rub their hands over your chest because we had chest hair, where the Japanese men have no hair on their chest. So that struck me as funny."

But what of the Japanese style of wrestling itself?

"It was a very physical form of entertainment in Japan. You better watch your ass over there or you'd get your ass beat," said Funk, a veteran of multiple tours of Japan. "They constantly had wars going on over there, they had the greatest competitors from the USA, but they clung to the athletic background. They liked the Hodges, the Huttons. What they wanted were great athletes that could perform in the ring."

And a different culture brings about different fan reaction, yet another thing Zbyszko found shocking. "It was weird, because even if (the Japanese fans) hated you they were so polite. You punched and kicked a Japanese guy and they would applaud. Things were so different. In America, you could hit someone with a low blow and get heat. If you hit someone in the balls in Japan, the crowd would laugh their ass off."

Whether home or abroad, constant travel has always been a part of the wrestler's life. And the life of his (or her) family. Jonard Solie, the son of legendary wrestling broadcaster Gordon Solie, explained a typical weekend for his father. "He would fly out to Atlanta Friday night, and do a show, and again Saturday morning, then he flew to Alabama to do another show, then back to Atlanta for a fourth show, then finally home."

But at least Gordon had the luxury of flying; most of the boys drove everywhere. "You'd live in your vehicle," Roop said. "I had a Volkswagen van. I should have bought a Corvette or something fast. Terry (Funk) drove with me once, and Terry liked to drive 90 MPH, and in my little VW van going 60 MPH he hated it. He never drove with me again."

PART 3:
The Kings of the Territories

If, as Terry Funk suggested, a "Wrestlers' Wrestler" is one who draws the biggest houses, then the most iconic world champions of the largest promotions certainly have to be included in the conversation.

From 1948 through the early 1960s, the NWA had almost complete control of the professional wrestling industry. Non-member promoters ran so-called "outlaw" shows in certain areas, but the NWA ruled the roost. The promotion had survived title controversies and disputes that had clouded the world title picture in the past, but the alliance was always at risk of coming apart at the seams as regional promoters jockeyed and politicked for their own agendas.

In 1960, frustrated with his inability to land a world title match against NWA kingpin Pat O'Connor, Verne Gagne and Wally Karbo took their stake in the Minneapolis Boxing and Wrestling Club and turned it into the American Wrestling Association. The AWA recognized O'Connor as its world champion, but gave O'Connor 90 days to defend his world title against Gagne. O'Connor and the NWA had no plans to do the match, so when the 90-day period expired, Gagne was declared AWA world champion.

The following year, Los Angeles promoters Gene and Mike LeBell organized Worldwide Wrestling Associates in Southern California, recognizing Édouard Carpentier as their world champion, as Carpentier had lost a controversial bout to Thesz. The WWA established a working agreement with the Japanese Wrestling Association, giving them a promising foothold in Japan and making the Southern California scene less dependent on the machinations of the NWA.

In 1963, Vince McMahon Sr. and Toots Mondt followed suit. When the NWA board approved the world title switch from Buddy Rogers to Lou Thesz (which took place on January 24, 1963, in Toronto), McMahon opted to transform his Capitol Wrestling Corporation into the World Wide Wrestling Federation. He recognized Rogers, who drew huge houses in the Northeast, as his first world champion

By the mid-1960s, the NWA's chokehold on wrestling was coming undone. While the WWA would cease operations and rejoin the NWA by the end of the decade, the AWA and WWWF would grow into prominent competitor promotions, eventually establishing a national presence on cable television.

As the NWA and its offshoots jockeyed for dominance, the credibility and drawing power of each company's world champion became increasingly important. These are the champions who carried the "Big Three" promotions on their backs from the 1960s into the expansion era of the 1980s.

VERNE GAGNE

An Olympic hopeful out of Minnesota, Verne Gagne was a major draw in the Midwest for three decades, but he was also one of the most influential promoters of the 20th century.

Born Laverne "Verne" Gagne on February 26, 1926, in Hennepin County, Minnesota, he grew up on the family farm and developed into an all-around athlete at Robbinsdale High School. He won regional and state championships in wrestling, and was also a star football and baseball player, being named to the All Minnesota football team in 1943. He was recruited and signed to play football for the University of Minnesota. He played both offense and defense for the "Golden Gophers," playing as both tight end and defensive end. He continued to wrestle collegiately, winning a Big Ten wrestling title at 175 pounds in his freshman year.

But in 1944, America was at war, and Gagne enlisted in the U.S. Marines to serve his country. He continued to play football for Lieutenant Colonel Dick Hanley at the El Toro Marine Corps station and returned to college in 1946, winning four Big Ten wrestling titles, a pair of NCAA titles, and an AAU championship in wrestling. He qualified for the 1948 Olympic with the U.S. Greco-Roman team, however the U.S. ultimately decided not to enter a Greco-Roman team, fearing the squad didn't have enough experience, and instead focused only on freestyle. Gagne was heartbroken.

After college, he was drafted by the Chicago Bears of the National Football League (16th round in 1947) but Bears owner George Halas didn't want his draft pick to continue wrestling as well as playing football. Gagne left the Bears and signed with the Green Bay Packers, but he was a wrestler at heart, and Minneapolis wrestling promoter Tony Stecher was working overtime to try to sign Gagne as a grappler. Forced to choose between the two sports, Gagne picked wrestling, which proved to be a wise choice. In 1949, Gagne made his professional wrestling debut in Texas and by November of the next year he was NWA junior heavyweight champion.

As an amateur wrestler, Gagne had no background in the art of submission wrestling, but he learned quickly and eventually adopted the sleeper as his primary finishing move.

After dropping the junior heavyweight title to Danny McShain, Gagne moved up to the heavyweight division and was groomed to be a contender for Lou Thesz's world title. In December 1951, *Ring Magazine* was predicting that Gagne would be the next NWA world champion. A handsome wrestling and football star from the heartland, Gagne seemed to have all the raw ingredients for the world title. "You take this kid Verne Gagne," Jim Londos said at the time, "well, he could have tied most of the wrestlers of 20 years ago in knots."

"(Gagne) and I worked a 'feud' for several years in the early and mid-1950s when he was the junior heavyweight champion, and those matches did big box-office wherever we appeared," Thesz wrote. "I guarantee you they wouldn't have drawn a dime if Verne hadn't been so credible. There was a personal competitiveness and pride there, too, unrelated to money or personality, and the fans could see it in our matches."

Wrestling proved to be a major draw on TV during the "golden age" of the 1950s, and Gagne became a big star on the DuMont Network, one of the early regional television networks out of Chicago. Promoter Fred Kohler produced *Wrestling from Marigold* on DuMont, and Gagne would quickly become his top star. But their relationship didn't start out particularly well.

"Fred Kohler didn't think he was big enough," Verne's son, Greg, said in an interview with SLAM! Wrestling. "He was the junior heavyweight champion down in Oklahoma at the time for the NWA. And he was about 215 (pounds). They brought him in Chicago and Fred told him about the big TV network and said, 'What I want you to do is we're going to dress you up what we think a Martian would look like and have you come out of the ceiling into the ring. We're going to lower you down."

Gagne, fresh off the Olympics, flat-out refused, offended by the gimmickry. "'You can line up everybody on the card and I will take on every one of them, one after another,'" Verne said, according to his son. "'If I can't beat them, I'll quit wrestling. But if you want me to go in the ring, I'm going in with my wrestling boots and my tights and if I can't make it as a wrestler like that, I'll give up the sport.'"

Because of his amateur credentials, the way he carried himself, and his refusal to rely on gimmicks and ballyhoo, Gagne presented himself as a credible athlete and he provided an authenticity that resonated with the viewing public.

Gagne was a handsome babyface who was as tough as the heels, who he regularly put in their place with his technical ability and million-dollar smile, and of course his famous sleeper hold. It was rumored that Gagne was earning upwards of $100,000 per year, an unheard-of amount in the 1950s.

On January 25, 1952, Gagne and Thesz wrestled to a 60-minute draw at the Amphitheatre in Chicago in front of an announced attendance of nearly 11,000 fans. That year, Gagne was also honored by the *Police Gazette* for his "contribution to clean and scientific wrestling" and was awarded a sterling silver belt in a ceremony broadcast on the DuMont Network. He was also named "Outstanding Professional Wrestler" of 1952 by the *Gazette*.

While Gagne was drawing big houses and winning accolades, he was the cause of dissension in the NWA offices. Gagne was heavily pushed by Kohler. Gagne was his top star, and Gagne's popularity in the Midwest was beginning to eclipse the popularity of Thesz. When Kohler introduced a U.S. title and made Gagne the new champion, some NWA power brokers saw it as diminishing the importance of the world title and of the NWA itself.

Between October 1953 and March 1954, Gagne headlined Madison Square Garden five times and proved to be a better draw than Thesz. But when the time came to take the belt off Thesz in 1957, the NWA selected Dick Hutton over Gagne. Gagne, however, did have an "unofficial" NWA world title run, beating Édouard Carpentier to win a disputed version of the championship (the title was fractured following a contested match between Thesz and Carpentier), but even that reign proved to be brief.

Whether it was due to politics, personalities, or circumstances, it was apparent that the NWA was not interested in making Gagne its kingpin. Gagne, in partnership with Wally Karbo, planned to form his own promotion; not just another NWA territory, but a full-fledged promotion independent of the almighty NWA. Gagne and Karbo bought into the Minneapolis Boxing and Wrestling Club and, in 1960, announced the creation of the American Wrestling Association. Gagne became the new champion.

Gagne held the AWA world title 10 times between 1960 and 1980, having memorable rivalries with Gene Kiniski, Dr. Bill Miller, the Crusher, Mad Dog Vachon, Nick Bockwinkel, and Dr. X. As both a draw and a promoter, he helped make the AWA a nationally recognized promotion, eventually landing a television deal with the newly established national sports network ESPN in the 1980s. Gagne, with his reputation among the boys, and his willingness to pay on par with his NWA rival for a lesser workload, was able to attract some of the biggest names in the business, many of whom he matched with himself as rivals for his beloved title. Gagne expanded the upstart promotion out of Minneapolis and into major hotbeds such as Chicago, Las Vegas, Denver, San Francisco, and Milwaukee. Gagne and Karbo also developed working relationships with major promotions in Houston and Memphis, to name just a few.

"Verne always had an intense tenacity," Nick Bockwinkel said in an interview with Scott Teal's *Whatever Happened To* newsletter. "He was very much a firebrand in the ring and he'd get frustrated very easily if things that he was trying to do weren't going as smooth as he would like them. What would happen was, he would get so mad at himself, and so angry, that he would trip and stumble and fall all over himself, because of the frustration he had mentally because of something that didn't go right."

Gagne was not only the face of the AWA from its inception through his in-ring retirement in 1981, but was also the trainer of legends. According to Greg, Verne trained a total of 144 wrestlers in an old barn with "no windows, second floor, one light bulb above the ring." Gagne could spot talent and had the ability to mold it into something special. He could bring out the best of his students' ability and find their strengths. He didn't just teach holds and try to create copies of himself. He trained tough guys like the Blackjacks Mulligan and Lanza, Dick the Bruiser, and Larry Hennig, and natural athletes such as Olympic-style weightlifter-turned-wrestler Ken Patera and amateur wrestling standout

The ageless Verne Gagne was the cornerstone of the AWA.

PHOTO BY GEORGE NAPOLITANO

Brad Rheingans, who in turn became one of the great trainers in the business. Gagne also created characters by turning Nebraska native and amateur wrestling standout James Raschke into the evil German Baron Von Raschke and the former Iranian Olympic wrestler turned U.S. Olympic wrestling assistant coach Hossein Khosrow Ali Vaziri into one of the most famous villains in wrestling history, the Iron Sheik. He also had a hand in training such Wrestlers' Wrestlers as Ric Flair, Bob Backlund, Curt Hennig, and Ricky Steamboat. He also fathered a son, Greg, who followed in his footsteps, first on the gridiron at the University of Minnesota and then into the wrestling ring. Greg Gagne found his greatest success in a tag team with Jim Brunzell known as the High Flyers.

Throughout the 1960s and 1970s, the AWA held its own against both the NWA and the WWWF, but the promotion was always somewhat hindered by Gagne's unwillingness to promote anyone on top for sustained periods of time other than himself. He was still promoting himself as world champion in his mid-50s. As Billy Robinson once said. "He was the promoter. He made himself the big star, like most of the promoters did in America." When he retired in 1981 (followed by a series of comebacks through the 1980s), he put the belt on Nick Bockwinkel, who was in his mid-40s.

As Vince McMahon began to popularize his gimmick-heavy, musclebound, rock-and-roll-infused brand of "sports entertainment," Gagne was slow to respond or follow suit. He wanted to present *wrestling*, and many of the wrestlers he pushed came either from the amateur mats or the football field. He wasn't particularly interested in entertainers. McMahon signed away many of Gagne's top young stars, and Gagne was simply unable to replace them. "Look at the guys Vince took from Verne and the AWA," said Larry Zbyszko, who would be the final AWA world champion when the promotion closed in 1991. "Vince took the Hulk (Hogan) and Mean Gene and Jesse (Ventura), Bobby Heenan. Verne built that talent."

Gagne tried to compete, giving the Road Warriors a massive push and trying co-promotional programs in the NWA-affiliated territories under the Pro Wrestling USA banner, but even with a high-profile spot on ESPN, the AWA was unable to compete.

Gagne was not only one of wrestling's top stars but one of its most successful promoters. He is one of only a handful of people to have been inducted into the WWE, WCW, and Professional Wrestling halls of fame, as well as the *Wrestling Observer Newsletter* Hall of Fame. He is also — ironically enough — a recipient of the Lou Thesz Lifetime Achievement award given by the Cauliflower Alley Club.

He died on April 27, 2015, at the age of 89 after a lengthy battle with Alzheimer's disease.

BRUNO SAMMARTINO

Ethnic heroes have always been big draws in the world of sports. Benny Leonard, for example, was the hero of Jewish immigrants during and after his reign as lightweight boxing champion of the world. To Jews everywhere, but especially in New York, Leonard represented them and their struggles; his victories were their victories and his wins filled them with pride. His fights would all be sell-outs, not just because he was champ (from 1917 to 1925) but because the people just wanted a glimpse of their hero.

It's no wonder wrestling promoters used the ethnicity angle ad nauseam. The gimmick frequently worked, and when it worked well, a promoter could catch lightning in a bottle, such as in the case of Jim Londos, "The Golden Greek," or Abe Coleman, "The Hebrew Hercules," sometimes known as "The Jewish Tarzan." But it can be argued that never in wrestling's long history has the "ethnic hero" been as successful, far-reaching, and long-lasting as it was with Bruno Leopoldo Francesco Sammartino.

Bruno Sammartino was born in Pizzoferrato, Abruzzo, Italy, the youngest of seven siblings, four of whom didn't survive into adulthood. By the time young Bruno was four years old, his father had left to set roots in the United States. He planned to send for his wife and children when his part of the American dream came to fruition. True to his word, the elder Sammartino did indeed send for his family to join him, but it took 11 years and World War II to end before the family would be reunited in Pittsburgh.

Those war years were very hard on Mrs. Sammartino and her children. They hid themselves in the Valla Rocca mountain and had to sneak into their German-occupied hometown for food and supplies. They were all sick and weak when they were finally able to go start their new life in America.

Fifteen-year-old Bruno arrived in Pennsylvania weak, malnourished, and unable to speak the language of his new country. This combination made the young immigrant a target for his fellow high school students. But the young Sammartino was nothing if not tough. Rather than hide from the bullies, Sammartino decided he would build his strength in an attempt to stop the bullying he and his siblings were enduring. He turned to weightlifting and was so dedicated to it that within just six years he almost beat out the legendary Paul Anderson, considered by many the greatest weightlifter of all time, for a spot on the 1956 U.S. Olympic team. Three years later, the 24-year-old Bruno set the world record for bench press (without elbow or wrist wraps), pressing an amazing 565 pounds.

Sammartino was developing a reputation in his local Pittsburgh area as a strongman and elite-level weight lifter. Local Pittsburgh broadcasting legend Bob "The Gunner" Prince invited Bruno onto his TV show to perform feats of strength. Luckily, one man who was tuned in to that show was Rudy Miller, a wrestling promoter who could see the potential in this immigrant strongman. On December 17, 1959, Bruno Sammartino made his wrestling debut. It only took 19 seconds for him to pin Dmitri Grabowski; a star was being made.

Bruno was signed by the Capitol Wrestling Corporation, led by Vince McMahon Sr., and was wrestling in Madison Square Garden by 1960. Buddy Rogers held the NWA world title at the time, and "The Nature Boy" had a massive following in the Northeast, where McMahon was based. Bruno knew that he wouldn't be pushed over the champ, so he gave his notice to McMahon and planned to go out west to work for Professor Roy Shire and his "outlaw" promotion, Big Time Wrestling. However, it never happened. While making his way to California, Sammartino ended up missing two shows he was booked for, one in Chicago and one in Baltimore. In his autobiography, Sammartino said he believed that this was a set-up by McMahon, who double-booked him, knowing he would miss a booking and be suspended. Set up or not, Bruno was indeed suspended not only in Illinois and Maryland, but also California, which agreed to honor the other states' decision to suspend.

Sammartino had no opportunity to work in the ring, so he returned home to Pittsburgh, where he found work as a laborer, a position he may have felt he would keep the rest of his working life. And it may very well have been if not for the advice of friend and fellow wrestler Yukon Eric.

Yukon Eric convinced Bruno to contact Frank Tunney, the promoter in Toronto. Toronto had a massive Italian immigrant population and Yukon Eric knew that Sammartino would get over big with them. He was young, strong, and one of their own, and he was now fluent in both English and Italian. Tunney knew a good thing when he saw it and took the chance of booking Sammartino, ignoring the suspension.

Teamed with "Whipper" Billy Watson, Bruno got his first big push in 1962, when the team won the international tag team title. Yukon Eric was right, and Tunney's risk paid off. It didn't take long for Bruno to become a star in Toronto. He received a pair of title shots against NWA world champion Lou Thesz in Canada, with the first match ending in a draw and the second seeing Sammartino dominate before going down to a fluky pinfall.

The NWA allowed these matches to happen for one reason. Toots Mondt and Vince McMahon Sr. had formed the WWWF, and NWA kingpin Sam Muchnick knew the draw of Bruno. Keeping Bruno in a program with the NWA champion kept the NWA strong and kept Bruno associated with the NWA instead of the new WWWF. McMahon was recognizing Rogers as WWWF champion, refusing to acknowledge the January 24, 1963, bout that saw Thesz beat Rogers for the belt in Toronto. "The Nature Boy" did better business in the Northeast, so McMahon wanted to keep him as champion.

However, Rogers suffered a mild heart attack and needed time away from the ring. The WWWF needed a new champ. McMahon turned to Bruno. McMahon and Mondt paid the fine to get Bruno's suspension lifted and matched him against the champ. On May 17, 1963, Sammartino defeated Rogers in just 48 seconds to win the WWWF title, submitting Rogers with a backbreaker. The match had to be quick by necessity to prevent any strain on Rogers's heart. This not only saved Rogers any stress, but also made Bruno somewhat of a folk hero. This great champion, a man who defeated Pat O'Connor for the NWA title and was as feared as anyone in the game, couldn't last one minute with Bruno.

Bruno would keep his title for a record seven years, eight months, and one day before finally dropping the belt to Ivan Koloff in Madison Square Garden. When Bruno was finally pinned, the crowd simply went silent, unable to comprehend that the mighty Sammartino had lost to "The Russian Bear."

The promotion was still successful, but McMahon wasn't generating the money he did with the Italian hero on top. His new babyface, Pedro Morales, had beaten Koloff for the belt. New York had a massive Puerto Rican population, but Morales wasn't drawing crowds the way Bruno had. McMahon asked Bruno to become champion again. Bruno was unwilling to do it. The strain and pressure of being champion for more than seven years had been exhausting. McMahon sweetened the deal by offering Bruno a higher percentage of the gate and a lighter workload. On December 10, 1973, Bruno won the title for a second time, beating Stan Stasiak for the belt.

By now Bruno was 38 years old, and during this title reign he suffered some serious injuries, including a fractured neck when Stan Hansen

Bruno Sammartino in his second reign as WWWF heavyweight champion.

PHOTO BY GEORGE NAPOLITANO

dropped him on his head during a botched bodyslam. Age and injuries made Bruno ask the boss to allow him to relinquish his title. His second title reign came to an end on April 30, 1977, when he dropped the belt to "Superstar" Billy Graham in Baltimore.

"Bruno got the job done every time he walked into the ring," said Baron Von Raschke, who challenged Sammartino for the world title in 1977. "He had his style and I had mine but we worked it out fairly well. Bruno came through Montreal one time when I was starting out and they had me work with him. Because I was Mad Dog Vachon's partner, I was over pretty good, but I was still very much a rookie. It was one of the nights I learned a big lesson. Montreal is mostly French and English, but there is also a large Italian population, and when Bruno was there that night there were a lot of Italians in the crowd. The promoter told me I should attack Bruno right away and just keep pounding on him. And not knowing any better, before the instructions were given and everything, I started to pummel him, got him down, bing bang boom. And as I was doing that, I noticed the front row was getting closer and closer to the ring. So we'd be up on our feet and I kept attacking him and the front row, all four sides was moving in, moving in, moving in. So Bruno whispers in my ear, 'You better lay off for a while.' So I took his advice and sure enough they backed up and sat down because we were very close to a big explosive riot in Paul Sauvé Arena."

According to the 2019 book *Wrestling in the Garden,* by Scott Teal and J Michael Kenyon, Sammartino headlined 130 main events at Madison Square Garden throughout his career, including 45 sell-outs, earning the Garden the sobriquet "The House That Bruno Built." In an example of the unsubstantiated hyperbole that can be found on the internet, those numbers have been reported on some websites as 211 main events and 188 sell-outs, though Teal and Kenyon's numbers are the real deal. Bruno also headlined three shows at Shea Stadium: a 65-minute draw against Morales in 1972 (in a rare babyface-versus-babyface title match), a grudge match against Hansen in 1976, and a steel cage bout against Larry Zbyszko in 1980.

"I've seen all of the champions of the last 40 or 50 years. If I was from another planet — and each time era is different, okay — but of all the eras, if Bruno Sammartino walked down to the ring and I was from another planet, I would know that he was the world heavyweight champion," said Kevin Sullivan. "The way he carried himself. The way he looked. The way he made it look legit. Bruno maybe was not the smoothest worker, but he sold out everywhere for the longest time. One of the things that I appreciate is great work and he's a great worker. Until you start filling up buildings consistently, you're a great technician. Buddy Rogers used to say, when guys gave excuses, like 'The Red Sox are in town today' and 'they got a fair going on' and 'there's a fishing tournament,' Buddy Rogers would say, 'If they wanna see you, Daddy-o, they'll climb over broken glass.' And that's the truth."

Bruno continued to compete at a reduced schedule, including a time-limit draw against NWA world champion Harley Race in St. Louis. He was dubbed "The Living Legend" and remained the most popular star in the WWWF. In his final major program, he feuded with Zbyszko, a young Pittsburgh grappler he had taken under his wing. When Zbyszko turned on Bruno, it gave him enough heat to last the rest of his career.

"The first couple days after the TV show (where Zbyszko's turn aired), I didn't believe how much heat I had. It was ridiculous," Zbyszko said. "Death threats and everything. But in those days it was different, the audience really believed. When Bruno fell down in the ring and was bleeding, people in the audience had heart attacks and died! People really loved him. They believed in him. He was a hero."

Bruno was a hero to so many, not just his Italian countrymen, but people across all ethnicities and races. He was a symbol of strength and determination. He was a superhero, yet he was also human. He had power and he had humility. He was a good guy that the people could believe in and kids could look up to. He was the model for all babyfaces to follow, from Hulk Hogan and Dusty Rhodes to John Cena and Roman Reigns.

Sammartino died on April 18, 2018, at the age of 82.

DORY FUNK JR.

"If anybody embodies Lou Thesz, it's got to be Dory Funk Jr. Smooth as silk."

That's how Jim Ross introduced Funk at the 2019 Cauliflower Alley Club awards banquet where Funk received the Lou Thesz Lifetime Achievement award, which was presented to him by the reigning NWA champion, Nick Aldis.

"He is one of the most admired and respected champions in the history of the business," Aldis said. "Dory Funk Jr. has been holding the door open (for younger talent) for years."

Born February 3, 1941, Dorrance was the first-born son of Amarillo, Texas–based wrestler and promoter Dory Funk, a young wrestler who had returned from World War II to start a family and career in the ring. He attended West Texas State University (now West Texas A&M University), where he played offensive tackle on the team that won the Sun Bowl in 1963. Groomed for the ring since he was a child, he made his pro wrestling debut that same year. Just four months later, he earned his first world title shot against AWA champion Verne Gagne.

Funk cut his teeth in the Amarillo territory before moving on to the Florida and Missouri territories, as well as tours of Australia for Jim Barnett and Japan for Giant Baba's All Japan Pro Wrestling. He was a magnificent scientific wrestler with an innate sense of timing and pace. From early in his career, he displayed a mastery of crowd control, building an audience to excitement, then bringing them back and building suspense and anticipation all over again. While technical wrestling was his forte, he didn't shy away from brawls. He was one of the few wrestlers that could go hold-for-hold with Gagne and Thesz, but could also throw hands with legendary brawlers like Stan Hansen and Bruiser Brody.

On February 11, 1969, Dory upended Gene Kiniski to win the NWA world title in Tampa, earning the victory with his signature finishing hold, the spinning toehold, applied after a series of seven consecutive bodyslams. Dory was the polar opposite of Kiniski — a humble, clean-cut technical fan favorite. He was exactly the infusion of youth and charisma the NWA needed at the time.

"I believe Junior was the greatest champ since Thesz. I really mean that, not just 'cause he's my brother," Terry Funk said. "But he could do it all. He should have been champ longer, but that's the business. Plus, he was much tougher than ya think. And smart. Junior could do it all."

Dory held the world title for more than four years, successfully defending the championship against a veritable Hall of Fame of title contenders, including Thesz, the Sheik, Johnny Valentine, Nick Bockwinkel, Billy Robinson, Harley Race, and many, many more.

Dory dropped the world title to Race in May 1973, just a couple months after suffering a separated shoulder and other injuries in an accident in his pick-up truck in which he swerved off the road and into a creek to avoid a cow in the road. Critics contend that the "pick-up accident" was a work, or at least embellished, and that Dory was feigning an injury to avoid dropping the world title to the NWA's chosen championship successor, Jack Brisco. Instead, he put over Race, who in turn put over Brisco. It proved to be Dory's one and only NWA world title run, though his little brother, Terry, won the belt in 1975.

After dropping the belt, Dory worked more in All Japan and — following the death of Dory Sr. — took the lead in booking American wrestlers for tours of All Japan, working as the business conduit between All Japan and the Amarillo office. Dory had three runs as NWA international heavyweight champion during the early 1980s and, along with Terry, formed the top *gaijin* (foreign) tag team in Japan.

In 1986, both Dory and Terry joined Vince McMahon's WWF. Renamed "Hoss Funk," Dory was out of place in the gimmick-heavy WWF. At 45 years old, his hairline was receding and he looked pale and pedestrian compared to the tanned bodybuilders running rampant in the

Terry Funk (standing) and Dory Funk Jr. (seated). In addition to being the only brothers to be NWA world champions, they also made a formidable tag team.

PHOTO BY GEORGE NAPOLITANO

federation at the time. Other than a *WrestleMania* 2 match against the Junkyard Dog and Tito Santana, his WWF run was largely forgettable.

After leaving the WWF, Dory continued to wrestle in Japan and Puerto Rico, as well as the independent circuit. In 1991, he established the Funking Conservatory professional wrestling school in Ocala, Florida. Dory brokered an agreement with the WWF a few years later, and several WWF prospects (including Kurt Angle, Edge, Matt and Jeff Hardy, and Mickie James) were sent to train under Dory at his Funkin' Dojo prior to making their WWF debut.

"I started training, really, with the West Texas kids," Funk said in a 2014 interview with *Pro Wrestling Illustrated*. "I trained Stan Hansen. A young guy you might have heard of, my brother Terry, I was involved with training him. Jumbo Tsuruta came over from All Japan, and I worked with him in preparation for his debut in 1973. I really enjoyed working for Vince and WWE as a trainer with the Funkin' Dojo. And I'm working with the stars of the future here with BANG! TV. The most satisfying thing to me is seeing the kids that I worked with and seeing them be successful in professional wrestling."

Dory had a run in ECW, teaming with his brother, Terry, in 1994, and unsuccessfully challenged Shane Douglas for the ECW world title in 1997. He also wrestled an exhibition match against Nick Bockwinkel at WCW Slamboree in 1993 and was a surprise entrant in the 1996 WWF Royal Rumble.

Remarkably, as of this writing in 2020, Dory still continues to compete. In February 2020, he wrestled a six-man tag match with Rick and Scott Steiner at the Funking Conservatory at the age of 79.

In addition to the Lou Thesz Lifetime Achievement award from the CAC, Dory has been enshrined in the WWF Hall of Fame, the *Wrestling Observer* Hall of Fame, the Professional Wrestling Hall of Fame, and the George Tragos/Lou Thesz Professional Wrestling Hall of Fame, and has received the Stanley Weston Award from *Pro Wrestling Illustrated*. As a wrestler, a trainer, and an ambassador for the sport of wrestling, Dory Funk Jr. has been one of the all-time greats.

"A wrestler's job for the promotion is to perform for the fans. Putting people in the seats, that's what it's all about," Funk said. "That part hasn't changed. It's still the same business that it was years and years ago. There are just different ways of accomplishing the same thing."

TERRY FUNK

What do you get when you combine a natural gift for performing, great athletic ability, and a father who was one of the roughest and toughest to ever get in a wrestling ring? You get a man who may very well be one of the most respected and admired men to ever put on the tights, a man whose career spanned more than 50 years, and who — in the final years of his career — took part in several insane hardcore matches men half his age couldn't handle. You get Terry Funk.

Born June 30, 1944, Terry was the second son of Dory Funk. Terry's life began in Hammond, Indiana, surrounded by wrestling and wrestlers. The young family traveled around the country while Dory developed his name and ability. Some of Terry's earliest memories were of the wrestling business.

"Gorgeous George use to come over to our trailer in Columbus, Ohio, when I was a kid when he would be coming back from a show," Funk remembered. "My mom would cook for him."

The family eventually planted roots in Amarillo, Texas, a location now synonymous with the Funk name. Terry and his older brother, Dory Jr., were both strong, athletic kids, playing football and competing in amateur wrestling. However, by the time they were teenagers, they were learning how to handle themselves in the professional style of wrestling, albeit not necessarily by their own choice.

"How many guys did I beat the shit out of that wanted to be wrestlers, I'm talking since I was 15 or 16 years old?" Funk said. "A guy would say he wanted to be a wrestler and my father would say, 'Well, go ahead and get in the ring with my kids. If you can beat either one of them, then maybe you can be a wrestler.' This is when I was 15 or 16!"

This introduction to the business may seem brutal or cruel, but to the Funk boys it was just normal life. Plus, they seldom lost these fights.

After high school, Terry followed in his brother's footsteps, first attending West Texas State University as a football player, then, at the age of 21, entering the world of professional wrestling. For the next half-century, Terry Funk was one of the hardest-working, tough-as-nails madmen to enthrall wrestling audiences around the world.

It would take an entire book to talk about Terry Funk's in-ring career, from being half of the first pair of brothers to win the NWA world title (which he accomplished by defeating Funk family rival Jack Brisco in 1975), to his massive appeal in Japan, to his days as a hardcore superstar. Needless to say, if there is anything you can accomplish in wrestling, Terry Funk did it, and often more than once.

Today, Dory Funk Jr. is remembered as the more technically skilled of the brothers while Terry is remembered as the unorthodox tough guy. This isn't exactly accurate, though. Terry was very skilled and had natural wrestling abilities, thanks to his amateur background, but he was so damn tough that it can be overlooked. "Terry Funk, that was another great performer, totally different style from his brother," said Buddy Colt. "Terry was more like Dory Sr. Rough and rugged style, but also a great worker."

Funk's impact on wrestling goes beyond just his in-ring ability and personal accomplishments as a promoter, performer, and trainer. He also became a mentor to many young wrestlers. In some cases, he may not have even realized it. "Any time you could be on a show with Terry Funk it was like school in session," said Bob Cook. "There are certain things you learn being around a guy like that that you don't even realize you're learning. You just soak it all in."

Even other second-generation wrestlers would learn things from Terry Funk that their lifetime around the business didn't teach them.

"Terry told me something that I never forgot," said Lanny Poffo, son of wrestler/promoter Angelo Poffo and brother of "Macho Man" Randy Savage. "I did a job for him in Madison Square Garden, on my second ever appearance in the Garden. He made me look so good I got over as if I had won. I didn't, but he made me look so good, just his effort, that's how great Terry is. He told me that it's more important to be peculiar than it is to be good. And when I became the Genius, that is the advice I kept in mind."

Inside the ring, Terry's list of feuds reads as a Who's Who of the history of wrestling. He had notable feuds with the likes of Jack Brisco, Harley Race, Ric Flair, Jerry Lawler, Hulk Hogan, Stan Hansen, Bruiser Brody, the Junkyard Dog, Ernie Ladd, Sabu, Tommy Dreamer, Cactus Jack (Mick Foley), and many more. The fact that Terry was able to work big draw angles with all these greats and was often one of their most memorable opponents is a true testament to his adaptability and versatility, in addition to his durability. He also earned respect. From the mid-1970s on, it was well known in the business that if you needed an angle to get over, Terry Funk was a man you could rely on to help sell it with his promos and matches, while being a true professional who could be trusted in the ring.

When Paul Heyman needed a veteran to serve as the locker room leader of his upstart promotion, Extreme Championship Wrestling, in the 1990s, he turned to Funk. Funk — almost a decade removed from his memorable 1989 "I Quit" match against NWA world champion Ric Flair, was called upon to headline ECW's initial foray into pay-per-view. As the run-down grizzled vet seeking a chance at redemption and glory, he was the sentimental favorite. He defeated Raven to win the ECW championship in April 1997 at the age of 52. Years later, Heyman awarded Funk a championship belt and the honorary title of "Lifetime ECW World Heavyweight Champion."

Terry Funk also had a career outside of the wrestling business. Hollywood came calling, and he answered. It started in 1978, when he was cast in the film *Paradise Alley*, Sylvester Stallone's first film as a director. This wrestling film was filled with pros in cameo rolls: Gene Kiniski, Ray Stevens, Dory Jr., Dick Murdoch, Ted DiBiase, and Bob Roop, to name just a few, yet Terry was given a major role as Frankie the Thumper, the main antagonist. Terry was a natural actor and was comfortable in front of the camera. Funk joined the Screen Actors Guild and had a side career in film and television. Some of his more notable roles were Sergeant Nuzo on the TV series *Tequila and Bonetti*; Prometheus Jones, the tough guy/town veterinarian on the series *Wildside*; Ruker in another Stallone film, *Over the Top*; and probably most memorably in the 1989 cult classic *Road House,* as Morgan.

But as much as Terry enjoyed acting, his true passion was wrestling, and he sacrificed a potential full-time acting career so he could get back in the ring. He "retired" so many times it became a running joke in the business because Funk kept coming back. He couldn't resist the siren's song of the ring. "I had a good time making movies and shows, but in my heart, I was a wrestler," he said. "I loved the boys. I loved the road. Hell, I even liked the crazy guys."

After more than 50 years in the business (his final match took place in 2017), Terry is now retired to his famous Double Cross ranch in Amarillo. His love of the business is still obvious to anyone lucky enough to talk to him. Terry Funk truly made the fans believe. How did he manage to be so believable? "I still believe in myself," he said. "I truly believe in Ricky Steamboat. I truly believe in Harley Race, Pat O'Connor, Lou Thesz. I believed. I believed and I still believe in Jerry Lawler. And I believe I am who I am. And I know, that is honestly the truth."

JERRY LAWLER

Jerry Lawler didn't need a "world championship" to become the King of one of the most enduring and robust territories in America. Lawler became a megastar in his native Memphis and the national promotions eventually came to the King's front door.

Lawler was born November 29, 1949, in Memphis, Tennessee. While he was a boy, his family moved to Amherst, Ohio, near Cleveland, where he became a lifelong fan of the Cleveland Indians and Cleveland Browns. He played football and baseball in high school, but his biggest accomplishments came not on the gridiron or the ball diamond but in the art classroom.

"All through school, I was drawing and painting," Lawler said in an interview with ObserverNewsOnline. "I knew I wasn't going to win any kind of sports scholarship, but I did win a full-tuition commercial art scholarship to the University of Memphis. When I first started attending wrestling matches, I started drawing some pictures of wrestlers and that's how I got my foot in the door with wrestling."

Lawler sent some of his illustrations to Memphis wrestling promoter Aubrey Griffith. Griffith liked the drawings and had them shown on television, eventually striking up a deal with Lawler to provide wrestling training in exchange for his art submissions. He trained under Memphis wrestling great Jackie Fargo and made his pro debut in 1970.

He captured some regional titles, but the feud that really put him on the map — and made his career — came in 1974, when he feuded with his mentor, Jackie Fargo, for the NWA Southern heavyweight title. On July 24, 1974, Lawler defeated Fargo for the championship and the title of "King of Wrestling." Lawler went all-in on the regal gimmick, adopting his signature crown and majestic robe.

"He was a great bump-taker," said Ron Fuller. "He took a lot of tremendous bumps, especially in his early days, before he had to back off from it a little bit. He was also really smart. He honed in quickly on how to call a match and the psychology of what goes on in the ring. Once you get a grasp of that, you can do anything — you can go heel, you can go babyface, whatever it is you want to do."

And go from babyface to heel (and back again) is something Lawler frequently and effortlessly did. By the end of 1974, he had turned babyface by splitting with nefarious manager Sam Bass. When he was a face, Lawler was absolutely beloved, by far the top hero in the territory. There were heel turns through the years, but Lawler always found a way to get the Memphis fans squarely in his corner when he wanted to, demonstrating a mastery of ring psychology and storytelling that wrestlers continue to study today.

"In the Memphis territory, Lawler understood what it took to be a top heel or a top babyface and he adjusted accordingly," said former referee Jimmy Korderas, who officiated many of Lawler's later matches in WWE. "Obviously he wasn't as technically sound as a Bret Hart or a Chris Benoit or Dean Malenko, but he knew how to engage an audience. He knew what he was capable of doing and didn't try to do more than that. He was also an entertainer. Maybe even before Vince (McMahon) got into 'sports entertainment,' you might make an argument that Jerry kind of saw the sports entertainment aspect of it before Vince did. He began coming out with the crown and the cape and the whole bit. He got the entertainment aspect and was able to capitalize on that, and that's what set him apart."

One of Lawler's signature mannerisms — one guaranteed to get a fan reaction — was to pull down the strap of his singlet when he was about to launch his comeback to finish the match. When the strap came down, "The King" was deadly serious. Lawler would rally with a series of fiery punches that would bring the fans into hysterics.

"As a performer, he was the best," said Al Snow. "He could sell anything. He could turn babyface to heel like nothing. And at no point, no matter how old he is and how many years people have been watching him, has he lost that ability to get a babyface over or to get heat on a heel."

Lawler had a stake in the Memphis office with partner Jerry Jarrett. The two had wrested control of part of the Tennessee territory away from promoter Nick Gulas, who planned on building the territory around his unproven son, George. Jarrett and Lawler established the Continental Wrestling Association, which thrived, while Gulas's NWA Mid-America company fizzled out by 1980. With Lawler and Jarrett taking turns with booking duties, Memphis became the last territory to succumb to the WWF's national expansion.

Lawler was introduced on the national stage courtesy of comedian and actor Andy Kaufman. Kaufman, a wrestling fan since childhood, was a fan of Lawler's. When the two were introduced by wrestling writer and photographer Bill Apter, they hatched a plan to do business together. As part of his comedy show, Kaufman had dubbed himself the "intergender heavyweight champion" and would wrestle women from the audience. It was pure pro wrestling heat, with Kaufman playing the role of arrogant misogynist to perfection and infuriating women with his insults and chauvinism.

As part of the storyline, Lawler took issue with Kaufman's behavior, igniting a war of words between the two, with Kaufman ridiculing Lawler and his "rube" Memphis fans. On April 5, 1982, "The King" and "The Comic" squared off in a one-on-one match at the Mid-South Coliseum. The match saw Lawler get disqualified by using a piledriver (followed by a second piledriver after the bell), which was banned as a dangerous move in the territory. Kaufman sold that Lawler had badly injured his neck with the move. The angle was hot enough for both Kaufman and Lawler to be invited onto *The David Letterman Show* as guests. Kaufman came on wearing a neck brace, while Lawler was roundly booed by the New York City studio audience. The segment went well at first until Kaufman insisted on an apology; Lawler responded with a stiff open-hand slap that send Kaufman sprawling to the floor. Kaufman responded by throwing a cup of coffee onto Lawler. And just like that, the Memphis wrestling territory was the hottest topic in the country.

For most of the 1980s, the biggest names in wrestling ventured to Memphis to face Lawler. Lawler won (and lost) regional titles every few weeks, including the AWA Southern heavyweight title, which he held 52 times between 1974 and 1987. On May 9, 1988, Lawler defeated Curt Hennig to win the AWA world title, with plans made to merge the CWA with the AWA and make a stand against the rapidly growing WWF. Lawler defeated World Class Championship Wrestling champion Kerry Von Erich (the once-powerful WCCW was in its death throes at the time) to unify those titles, but a unified AWA/CWA/World Class never panned out. The CWA pulled out of the AWA and Lawler was stripped of the world title.

Lawler and Jarrett recovered by forming the United States Wrestling Association, having bought into Fritz Von Erich's WCCW. The USWA set out to run shows in Tennessee and Texas, but that fell apart a short time later when the Von Erich family withdrew their organization and unsuccessfully tried to relaunch World Class. In 1992, Lawler and Jarrett brokered a talent exchange with the WWF that saw Lawler join the WWF as a heel color commentator and part-time wrestler, while remaining a babyface in the USWA in Tennessee.

The move to the WWF gave Lawler a new lease on life. He had a classic feud with Bret Hart and established himself as one of the voices of the company, along with play-by-play man Jim Ross. He continued to wrestle periodically for WWE through 2012, when he suffered a heart attack during a live broadcast of *Monday Night Raw*, having wrestled a tag team match with Randy Orton against CM Punk and Dolph Ziggler earlier in the night. Despite that incident, he continued to wrestle on the independents and — as of this writing — he's still active on the indies at the age of 70.

With more than 150 championships to his credit, Lawler has proven to be one of the most versatile and adaptable wrestlers of all time.

HARLEY RACE

Harley Race was tougher than a $2 steak and meaner than a junkyard dog. The self-professed "Greatest Wrestler on God's Green Earth" proudly carried the NWA world championship seven (or eight, depending on whether you count his three-day international run in 1984) times between 1973 and 1984.

Bobby Heenan once said, "The only two men in the world that Andre the Giant feared were Haku and Harley Race." Whether or not that's true only Andre would know for sure, but Andre was certainly willing to let Race bodyslam him, an honor he reserved only for a handful of opponents, especially later in his career.

Race overcame polio as a child, got expelled from high school for punching the principal, and recovered from a car crash that nearly put him in a wheelchair for life just one year into his burgeoning wrestling career. And that's just the tip of the iceberg. Stories about "Handsome" Harley's antics and exploits are part of the oral history of pro wrestling, from allegedly brandishing a gun in the locker room to teaching lessons to loudmouths in gin mills.

"God, Harley scared everybody," said Jonard Solie, son of veteran wrestling announcer Gordon Solie. "I would hear stories about him in bars back in Missouri and — wow. I'm not sure how true they were, but they were believable enough to scare everyone who heard them."

"Those stories you hear about how tough Harley Race was, I mean out of the ring, they're all true," said Paul Orndorff. "He was good — real good — and he was tough. You had to be then. If you weren't tough, you weren't going to make it."

"Harley had some shooting skills in that he was able to take care of himself," said Ron Fuller. "He wasn't known for shooting, but he was known as a brawler who would get things done. Whatever he had to do, he'd do it."

"Harley wasn't just tough. He could kick anybody's ass," Terry Funk said. "But just being a tough guy didn't get him to where he got. Harley got to the top the same way Lou Thesz did, or Danny Hodge, Pat O'Connor, Dory, or Jack Brisco did. He could wrestle and he could hold his own no matter what anyone threw at him. And he was so professional that he knew what was good for business."

"Handsome" Harley Race: as gritty and tough as they come.

PHOTO BY GEORGE NAPOLITANO

Born April 11, 1943, in Maryville, Missouri, Race was the son of sharecroppers who impressed upon him at a young age the value of hard work. After being suspended from school at 15 ("I was barred from school property until I apologized . . . I'm not the apologetic type, so it would become a lifetime suspension," he wrote in his 2004 autobiography, *King of the Ring: The Harley Race Story*), he landed a job working on a farm belonging to Stanislaus and Wladek Zbyszko. A wrestling fan as a child, Race felt the pull of the ring, and began training under the Zbyszkos.

"Mostly what they taught me were submission holds," he wrote. "They'd put me in one and say, 'Try to get out.' The more I tried, the more I wore myself out or hurt myself."

Race got hired by St. Joseph, Missouri, promoter Gust Karras, who assigned him odd jobs with the company, including driving the 800-pound Happy Humphrey, who was simply too large to get behind the steering wheel. He wrestled his first match in 1960, then moved to Nashville, where he wrestled under the name Jack Long. But, barely a year into his career, he was in a horrific car accident that killed his pregnant wife, Vivian. The doctors said he was at risk of having his leg amputated and that he was unlikely to be able to walk again. Resolute, Race told the doctor he would send him tickets to his next match.

True to his word, Race made a full recovery and returned to the ring. He began wrestling under his given name while working in the Amarillo territory in 1964 and formed a tag team with Larry Hennig. Race and Hennig held the AWA tag team title and had a lengthy feud with Verne Gagne on top.

After that stint in the AWA, Race moved back to the NWA, winning the NWA Missouri title in 1972. On May 24, 1973, Race defeated Dory Funk Jr. to win the NWA world title in Kansas City. Race was selected by the NWA as a worthy and credible champion when Funk balked at dropping the title to fellow babyface Jack Brisco. Race held the belt for two months before doing the favors for Brisco in Houston. He also bought into the Kansas City and St. Louis territories.

Race regained the title on February 6, 1977, with a win over Terry Funk in Toronto. This time, he held the world title for two and a half years, losing it to Dusty Rhodes in 1979. Though others like Rhodes, Giant Baba, and Tommy Rich held the title for brief runs, Race was the flagbearer of the NWA from 1977 through late 1983, when he dropped the belt to Ric Flair in a steel cage match as the main event of the first *Starrcade* supercard. It was a passing of the torch from the Race era into the Flair era, one that Flair didn't take for granted.

"Without Harley Race, there was no Ric Flair," Flair tweeted following Race's death in 2019.

Jim Cornette considered Race to be one of the best bump-takers in the business and praised his body control.

"Harley's bumps were always perfect," Cornette said on the *Jim Cornette Experience* podcast. "They were wild all over the place. They were backwards over the top rope and this and that, the big backdrops, whatever. They were perfect. When he got bodyslammed and he'd go up higher than anybody else, and with that body, and that body weight, and that fucking physique. Or when he'd take a backdrop and he'd get backdropped higher than anybody else. He would always land perfect. Every inch of his body from his shoulders to his hips, and then the flat of his feet would land at the same time. Bam! Kids in wrestling school, if you take a bump and it goes 'clomp, clomp,' you've fucked up. If you take a bump and it goes 'Bam!' you've done it right because you've hit everywhere at the same time. You've dispersed the shock. If Harley took a headlock takeover, he would fucking throw his body. He would push off with his left foot and he would throw his right leg straight up in the air. That way, his body had to follow. And he would land perfectly on the other side and over his opponent. . . . He was an incredible fucking worker and was always in control of himself."

In 1986, Race shocked the wrestling world by leaving the NWA for the WWF. To many, he seemed to be a fish out of water; a legit 43-year-old tough guy in a rival company populated by bodybuilders, cartoon characters, and gimmick acts. But Race considered the WWF to be a new challenge and he went into it with gusto. After winning the King of the Ring tournament, he became "King" Harley Race, complete with regal purple robes and a gaudy crown. He had a match at *WrestleMania* III, beating the Junkyard Dog, and had a series against WWF world champion Hulk Hogan in early 1988, but an abdominal hernia effectively spelled the end of his WWF run.

He continued to wrestle periodically, including stints in the AWA and World Championship Wrestling, then settled into a role as a manager, guiding both Lex Luger and Big Van Vader to the world title. He opened and operated World League Wrestling and the Harley Race Wrestling Academy and had a hand in training dozens of wrestlers, including Trevor Murdoch and Tommaso Ciampa. At his school, he stressed the fundamentals of mat wrestling as well as the importance of showmanship.

"The longer your body is on the mat, the longer you are in the business," he said in a 2005 interview with the *Des Moines Register*. "If your background is in basic mat wrestling, you can wrestle anybody.

"You go in the ring and you're the band director," he said. "You're not part of the audience or part of the band. What you create in your mind is what makes people get behind you or go against you."

Race died of lung cancer on August 1, 2019. He was 76.

DUSTY RHODES

"I admit, I don't look like the athlete of the day is supposed to look. My belly is just a little big. My heinie is just a little big. But, brother, I am bad and they know I'm bad."

The "son of a plumber" was wrestling's working-class hero of the 1970s and 1980s. One of the most charismatic wrestlers ever to lace up the boots, Rhodes was a three-time NWA world champion and a successful and influential booker with Jim Crockett Promotions.

Virgil Runnels Jr. was born on October 11, 1945, in Austin, Texas. A wrestling fan as a child, he adored Sweet Daddy Siki and Thunderbolt Patterson. He graduated from Arlington High School and went on to play baseball and football at West Texas State University. He earned a spot on the Hartford Charter Oaks in the short-lived Continental Football League, but when the team folded, he decided to give wrestling a try. He started up in the Boston area for Tony Santos's Big Time Wrestling promotion in 1967 before moving back to Texas where he worked for Fritz Von Erich. There he adopted the name Dusty Rhodes, inspired by the character Lonesome Rhodes in the movie *A Face in the Crowd*.

In 1968, he began teaming with fellow Texan Dick Murdoch in the Kansas City territory. As the Texas Outlaws, Rhodes and Murdoch became one of the area's top heel teams. Over the next few years, the Outlaws made the rounds, with stops in Texas, Michigan, Florida, Australia, and Japan. Working tags with Murdoch helped Dusty understand the nuances of wrestling psychology and getting a reaction from the fans.

"The fans, the audience, the universe, they're not going to let you come back until you're ready. It's like tuning a guitar by ear," he told SLAM! Wrestling. "I know that Murdoch and myself in a tag match, when it would be time for the babyfaces to make their comeback, if they, the fans — Murdoch taught me this — if they weren't ready, he'd cut them off. He'd just cut them off until it was right for that huge explosion at the end of the movie. There's a fine line there. You can sell your ass off to where they wanted you to come back, but you went too far to where you just died and they've lost interest in you. That's the art of the game."

In 1974, Rhodes had a babyface turn while working a tag match with Pak Song against Eddie and Mike Graham in Florida. After subtly teasing dissension with Song and manager Gary Hart throughout the match, Song "accidentally" hit Rhodes with a chop aimed for Eddie Graham. Rhodes fell to the floor. When he regrouped, he re-entered the ring, glared at Song, did a quick Ali shuffle, and then tore into his tag team partner, throwing some shots at Hart for good measure. The fans came unglued. Dusty Rhodes, "The American Dream," was a bona fide fan favorite.

"I met Dusty Rhodes in Florida with Eddie Graham's promotion," said Koko Ware. "Dusty Rhodes was the Hulk Hogan back then. He had all of the charisma. The Dream could talk. His gimmick wasn't wrestling. He didn't wrestle much at all, it was mostly just punching and kicking. He wasn't the kind of guy who was going to put holds on you. But the fans just loved him. I never had any problems with the Dream. He was always a hell of a guy to me."

The key to Rhodes's popularity was his blue-collar ethos. In an era where wrestlers — and athletes in general — were getting bigger and more muscular, Rhodes looked a guy you'd bump into at the corner bar. But he talked like street preacher. He was a jive-talking, booty-shaking character who was simply larger than life. "I just thank God that there are people like yourself (who) come out to see 'The American Dream,' because when I was growing up I sure didn't think that 265 pounds of blue-eyed soul would captivate a country like I have," Rhodes said in a WWWF television interview at the time.

Rhodes bounced between the NWA territories and the WWWF in the late 1970s and early 1980s. He feuded with WWWF world champion Billy Graham, headlining Madison Square Garden twice. On August 21, 1979, he defeated Harley Race to win the NWA world title in Tampa, but he dropped it back to Race just five days later in

Orlando. Two years later, he scored another win over Race in Atlanta for his second world championship. Three months later, he lost the belt to Ric Flair in Kansas City.

In an example of what would later come to be known as the "Dusty finish," Rhodes — wrestling under a mask as the Midnight Rider — appeared to have won the world title for the third time in 1982. In the storyline, Rhodes had been suspended in Florida and, coincidentally, a masked man with the exact same physique and lisp appeared on the scene. The Rider scored a win over Flair, but acting NWA President Bob Geigel declared that the Rider would have to unmask or return the title. The championship was returned to Flair, but the Dusty finish (where a challenger appears to have won a title only for the decision to be overturned later) made fans clamor for the rematches, ensuring the feud had staying power. Effective in small doses, the Dusty finish became as played out as a cheesy M. Night Shyamalan twist by the end of the 1980s.

Rhodes settled in as booker and headliner for Jim Crockett Promotions, a position which frequently put him in the crosshairs of wrestlers who felt he was pushing himself too much. Yet it's hard to argue Rhodes's popularity and drawing power at the time. He was voted Best Babyface (1980), Most Charismatic (1982), and Best Booker (1986) by readers of the *Wrestling Observer Newsletter*, but he was also voted Most Overrated (1987 and 1988) and Readers' Least Favorite Wrestler of the year (1987 and 1988). His booking had become stale and he became a polarizing figure.

His famous 1985 "Hard Times" interview still stands as one of the most powerful and captivating wrestling promos of all time. In that three-and-a-half minute classic, Dusty accused Ric Flair of "putting hard times on Dusty Rhodes and his family" and segued into the hard times that the unemployed American textile workers and auto workers were facing. "'Nature Boy' Ric Flair, the world title belongs to these people (the fans)," Rhodes said, with the fiery passion of a preacher. "I'm gonna reach out right now. I want you at home to know, my hand is touching your hand . . . the love that was given me, I will repay you now because I will be the next world's heavyweight champion."

On July 26, 1986, "The Dream" won the NWA world title for the third time, beating Flair at the Great American bash. Again, his reign would be brief — he dropped the belt back to Flair just two weeks later in St. Louis. Rhodes moved on to feuds with Tully Blanchard and the Four Horsemen, but was fired after an angle he booked — where the Road Warriors gouged his eye bloody with a metal spike — violated the standards of Turner Broadcasting System, which had purchased Jim Crockett Promotions.

In 1989, Rhodes turned up in the WWF. In an attempt to make the former booker for the rival NWA look foolish, the WWF front office dressed Rhodes in a polka-dotted outfit and cast him as a working-class clown. Rhodes went into the gimmick with gusto, however, and managed to get over in the WWF, having memorable feuds with "Macho King" Randy Savage and "The Million Dollar Man" Ted DiBiase.

Rhodes left the WWF in 1991 and returned to WCW, where he served, at various times, as a member of the booking committee, a manager, and a color commentator, still donning the tights from time to time. He did a stint in ECW in 2000, returned to WCW before the company folded, did some time on the independents, and landed in Total Nonstop Action in 2003, where he took on booking duties behind the scenes and served as an on-air authority figure.

Rhodes returned to WWE in 2005 as a member of the creative team and made periodic appearances on TV. He became the head writer and creative director for NXT, WWE's developmental program, and became a father figure and mentor to a new generation of up-and-coming talent.

Rhodes died on June 11, 2015, after a lengthy illness. He was 69. Two months after his death, WWE announced that an NXT tag team tournament would be named the Dusty Rhodes Tag Team Classic in his honor. His sons, Dustin and Cody, have both had successful careers in wrestling, with Cody playing a vital role in helping to launch All Elite Wrestling in 2019.

BOB BACKLUND

"Maybe he didn't look it, but man, he was tough. He could make you scream with an armbar."

That's how Paul Orndorff described Bob Backlund, the All-American boy who carried the World Wrestling Federation from 1978 to 1983.

In the often flamboyant and over-the-top world of wrestling, Backlund was a throwback to a bygone era. A clean-cut, almost youthful-looking boy next door, he used his speed, freakish athleticism, technical wrestling ability, and intense determination to win over the hearts of fans around the world as well as multiple championship titles along the way.

Robert Backlund was born August 14, 1949, in Princeton, Minnesota. He began his wrestling journey at Princeton High School, where he was a state finalist in wrestling. At Waldorf Junior College in Iowa, he played football and earned All-American honors in wrestling. At North Dakota State, Backlund won the NCAA Division II title at 190 pounds, and finished fifth in the heavyweight division the following year. Backlund graduated with a degree in physical education, but the young redhead still had wrestling on his mind and in his heart.

Backlund was trained by fellow Minnesotan Eddie Sharkey and made his professional debut in 1973 in Verne Gagne's AWA. Despite not having a flashy gimmick or name, Backlund nonetheless became a fan favorite; his pure technical ability and boy-next-door appeal won the people over. Within a year, Backlund left the AWA to begin crossing the United States with the NWA, including a stop in Western States (Amarillo) for Terry and Dory Funk Jr., where he would win his first of many titles, defeating Terry Funk for the NWA Western States heavyweight title.

"Backlund got over fast, and he was a hell of a wrestler," Funk remembered. "We had Karl Von Steiger. He was doing this German angle, kind of mean, got lots of heat. So I get Backlund over, he gets Von Steiger over, and they kept going at it. I went to work with Dusty in Georgia, and then next thing I knew, Backlund was there in Georgia with me."

On April 23, 1976, Backlund defeated Harley Race to win the NWA Missouri heavyweight title, which was widely considered to be a stepping-stone to the NWA world championship. He held that title for 217 days before he dropped it to Jack Brisco. This run set Backlund up for his greatest in-ring success. In 1976, the "City That Never Sleeps" came calling and Backlund found his way to the WWWF. There, he was teamed with manager "Golden Boy" Arnold Skaaland, himself a former WWWF tag team champ (he held the WWWF U.S. tag title with Spiros Arion in 1976). With Skaaland in his corner, Backlund began a feud with champion "Superstar" Billy Graham. He defeated Graham to win the world title on February 20, 1978, at Madison Square Garden.

Personality-wise, Backlund and Graham were polar opposites. Graham, a bodybuilder draped in outrageous tie-dyes, was one of the best promo men of his era. Backlund was a soft-spoken, no-frills grappler. It was a natural rivalry, but one that represented a persistent challenge Backlund would face in the years to follow. As the WWWF continued to push wrestlers with overblown gimmicks (Graham, the Wild Samoans, Jimmy Snuka, Sgt. Slaughter, George "The Animal" Steele, the Iron Sheik) Backlund looked bland in comparison. Similar to the backlashes against Rocky Maivia, John Cena, and Roman Reigns decades later, a vocal minority of fans came to resent Backlund's success. Still, McMahon kept Backlund as his world champion for more than five years (a "phantom title change" to Antonio Inoki took place in Japan in 1979 but was not acknowledged in the U.S. at the time).

While he had his critics, Backlund helped bring the WWF out of the 1970s and into the 1980s, introducing a faster-paced, more athletic championship match in a company that had been dominated by plodding superheavyweights.

As 1983 drew to a close, McMahon decided on making Hulk Hogan the flagbearer of the WWF. McMahon asked Backlund to turn heel to set up a babyface Hogan win for the title. Backlund refused, unwilling to sully the sportsman-like image he had built up, and instead dropped the world title to the Iron Sheik, a former Amateur Athletic Union Greco-Roman wrestling champion in 1971. Backlund believed losing to a legitimate wrestler like the Iron Sheik would be a more fitting end to his run.

After losing the title to Sheik in December 1983, Backlund left the WWF. After a brief stint in the short-lived Pro Wrestling USA promotion, he retired in 1985, and eventually became a high school wrestling coach. He did, however, make a handful of returns to the ring, mostly in Japan, where he worked a few "shoot-style" matches for the Universal Wrestling Federation and the Union of Professional Wrestling Force International promotions.

In 1992, Backlund made an unlikely return to the WWF. This time, he was willing to go heel. In 1994, he turned on Bret Hart after losing a clean, technical match, locking Hart in his crossface chicken-wing submission lock. The All-American degenerated into the raving Mr. Backlund, a cocky, bowtie-wearing sadistic loudmouth. Ironically, while Backlund was past his prime as an athlete (yet still in remarkable physical condition, as illustrated by his record-setting 61:10 showing in the 1993 Royal Rumble), he finally hit his stride as an entertainer. Backlund beat Hart to win the world title for the second time on November 23, 1994. This time, he proved to be a transitional champion, losing the belt just three days later to Diesel (Kevin Nash) in an eight-second match at Madison Square Garden.

Backlund was inducted into the WWE Hall of Fame in 2013. After his retirement, he settled into a role as a goodwill ambassador for WWE, and had a brief return as the manager of Darren Young in 2016.

Bob Backlund was the perfect mix of "old school" shooter and 1980s wrestling superstar performer, and he ruled on top of the wrestling world as it was going through its evolution from one style into the next. There was nobody who could have been a better bridge between the two, and luckily both generations got to fully appreciate the wrestling genius of Bob Backlund.

WRESTLING TAKES HOLLYWOOD: THE WRESTLER AS CROSSOVER CELEBRITY

According to *Forbes*, the highest-paid Hollywood actor of 2020 made a remarkable $87.5 million between June 2019 and June 2020. That actor was Dwayne "The Rock" Johnson. Yes, this third-generation professional wrestler crossed over into mainstream pop culture, his films have grossed almost $14 billion worldwide, and he is considered one of the most recognizable men in the world, all this before the age of 50. Dwayne Johnson is arguably the most successful professional wrestler to cross over into mainstream celebrity, but he is far from the first.

It can be argued that being an elite-level pro wrestler itself makes you a celebrity. You are on television on a regular basis, you have fans all over the world. Your likeness is on posters and toys, and everywhere you go there are people who want an autograph, or photo, or just to shake your hand. So wrestlers are indeed celebrities, are they not? Yes, to an extent. Wrestling is a niche market, albeit a large one, but outside the community of fans, even the biggest stars in the business are widely unknown by the rest of society. We are going to take a look at some of the wrestlers who were able to gain success beyond the mat and a level of recognition outside of the fan base. In some cases, their fame overshadowed their wrestling careers, like the aforementioned Dwayne Johnson — there are millions of his fans who never knew the wrestling exploits of the Rock. Some of the men we'll meet in this chapter were bona fide stars, others were successful outside of wrestling but far from household names. And we will even look at a few who had such success as a wrestler alone that they became part of pop culture itself. Our first stop: Hollywood.

Wrestlers and movies have had a long relationship. Victor McLaglen was an accomplished boxer and pro wrestler before his breakthrough role as Charles Hinges in the 1924 film *The Beloved Brute*. McLaglen went on to win the 1935 Academy Award for Best Actor for his role in *The Informer*, and he starred opposite John Wayne as Squire Danaher in *The Quiet Man* (one of several movies he did with the Duke) in 1952.

In the 1930s, several wrestlers were cast in films, often playing themselves, such as Stanislaus Zbyszko in 1932's *Madison Square Garden*. Zbyszko appeared alongside many real figures also playing themselves, including boxers Jack Johnson, "Sailor" Tom Sharkey (who turned to pro wrestling when New York banned prizefighting), Billy Papke, and Tommy Ryan. To put this in perspective, in 1932 boxing was arguably the biggest sport in America, rivaled only by baseball. Zbyszko was a big enough name to be featured alongside these men, who were considered legends at the time. In fact, Stanislaus Zbyszko was such a popular figure that 45 years after he retired, a young wrestler named Larry Zbyszko took his surname as his own ring name.

"The name Zbyszko, that was Bruno's idea," Larry Zbyszko (born Lawrence Whistler) said. "I was Polish anyway. And in those days, the early '70s, the name was still known, people would come up to me and think Stanislaus was my grandfather." And asked if he told them he was: "Certainly, back then, yeah!"

Occasionally, professional wrestlers would become full-time character actors, such as Mike Mazurki. If the name doesn't ring a bell, anyone who is a fan of old films or old television shows has seen his face countless times. Mazurki appeared in well over 100 films, including classics such as *Some Like It Hot*, *Dick Tracy* (both the 1945 and 1990 versions), *Samson and Delilah*, and *The Thin Man Goes Home*. On the small screen, Mazurki had guest spots on *Gilligan's Island*, *The Munsters*, *Bonanza*, and *The Untouchables*, to name just a few. To the wrestling world, Mazurki is probably best known for his unmistakable cauliflower ears. Mazurki's swollen ear is the logo for the Cauliflower Alley Club, the organization he co-founded and served as the first president of back in 1965.

Another wrestler who had a long film career was "The Super Swedish Angel" Tor Johnson. Johnson became a B-film icon thanks to his appearance in three of Edward D. Wood Jr.'s films: *Bride of the Monster* and *Night of The Ghouls*, in which Tor plays the mute, hulking Lobo; but most famously *Plan 9 from Outer Space*, in which Tor plays Inspector Daniel Clay, who is killed and resurrected by the aliens as a mute zombie with a gaping mouth and facial scar. Thanks to his character in *Plan 9 from Outer Space*, the Don Post mask studio created a Tor Johnson Halloween mask in 1964. The mask was so successful, it remained in production every year until 2012 and is one of the best-selling masks of all time. The 400-plus-pound Johnson appeared in dozens of movies and television shows, even once as a contestant on Groucho Marx's quiz show *You Bet Your Life*. In an interesting casting choice, in the 1994 Tim Burton biopic of Edward D. Wood Jr., Tor Johnson was portrayed by another professional wrestler, George "The Animal" Steele.

Don Stansauk (Hard Boiled Haggerty) and Douglas A. Baker (Ox Baker) were also respected wrestlers who became better known as character actors.

Haggerty began his athletic career as a professional football player, drafted by the Detroit Lions and later traded to the Green Bay Packers. He began his wrestling career after two years with the Packers, and he traveled through multiple NWA territories, including Hawaii, Minneapolis, World Class, and Maple Leaf Wrestling, and even spent some time in the AWA in the early 1960s. But it was a small role in the 1969 musical western *Paint Your Wagon*, starring Lee Marvin and Clint Eastwood, that made Haggerty, billed as H.B. Haggerty in the credits, decide on a new career path. A film career was about to take precedence over a ring career. He appeared in a plethora of films and television shows over the next 29-plus years, including *Foxy Brown*, *The Four Deuces*, and even *The Muppet Movie*. His small-screen credits include *Happy Days*, *Kung Fu*, *The Love Boat*, *Adam-12*, *Baretta*, *Columbo*, and many others. He worked in film consistently until his death in 2004.

Ox Baker, on the other hand, worked in show business less than Haggerty did, but thanks to his unforgettable look and menacing screen presence, he is and will forever be remembered for his screen appearances. However, Baker's wrestling accomplishments are not to be overlooked.

He wrestled throughout the NWA territories, had a successful AWA run, and had a few runs in the WWWF, as well as stops in Stampede Wrestling and the World Wrestling Council in Puerto Rico.

Baker's legend as a "killer" stems from the fact that not one but two of his opponents died after matches with him. In 1971, Baker, along with his tag team partner the Claw, took on Cowboy Bob Ellis and Alberto Torres for the AWA Midwest Tag Team title. Three days after the match, Torres passed away. The actual cause of death was a ruptured appendix, but the wrestling promoters claimed it was Ox Baker's famous Heart Punch that killed Torres. Just over a year later, Baker faced Ray Gunkel. Gunkel suffered a blood clot, which led to a fatal cardiac arrest in the locker room following the match. Again, Baker was "blamed" for the death. Why let a good angle go?

The publicity of his opponents' passing and Baker's frightening appearance made him a natural fit for movies. His appearances in Jackie Chan's *The Big Brawl* and the classic *Escape from New York* forever put Baker in the annals of great movie "bad guys."

Of course, it is impossible to talk about wrestlers in movies without at least mentioning El Santo, the great Mexican *luchador enmascarado*. El Santo appeared in more than 50 films over four decades and became a national hero in his native Mexico. El Santo was born Rodolfo Guzmán Huerta in 1917. One of four brothers to become professional wrestlers (his brothers were known as Black Guzmán, Pantera Negra, and Jimmy Guzmán), Rodolfo wrestled under many names in the 1930s and early 1940s before he adopted the silver mask and the name that would become legend. On June 26, 1941, El Santo was "born" and quickly became a hero in the ring. By 1952, El Santo was so beloved that José G. Cruz started a comic book based on the *luchador*, which became a top seller and made El Santo even more popular in his country.

It was only natural to want to put the masked hero into a movie, and a film entitled *The Man in the Silver Mask* was proposed to El Santo, but El Santo didn't have faith in the project and declined. It wasn't until 1958 that the wrestler agreed to appear in a film — two, actually. The films *The Evil Brain* and *The Infernal Men* would star fellow wrestler Fernando Osés, with El Santo as his sidekick. The two portrayed masked policemen. But when the producers couldn't find a distributor, the movies were shelved. Three years later, after the release of El Santo's first starring role in *Santo vs. the Zombies*, the popularity of El Santo was so great that those first two films were released (but with new titles using El Santo's name) as *Santo vs. the Evil Brain* and *Santo vs. the Infernal Men*. El Santo's character was now established as a professional wrestler who happens to be a superhero when not in the ring. These films were so popular in Mexico that El Santo himself became more legend than man. He was never seen without his famed silver mask and was even buried in it when he passed away in 1984. And a statue of the hero now stands in his hometown of Tulancingo.

One of El Santo's son's followed in his footsteps, even portraying the legendary Santo in a 2001 film entitled *Infraterrestre*. And in 2016 his own grandson adopted the *luchador* name of El Santo Jr., carrying on the family name. El Santo was not the first *luchador*, but he did pave the way for a new type of superhero *luchador*, including such names as Mil Máscaras and Blue Demon.

Robert Remus, better known as Sgt. Slaughter, was able to parlay his wrestling fame into another area of pop culture. Sgt. Slaughter was made a character in the successful comic book, animated series, and toy line of G.I. Joe. There is a generation of kids in the United States who know Sgt. Slaughter the G.I. Joe figure more than Sgt. Slaughter the professional wrestler.

The magical 1980s World Wrestling Federation success afforded several performers the opportunity to cross over into the mainstream. Cindy Lauper and MTV played a large part in this, first with the appearance of Captain Lou Albano in Lauper's video for the hit song "Girls Just Want to Have Fun" (and his appearances in three other Lauper videos). This pairing led to the "Rock and Wrestling Connection," but it also made Albano a bit of a crossover success for a short period of time. Captain Lou had been a figure in the world of professional wrestling from as far back as 1953 and had massive success as both in-ring performer and manager, but the 1980s were an especially good time for him. Not only was he appearing in videos in heavy rotation on the new MTV, but he was cast in several Hollywood films, such as *Wise Guys* with Danny DeVito and *Stay Tuned* with John Ritter. Albano had guest spots on megahit TV shows like *Miami Vice* and *227* and a regular spot in the game show *Hollywood Squares*. The Captain was even given his own TV show, *The Super Mario Bros. Super Show!* Albano, a loud-mouthed, brash heel, was cast as the lovable Nintendo mascot Mario on a children's show. Albano also had a starring role in the cult wrestling classic *Body Slam*, starring Dirk Benedict of *The A-Team* and *Battlestar Galactica* fame and fellow wrestlers the Tonga Kid and Roddy Piper.

Piper himself was able to gain some crossover success starring in the John Carpenter film *They Live*. Piper, unlike most wrestlers-turned-actors up to this time, gained critical acclaim for his performance. He followed this up with some less appreciated film roles, such as in *Hell Comes to Frogtown*, as well as guest spots on television shows such as *The Outer Limits*, *Robocop*, *It's Always Sunny in Philadelphia*, and *Walker, Texas Ranger*, to name a few. Piper was a natural performer and may have gone on to greater success as an actor, but he sadly passed away at the far-too-young age of 61.

There were others who had varying degrees of success on both the big and small screen. Terry Funk appeared in multiple television and film roles, including those in *Road House*, *Over the Top*, and *The Ringer*. Randy "Macho Man" Savage was famous enough to become a pitchman for Slim Jim beef jerky. Among those of us who were around in those days, who can forget the "Oh yeah, snap into a Slim Jim" commercials? And Andre the Giant appeared in TV shows like *The Six Million Dollar Man* and most memorably in *The Princess Bride*, a role Andre was so proud of that, according to Terry Funk, "If you were traveling with Andre after that movie came out, he would ask every time you were in the van with him, 'Terry, want to watch my movie?' And he would throw the tape on."

But Terry, Randy, and Andre were far more famous for their wrestling careers than their outside ventures, with the possible exception of *The Princess Bride*, which was voted the 84th-best screenplay of all time by the Writers Guild of America.

Every now and then, someone will come along who transcends their profession. Muhammad Ali in boxing, for example. And Ali credited a professional wrestler as helping to create his early public persona. In a 1969 interview with Hubert Mizell, Ali recalled, "(I got it) from seeing Gorgeous George wrestle in Las Vegas. I saw his aides spraying deodorant in the opponents' corner to contain the smell. I also saw 13,000 full seats. I talked with Gorgeous for five minutes after the match and started being a big-mouth and a bragger. He told me people would come to see me get beat. Others would come to see me win. I'd get 'em coming and going."

George Wagner was a talented amateur wrestler who turned pro in the 1930s to moderate success — that is, until 1941. In that year, the "character" of Gorgeous George was born. George would wear flamboyant capes and robes, throw golden bobby pins from his bleached-blond hair to the crowd, and was escorted to the ring by a valet, who would hold the ropes open for him and spray the ring, and his opponent, with perfume, as to not offend George. He was crass and obnoxious, not to mention overtly effeminate, an unbelievably daring move in the 1940s. He would enter the ring to the strains of "Pomp and Circumstance" (later taken by Randy Savage, along with the fancy robes; Savage, in a way, was the masculine version of George) and had an uncanny way of making the crowd despise him.

Gorgeous George really was instrumental in popularizing theatrics to the world of professional wrestling. He was selling out wrestling cards and was well known in the business. Then, in 1947, something happened that would change the course of professional wrestling forever. On November 11, 1947, Gorgeous George appeared on national television and became an overnight superstar. Greg Howell wrote on his fascinating website Greatest Television Events and Iconography, "Gorgeous George is credited as one of the most important early TV stars to push TV sales into American homes. Some dealers believed Gorgeous George was selling as many TVs as Milton Berle, Howdy Doody, and Kukla, Fran, and Ollie."

Gorgeous George had become an A-list celebrity, rubbing elbows with stars like Bob Hope. He has been named as an influence by stars such as James Brown and Ali. Even Bob Dylan claimed meeting Gorgeous George changed his life. In his memoir *Chronicles: Volume One*, Dylan says, "He winked and seemed to mouth the phrase, 'You're making it come alive.' I never forgot it. It was all the recognition and encouragement I would need for years."

It would be more than a generation before another professional wrestler became as much of an icon as George, and that man may have even surpassed George's level of stardom. He was a bronzed god. A blond-haired bass guitar player named Terry Bollea.

Bollea started his wrestling career in his native Florida. Trained by Hiro Matsuda and encouraged by the Brisco brothers, Jack and Jerry, he went to work for Mike Graham. Those early years saw him search for an identity, trying the masked route as "The Super Destroyer," joining the Alabama territory as Terry Boulder, and eventually Jerry Jarrett's Memphis territory as Sterling Golden. Terry Funk introduced him to Vincent J. McMahon, who renamed him Hogan and gave him a run as a heel, facing the likes of champion Bob Backlund and Andre the Giant. Funk also took the newly named Hulk Hogan to Japan, where he started to show signs of the star that was to come. Hogan was over huge in Japan and was soon offered a role as an egotistical heel wrestler who faces Rocky Balboa in a charity match at the beginning of *Rocky III*. Accepting this role put Hogan on the "outs" with McMahon and Hogan joined Verne Gagne's AWA, where he made the transformation to babyface. Then, as they say, history was about to change.

In 1982, Vincent Kennedy McMahon bought the WWF from his father. He knew he needed a face for his expanding company. McMahon recognized that cable TV was about to change the business, and if he could find a marketable figure, he would be the one to break through and go nationwide. Bob Backlund was a capable champion, and respected, but McMahon knew he needed something far more colorful to sell his new vision of wrestling. He lured Hogan away from Gagne on the promise of making him champ, and by 1984 his promise came true. It was a turning point in wrestling history.

"Hulkamania" was born, and for the next several years it truly was an unstoppable force. Hogan crossed over into the mainstream like no wrestler before, even more so than Gorgeous George. People who never saw a wrestling match in their lives knew and loved Hulk Hogan. He became a talk show fixture appearing with Johnny Carson, Jay Leno, Arsenio Hall, Joan Rivers, and on and on. He was on the cover of almost every magazine on the newsstand at one time or another, and was the first ever pro wrestler on the cover of *Sports Illustrated* (Danny Hodge made the cover of *SI* in 1957, but that was by virtue of his amateur success prior to his pro career). He was given his own Saturday morning cartoon series and appeared in numerous films, including *No Holds Barred*, *Gremlins 2*, *Santa with Muscles*, *Mr. Nanny*, and *Suburban Commando*, all this while maintaining a presence as the face, and champion, of the WWF. There were endorsements for everything from breakfast cereal to vitamins, dolls, T-shirts, Halloween costumes, posters, and just about anything else you can imagine. If you needed to sell a product in the mid to late 1980s, Hulk Hogan was your go-to.

"The Hulkster" referred to children as his "little Hulkamaniacs" and he became the most requested celebrity to the Make-A-Wish Foundation in the 1980s, beating out the likes of Madonna, Michael Jackson, and Michael Jordan. His motto of "Train, say your prayers, and eat your vitamins" was better known to the youth of America than First Lady Nancy Reagan's "Just Say No" campaign.

Hogan also changed the business side of wrestling by becoming its first pay-per-view star. Pay-per-view was the offspring of closed-circuit events, usually championship boxing matches, held in theaters. When cable technology caught up, this could now be done on a home-by-home basis. Again, it was mostly major boxing events that could convince people to pay extra to watch something on TV, but Vince McMahon took a gamble, and on the back of Hogan, *WrestleMania* was a major success. And it continues to be to this day.

Hogan learned, however, that with mainstream success comes mainstream attention. He was sued for $5 million by comedian Richard Belzer when he applied a modified guillotine choke to Belzer while appearing on the talk show *Hot Properties* in 1985 (it was settled out of court). His name was dragged through the mud in 1994, when he testified that he had regularly used anabolic steroids (after having publicly denied the accusation on an appearance on *The Arsenio Hall Show*). And he was widely criticized in 2012 when a sex tape went public that included Hogan making offensive racial comments.

It wasn't easy for Terry to become Hulk Hogan full time, as Terry Funk, a man who was instrumental in helping him make that transformation, expressed.

"I'm going to tell you something about Hogan, he was the right choice, I really mean it," Funk said. "He was Terry Bollea, and he had to do a lot of things to become Hulk Hogan, the number-one wrestler.

And sometimes the things he had to do were not that good. . . . He sold his soul while filling his pockets with money. And would I have done the same thing? Honestly and seriously, you bet I would have. And for all those things, he was a hero to the kids, he was great for the kids, and he was good to them, so overall, Hogan was good for the business."

Hogan remains a celebrity both in and out of the wrestling ring today. He even had a successful "reality" TV show centering on his home life. But in those years between 1984 and 1988, Hulk Hogan and "Hulkamania" ruled the world, making a professional wrestler one of the most famous people on the planet. The character of "The Hulkster" was a role model to children everywhere and loved by wrestling fans the world over. He was synonymous not only with wrestling but with what being a "real American" was. He was a superhero come to life. And for a generation of kids, Hulk Hogan was who they wanted to be like. His was a star the likes of which is seldom seen.

PART 4:
The Supercard Era

By the early 1980s, Vince McMahon Jr. had begun to turn his attention beyond his family's regional stronghold in the Northeast and yearned to expand his World Wrestling Federation nationally. The emergence of cable television gave him an outlet as he was able to maneuver his programming into other television markets and give fans a taste of his brand of sports entertainment. Targeted live shows would follow as he dipped his toes into the NWA territories, followed by talent raids to bring the top-drawing stars in the major territories under the growing WWF umbrella.

But the growing field of pay-per-view programming offered another potentially lucrative revenue stream. Closed-circuit programming had been around since the 1970s, which allowed a sporting event to be broadcast before paying remote audiences, usually at a movie theater or smaller auditorium. More than two million Americans had watched the 1976 donnybrook between Muhammad Ali and Antonio Inoki on closed-circuit. At $10 per head, that fight grossed $20 million on closed-circuit theater revenue alone. The advent of pay-per-view — where a live event was purchased through a cable provider and available for viewing from the comfort of home — was a game-changer.

On September 16, 1981, Sugar Ray Leonard fought Thomas Hearns for the welterweight boxing championship, which aired on pay-per-view. Boxing had taken the plunge; wrestling was quick to follow.

On November 24, 1983, Jim Crockett Promotions presented *Starrcade*, its first attempt at a supercard airing on closed-circuit in select markets. The event featured the top names in several of the regional NWA territories, headlined by the world title match between Harley

Race and Ric Fair. By 1985, McMahon had gotten into the game with the first *WrestleMania* (featuring the team of Hulk Hogan and actor Mr. T against Roddy Piper and Paul Orndorff), attracting more than one million viewers on closed-circuit, on top of a sold-out house at Madison Square Garden.

On November 7, 1985, the WWF offered its first true pay-per-view event. The Wrestling Classic featured a 16-man tournament (won by The Junkyard Dog) and a WWF world title match between Hogan and Piper. As the 1980s progressed, both the WWF and Jim Crockett Promotions continued to expand their pay-per-view offerings. Weekly television programming built angles to build blow-off matches on pay-per-view, with live events featuring rematches from the PPVs or build-up matches geared towards the next pay-per-view card.

The PPV era allowed many territorial stars to be seen by national viewing audiences. As a result, the 1980s was something of a chemistry experiment. A WWF or NWA PPV could feature the light heavyweight, high-workrate style that was in fashion in Stampede; the scientific wrestling that was popular in Florida; the brawling of Memphis; the giants, ethnic stars, and novelty attractions of the Northeast; and the Southern-style rasslin' of the Mid-Atlantic, all packaged together like a Frankenstein's monster made from a dozen different bodies.

The wrestlers who were able to thrive against such diverse talents and styles were truly exceptional and they left an indelible stamp on wrestling history.

RICKY STEAMBOAT

Arguably the best pure babyface of all time, Ricky Steamboat was unquestionably one of the smoothest and most graceful athletes ever to lace up a pair of boots.

For Ric Flair, there's no question that "The Dragon" was wrestling's all-time best good guy. "Steamboat! There will be arguments about this, but not many that can stand," Flair said in a 2018 interview with WWE .com. "I don't think anybody had better matches in the history of the business than Steamboat and I had."

Randy Savage might have had a different opinion.

In 1989, Flair and Steamboat had a trilogy of matches for the NWA world title that set a new standard of excellence in wrestling. But two years earlier, Steamboat and "Macho Man" Randy Savage tore the roof off the Pontiac Silverdome and delivered the first truly classic *WrestleMania* match.

The Savage/Steamboat Intercontinental title match at *WrestleMania* 3 was voted Match of the Year by readers of both the *Wrestling Observer* and *Pro Wrestling Illustrated*. Savage, a notorious perfectionist, insisted that the match be scripted out move by move ahead of time, which was a rarity at the time.

"We were using the yellow legal pad and writing down steps," Steamboat said in a 2017 interview with ESPN.com. "And it got into like 100-something steps. Finally, when we got the match top to bottom, we would then meet and quiz ourselves, and I would say, 'OK, I'm at step No. 55, it's this and this. Now tell me the rest of the match.' And he would go, 'Step No. 56 is this, and No. 57 is this.' We would go back and forth.

"I believe we sort of changed the course of (history) in terms of setting up matches, and we did it with all of the false finishes in that match. We had 22 finishes in a match that went just shy of 15 minutes. So it seems like we were trying to cover and beat each other every 45 seconds."

The rivalry between Ricky "The Dragon" Steamboat and "The Macho Man" Randy Savage is considered one of the greatest feuds in wrestling history.

PHOTO BY GEORGE NAPOLITANO

Savage/Steamboat was a grudge match played out before a record-breaking 78,000 fans (a number inflated to 93,173 by the WWF). The main-event spectacle of Hulk Hogan versus Andre the Giant was the draw, but the Intercontinental title bout delivered the goods.

Two years later, Steamboat found himself in the rival Jim Crockett Promotions, coming in as the surprise tag team partner of "Hot Stuff" Eddie Gilbert and scoring a pinfall over Flair in a tag team bout. On February 20, 1989, Steamboat defeated Flair to win the NWA world title. He retained the title in New Orleans in a best-of-three falls match on April 2, 1989, that aired on SuperStation TBS against *WrestleMania* V, which was airing on pay-per-view. On May 7, 1989, Flair beat Steamboat to regain the NWA title. All three matches were given five-star reviews by the *Observer*.

"Ricky's matches with Flair were incredible. They were that generation's Funk/Brisco," said Kevin Sullivan.

Flair moved onto a feud with the returning Terry Funk. Steamboat had a brief feud with Lex Luger and then left the NWA by year's end.

Despite wrestling some of the most critically acclaimed bouts of the late 1980s, Steamboat never received a sustained push in either the WWF or the NWA. As the WWF was looking to push him as IC champion and position him as the company's number-two babyface behind Hogan, Steamboat requested time off to spend with his family and newborn son, effectively killing his push. A contract dispute prematurely ended his 1989 NWA run. But these flurries of greatness, followed by disappearances, only added to the Dragon's mystique with fans.

Ironically enough, the career babyface was born with a name that perfectly suited a heel — Richard Blood. The son of an English father and Japanese mother, Blood was a state champion wrestler in high school. He attended Verne Gagne's training school and made his pro debut in the AWA in 1976. When he went to work in Florida, promoter Eddie Graham changed his name from Blood to Steamboat due to his strong resemblance to Sammy Steamboat, a Hawaiian wrestler from the 1950s and 1960s who had been Graham's tag team partner.

With his good looks, bodybuilder physique, and humble demeanor, Steamboat became a popular babyface and moved on to Jim Crockett Promotions where he was set up as Wahoo McDaniel's protégé. He defeated Flair for the NWA Mid-Atlantic Television title, and the two had chemistry right off the bat (particularly with Steamboat's signature deep arm drags), clashing multiple times throughout the late 1970s and early 1980s.

Steamboat and Flair were diametrically opposed as characters, but they were also brilliantly able to play off one another athletically. Steamboat was a masterful seller and managed to make his opponent look like a sadistic monster.

"A lot of times when I watch a movie, I'll pull myself away from the storyline just to watch the actor work, to watch how he cries, watch how he gets pissed off — the emotions, the facials. I remember doing that a lot throughout my career, which helped me become a babyface salesman, selling in the ring," Steamboat told ESPN.com. "I've watched *Raging Bull* a dozen times, watching (Robert) DeNiro getting his ass handed to him each time during those fight scenes because it looked so real."

Steamboat and tag team partner Jay Youngblood became the NWA's top babyface tag team, capturing both the Mid-Atlantic and NWA world tag titles multiple times. In 1985, Steamboat jumped to the WWF, where he was given the nickname "The Dragon" and repackaged as a martial artist, playing off his Japanese ancestry. After winning a feud against Jake "The Snake" Roberts, Steamboat faced Intercontinental champion Savage on the January 3, 1987, edition of *Saturday Night's Main Event*. During that match, which aired nationally on NBC, Savage attacked Steamboat's throat with the ring bell. Steamboat suffered a "crushed larynx" in storyline, setting the stage for the big grudge match at *WrestleMania* III.

Steamboat beat Savage for the IC title at *'Mania*, but on June 2, 1987, he dropped the belt to the Honky Tonk Man in Buffalo, New York, in a stunning upset. After his requested break to spend time with his family, he returned and was entered into the tournament for the vacant world title at *WrestleMania*, but fans hoping for a *WrestleMania* rematch between Steamboat and Savage (now a babyface) were disappointed, as Steamboat was eliminated with an opening round loss to a past-his-prime Greg Valentine. He was gone from the WWF a short time later.

After his 1989 NWA run and classic trilogy with Flair, Steamboat did a stint in New Japan before returning to the WWF as a literal fire-breathing dragon, a cartoonish take on his nickname, and quite possibly an attempt by the office to make him look foolish after his NWA run and after having chosen family over the IC title four years earlier. By the end of 1991, he was in World Championship Wrestling, where he worked programs with Steve Austin, Rick Rude, and Paul Orndorff, and teamed with both Dustin Rhodes and Shane Douglas.

Steamboat retired in 1994. He was inducted into the WWE Hall of Fame in 2009 and came out of retirement to wrestle a match with Chris Jericho at *WrestleMania* 25, along with partners Jimmy Snuka and Roddy Piper.

RICKY MORTON

When it came to taking a whipping, no one did it better than Ricky Morton.

Collectively, Morton and partner Robert Gibson formed the Rock 'n' Roll Express, one of the most successful and influential tag teams of the 1980s.

While Morton had a fiery offense and charisma to spare, the Nashville native excelled in selling a beating. The typical R 'n' R Express match formula saw Morton and Gibson establish the upper hand early through teamwork and precision double-team attacks until the heels finally levelled Morton with a cheap shot. From there, the heels would apply the heat, savaging Morton until he was finally able to make the hot tag to Gibson.

It's a basic formula, but it worked because Morton was an absolute master at selling and rallying the fans behind him.

"He's a phrase in wrestling terminology now. Instead of 'moves like Jagger,' it's 'selling like Ricky Morton,'" said Jim Cornette on the *Jim Cornette Experience* podcast.

"If not the greatest babyface of all time, Ricky was definitely one of the greatest babyfaces of all time because of the way he sold, and not just the way he sold, but his facial expressions as he was selling," said Kevin Sullivan. "I was at a battle of the bands once and one of the bands broke out in a song called 'Sell, Ricky, Sell,' and it was about Ricky Morton. I almost died."

The son of wrestler Paul Morton, Ricky broke into the business in 1978 under the tutelage of his father and Ken Lucas, who proved to be a major influence on the fledgling rock 'n' roller.

"Jack Brisco put Ken Lucas in the top three babyfaces he ever worked with. Think about that!" Sullivan said. "So Ricky partnered up with Ken

*One of the best babyfaces-
in-peril of all time, Ricky
Morton.*

PHOTO BY HOWARD BAUM/HARD-WAY ART

when he was young. And Ricky is a second-generation wrestler. Those second-generation guys have a step up on guys coming into the business. They've been around it their whole life, training with their dad from when they were young."

"Ricky was a natural talent, but he learned a lot from Sonny King and Ken Lucas," said Morton's longtime friend Koko Ware, who called Morton his "brother from a different father and mother." "Going on the road with those guys, listening to the stories. Those guys took him under their wings. And one day, Ricky pulled it all together for himself. And when Jerry Lawler gave him and Robert Gibson a gimmick and made them the Rock 'n' Roll Express, they were off and running."

Morton and Gibson began teaming in 1983 in Mid-South Wrestling, adopting the name the Rock 'n' Roll Express and borrowing the long hair, bandannas, and spandex made fashionable by the "hair metal" rock bands of the era and showcased on the hot new cable TV channel MTV.

After winning the Mid-South Wrestling tag team title three times, the Express moved to Jim Crockett Promotions, where they defeated Ivan Koloff and Krusher Kruschev to win the NWA tag team title on July 9, 1985. Morton and Gibson would hold the NWA tag belts four times between 1985 and 1987, feuding with the Midnight Express, the Russians, and the Four Horsemen.

"When he was selling for you it looked like he had real tears," said Barry "Krusher Kruschev" Darsow. "Everyone believed he was really hurt. He could do anything a heel asked for and more. Also he was a great guy."

Undersized by the standards of the day and blessed with youthful good looks and a willingness to bump with gusto, Morton was a natural underdog who was able to take a thrashing from larger, older opponents and keep coming back for more.

A typical R 'n' R Express match saw Gibson start out and get the best of his opponent with some armdrags or a Beell throw out of the corner. Morton would tag in and dazzle with some flying headscissors or other flashy attacks until the inevitable cut-off where the heels would take over.

As the rulebreakers battered Morton with forearms or stomps, Morton would writhe on the canvas, his face registering agony with every blow. Instead of lying limp on the mat, he would turn his body towards the fans on all four corners of the ring, his right arm reaching out as if instinctively reaching for his partner but also drawing in the fans, inviting them to "tag in" themselves and pulling them into the match.

After a bit of a mugging, Morton would rally with fiery right hands and a spurt of energy, his bleached blond hair flowing behind him, only to get cut off by the villains and begin the process over once again.

"Working against Ricky was a joy," said "Outlaw" Joel Deaton, who faced the Rock 'n' Roll Express multiple times in both Jim Crockett Promotions and All Japan Pro Wrestling. "It was so easy. All you had to do was put your hands on him and the people would go nuts. When you're a heel and you're working a babyface that's really over like that, it makes it so easy."

Neil Young sang "rock and roll will never die" . . . and the Rock 'n' Roll Express has proved him right, chugging along through the years and collecting championships into the 2020s. The duo was inducted into the WWE Hall of Fame in March 2017, with their "arch-nemesis" Jim Cornette doing the honors of inducting them.

Morton has also served as a guest instructor at the WWE Performance Center, passing on his talent for selling and the intricacies of tag team wrestling to the next generation of aspiring wrestlers.

"Ricky has been around forever and he still draws money," Sullivan said. "He was something special and he still is."

In 2019, Morton and Gibson made appearances in AEW. In October 2019, they defeated Royce Isaacs and Thomas Latimer to win the NWA tag team title, 19 years after their last NWA tag title run. Long live rock, indeed.

BRAD ARMSTRONG

*"I can't tell you how many booking meetings I sat in
where we needed to get a guy over and had to figure out
'Who are we going to put him with?' My answer always
was 'Put him with Brad Armstrong. Brad will get him
over.' . . . You can't do a book on 'Wrestlers' Wrestlers'
without doing a chapter on Brad Armstrong."*

—Former WCW booker Kevin Sullivan

As an in-ring performer, Brad Armstrong is almost universally hailed by his peers as one of the all-time greats, but despite his excellence, he never received a true push on the national stage.

Born June 15, 1962, Brad (Robert Bradley James) was the second of four sons born to "Bullet" Bob Armstrong and his wife, Gail.

Brad cut his teeth in the Gulf Coast region, debuting in 1980 as a babyface in Southeastern Championship Wrestling. A good-looking second-generation competitor with exceptional balance and an impressive physique, Armstrong worked up the ranks in the lightweight division, winning the NWA Southeastern U.S. junior heavyweight title in 1982. He was named Rookie of the Year by the *Wrestling Observer* (a distinction he shared that year with Brad Rheingans) and was voted Rookie of the Year by readers of *Pro Wrestling Illustrated* in 1982.

In 1984, Brad moved to Georgia Championship Wrestling, where he won the prestigious NWA National title in stunning fashion on February 18, 1984. Armstrong entered the match against champion Ted DiBiase wearing a mask and warm-ups (to hide his physique) as "Mr. R," thought by most to be Tommy Rich, who had been suspended by the promotion. DiBiase pulled off the mask, expecting to see Rich, but was surprised to find Armstrong under the hood, and then distracted when a smiling Rich emerged from backstage, waving at the future "Million Dollar Man." Armstrong capitalized with a quick roll-up to win the title. It wouldn't be the last time Armstrong was put under a mask.

Armstrong enjoyed two brief reigns as national champion in 1984 and had a one-month run as the Mid-South North American champion in December 1984 into January 1985. He made it to the finals of a tournament to crown the first All Japan Pro Wrestling junior heavyweight champion in July 1986, succumbing to Hiro Saito in the championship round.

Still, sustainable singles success eluded Armstrong. In 1986, in Bill Watts's UWF, he reunited with occasional Southeastern tag team partner "White Lightning" Tim Horner and was slotted in lower-card tag bouts in both the UWF and Jim Crockett Promotions, which eventually bought the UWF in 1987. The Lightning Express was relegated to

"Brad was so smooth. He almost made it look too easy." Brad Armstrong with his father, "Bullet" Bob Armstrong.

PHOTO BY GEORGE NAPOLITANO

opening matches and the undercard, despite impressive showings against such teams as the Midnight Express and the Sheepherders.

"He never got the real push but he was versatile and could go with anybody," said Sheepherder Luke Williams.

Still, Armstrong was a go-to guy who could make champions look strong. He received numerous title shots against all of the singles champions in the company (including several world title shots against Ric Flair) despite having a mediocre win-loss record.

A few half-hearted attempts at repackaging Armstrong were made, including brief runs as "The Candy Man" (wearing red-and-white pin-striped tights and tossing candy to kids at ringside), "Arachnaman" (a low-budget Spider-Man rip-off), "Fantasia/Badstreet" (a masked Freebird), and — in the late 1990s — as "Buzzkill," a hippie-dippie, low-rent version of Road Dogg, the character portrayed by his brother Brian in the WWF. Every gimmick flopped. Ironically, Armstrong never got a chance to show off his real-life personality.

"If the Brad Armstrong from behind the scenes had been the Brad Armstrong that you saw (on television), he would have been a huge star, because he was the funniest, wittiest, smartest, quickest guy that I ever met in my life," said Kevin Sullivan, who faced Armstrong numerous times throughout the 1980s and was one of Armstrong's biggest advocates as booker in World Championship Wrestling. "Technically, there wasn't anybody as solid as Brad in that era. Brad was a solid, solid performer.

"Ric Flair said has said he was one of the five best babyfaces he ever worked with, and just think about the list of guys that Ric has worked with," Sullivan said. "Brad was terrific. I mean, Brad was so smooth. He almost made it look too easy."

Jim Ross offered a similar sentiment in a blog post from 2012. "Behind the scenes, Brad Armstrong was one of the funniest, most personable men I've ever met in the business," Ross wrote. "He could light up any locker room and seemingly got along with everyone. If someone had an issue with Brad Armstrong, they really needed to take a long look into a mirror.

"One of the greatest things someone in our business can say of any wrestler is that said wrestler could have a good match with anyone, no matter who. Brad Armstrong certainly fits on a rather short list of wrestlers that could literally have a good match with anyone. I've called hundreds of Brad Armstrong bouts, in singles and in tags, in main events and in prelims, and I never saw him have what would be perceived as a 'bad match.' Not one time."

Armstrong went on to work as a trainer, producer, and occasional announcer for WWE and continued to wrestle on the independents until 2011. He appeared at WWE's 2011 Hall of Fame ceremony to induct his father, "Bullet" Bob.

Armstrong died in his home in Kennesaw, Georgia, on November 1, 2012, at the age of 50.

"Brad Armstrong could work with anybody. The guy was as smooth as silk," said Steve Austin in the 2013 edition of his autobiography, *The Stone Cold Truth*. "He was like Ricky Steamboat, in a way — another guy you went out there with and never had to say a word to. He knew the finish and how to get there. I knew how good he could be. I'd call all the spots in the ring and we'd just wrestle."

BARRY WINDHAM

*"I watched a ton of Barry Windham growing up. I thought
he was the cat's pajamas. When I worked him (in 2010),
he was older. He didn't want to do a lot, but what he did
was terrific. It's quality over quantity. Do you want to eat
six ounces of filet mignon or a 20-pound bag of shit?"*

—Sinn Bodhi

It's safe to say most people who grew up watching wrestling in the 1980s watched a ton of Barry Windham. No matter where you were located or what territory you watched, Barry Windham eventually showed up there and he always made a statement everywhere he went.

From his early start at the age of 19 in Texas, through the glory days of Florida Championship wrestling, with stops in the exploding WWF, the AWA, multiple NWA territories, and a controversial "world" title run in WCW, Windham was a star everywhere he went, albeit a shooting star as he never seemed to stay in one place for too long.

The son of legendary tough guy Blackjack Mulligan, and trained by his father and Harley Race, Barry Windham followed in his father's footsteps but he took a much different approach. Blackjack was pure heel — black hat, boots, a snarl, and an air of ferocity, while his son emerged as a blond-haired babyface. A six-foot-six all-American boy.

Windham was popular as a singles wrestler as well as a fantastic tag team competitor, teaming with former Syracuse University inter- collegiate heavyweight amateur champion Mike Rotunda, who was his real-life brother-in-law, having married Windham's sister, Stephanie, in

1976. One of his main rivals was Kevin Sullivan and his army. While Sullivan's wars with Windham heated up Florida rings throughout the early 1980s, in real life, Sullivan considers himself one of Windham's biggest fans.

"To me, Barry Windham was one of the greatest babyfaces of his generation," Sullivan said. "His matches with Flair in Florida were legendary. It's passé today, but they would do 60 minutes one week and the next week they would go 90 minutes. Today, it's next to impossible to keep people for 20 minutes. Barry just had that really athletic physique at the time. He should have played in the NFL. He should have been drafted. He was one of the greatest wide receivers in college (at West Texas State University). When it came to wrestling, he would go over the top rope and sometimes not even grab the top rope. And when he made the comeback, he made a huge comeback."

Windham and Rotunda won the Florida U.S. tag team title three times in 1984 and signed with the WWF in October of that year. As a pair of all-American boys, they were given the name the U.S. Express. In January 1985, they defeated Dick Murdoch and Adrian Adonis to win the WWF tag team title. They were then slotted into a program with the anti-American team of Nikolai Volkoff and the Iron Sheik. With the now-fan-favorite captain Lou Albano as their manager, the U.S. Express became one of the hottest acts in the WWF. They dropped the belts to the Sheik and Volkoff at the first *WrestleMania*. They regained the belts later that year, then dropped them to Brutus Beefcake and Greg Valentine.

And, a short time later, Windham simply vanished from the WWF. It was a head-scratcher. Windham had size. He had charisma. He had incredible athletic ability. In short, he had every attribute the WWF prized. But he disappeared from the WWF seemingly overnight. He resurfaced in the NWA and, in 1986, had a career-making feud with NWA world champion Ric Flair. His February 14 "Battle of the Belts 2" bout against Flair received five-star recognition by *Wrestling Observer Newsletter* publisher Dave Meltzer, making it one of only a dozen matches to receive the coveted five-star rating that decade.

But, while Windham was taking Flair to the limit night after night, the NWA never pulled the trigger and made the handsome, blond babyface from Sweetwater, Texas, the world champion.

"He was, at one point, probably the best in-ring performer in the business," said Jim Cornette in a 2017 edition of his *Cornette's Drive-Thru* podcast. "But, at the same time, while he was always featured as a star, he was never featured as *the* star."

"He was a ballet dancer at that size," Cornette said. "He was just amazing. Fluid and coordinated. He was going to be, several different times, world champion. I've heard — like Flair I heard one time said, I've heard other people say — they weren't sure if he wanted it."

Being world champion meant carrying the load for the company. It meant you were responsible if attendance dropped. It meant that everyone was gunning for you and your spot. Depending on who you talk to, either Windham wasn't interested in being the top dog or the promoters didn't feel he could carry the load. He was athletic without having the bodybuilder physique that was in vogue at the time. He was a competent promo man, but not one of the elite. He was a perfect contender, but a very imperfect champion. But, from bell to bell, he was one of the best in the game.

Windham went on to team with Ron Garvin, winning the U.S. tag title twice and feuding with the Midnight Express. When Garvin reunited with his storyline "brother" Gorgeous Jimmy Garvin, Windham was paired with Lex Luger. Windham and Luger won the NWA tag title from Tully Blanchard and Arn Anderson in March 1988, but one month later, they dropped the belts back to Tully and Arn when Windham turned on Luger and joined the Horsemen. As a heel, Windham adopted his father's claw hold as his finisher of choice. He had an impressive run as U.S. champion and had a bloody feud with Dusty Rhodes before dropping the belt to Luger in February 1989.

In the summer of 1989, Windham turned up in the WWF as "The Widowmaker." His previous stint (and tag championships) with the company were acknowledged. By fall, "The Widowmaker" was again gone from the WWF. He returned to World Championship Wrestling and rejoined the Horsemen in 1990. In 1991, the WCW world title was vacated when Ric Flair was fired from the company. Windham faced Luger in a steel cage match for the vacant title at the 1991 Great American Bash in Baltimore, with Luger turning heel and winning the belt. Ironically, Flair had offered to drop the belt to Windham before he was fired.

It wasn't until 1993 that Windham had a run as NWA champion, but by that time, WCW had instituted its own world title and, despite its history, the NWA title was rendered virtually meaningless. Windham defeated the Great Muta for the NWA belt in February 1993 and held it for five months, losing it to Flair in July 1993. Knee injuries and subsequent surgeries limited his time in the ring in subsequent years, and weight gain and ring rust took their toll. He had brief runs in the WWF as the Stalker (yet another new persona) in 1996, and as one-half of the New Blackjacks (with Justin "Hawk" Bradshaw) in 1997–98, then again returned to WCW as a member of the West Texas Rednecks. Barely used in WCW, he was released in 1999, and spent the next decade making appearances on the independents and settling into semi-retirement. He was inducted (as a member of The Four Horsemen) into the WWE Hall of Fame in 2012.

From 1982 through 1987, Windham was one of the best all-around wrestlers in the game. Had he had the promo ability of Ric Flair or a physique like Hulk Hogan's, he could have been the biggest star of the 1980s.

CURT HENNIG

Just how good was Curt Hennig? Good enough to warrant a gimmick like "Mr. Perfect" . . . and actually make it work. That's how good Curt Hennig was.

"Curt was one of the greatest athletes to ever put on a pair of wrestling boots," Bret Hart said in a 2016 interview with *Sports Illustrated*. "You could wake me up at four in the morning and I could wrestle Curt Hennig for an hour and have a five-star match. He was so safe in his matches, and logical. He didn't waste a lot of moves. Every move made sense. There was a reason why he did it, and it fit into the theme of the whole storyline. A lot of wrestlers would be better off today if they watched Curt Hennig. It's not about what you do, it's how you do it."

"He's the kind of guy that guys liked to work with because if you went to slam him, you never felt his weight. If he punched you, you never felt the punch. If you drop down and go to hip-toss him, he's right there . . . Everything that you do is smooth because of what he's doing," said Jim Cornette in a 2018 edition of the *Cornette's Drive-Thru* podcast.

Curt was born on March 28, 1958, in Robbinsdale, Minnesota, the son of Larry "The Axe" Hennig, a top star in the AWA. Robbinsdale spawned more wrestlers than Parts Unknown. Verne Gagne, Greg Gagne, Rick Rude, Nikita Koloff, Barry Darsow, "Berzerker" John Nord, and Tom Zenk are just some of the pro wrestlers who grew up the tiny town of about 16,000 residents.

With the Hennig bloodlines and whatever was in the water in Robbinsdale, it was probably only a matter of time that young Curt would succumb to the lure of the squared circle. A standout amateur wrestler in high school, Curt trained under his father and Verne Gagne and made his pro debut in January 1980. He spent two years in the AWA before trying his hand in the WWF, where he worked undercard bouts, sometimes teaming with a fellow young second-generation competitor, Eddie Gilbert. He moved on to Don Owen's Pacific Northwest territory, winning the tag title three times, with his father, Buddy Rose, and Scott McGhee.

He jumped back to the AWA in 1983. He was still adding body mass, but at six-foot-two and with the Hennig pedigree, he was being groomed for the main-event level. In January 1986, Hennig teamed with Scott Hall to win the AWA tag team title from "Gorgeous" Jimmy Garvin and "Mr. Electricity" Steve Regal, a title his father had won on four occasions. Hennig and Hall dropped the tag belts to Buddy Rose and Doug Somers four months later in controversial fashion, dropping the belts on a DQ decision. Following their loss, Hall and Hennig went their separate ways, with Hall ultimately leaving the company for Jim Crockett Promotions. Hennig was slotted into a babyface-versus-babyface program with AWA world champion Nick Bockwinkel. Hennig wrestled the champion to a 60-minute draw on New Year's Eve 1986 in a match televised nationally on ESPN, solidifying the second-generation competitor as a legitimate title contender and bona fide singles star. But, as 1987 rolled on, Hennig was unable to wrest the belt away from Bockwinkel, and frustration set in.

On May 2, 1987, Hennig finally beat Bockwinkel for the AWA title after accepting a roll of dimes from Bockwinkel's arch-rival, Larry Zbyszko, and KO'ing the champ with the foreign object in his fist. Hennig truly excelled as a heel, exhibiting a cool, cocky swagger that would eventually take him to the WWF.

"His style at the time was to make the babyfaces shine by taking big bumps," wrote Dave Meltzer in his book *Tributes II: Remembering More of the World's Greatest Professional Wrestlers*. "Often compared with Flair, Hennig was bigger and came across more athletic and took more outlandish bumps but didn't have Flair's charisma. While many of Flair's big moves were spots that you could see coming, Hennig's knack in his big spots was that fans didn't see where the spot was going. Two of his trademarks were where he begged off backwards, and not seeing where he was, would crotch himself on the ringpost, and then

"Exotic" Adrian Street in all his
outrageous glory.

Ric Flair incapacitates "The American
Dream" with a chinlock.

Jerry "The King" Lawler was a master of ring psychology and had one of the best worked
punches in the game.

ABOVE: *WWF world champion Bob Backlund shakes hands with North American champion Ted DiBiase.*

PHOTO BY GEORGE NAPOLITANO

LEFT: *A bloody Ric Flair struggles to escape a sleeper applied by Barry Windham.*

PHOTO BY GEORGE NAPOLITANO

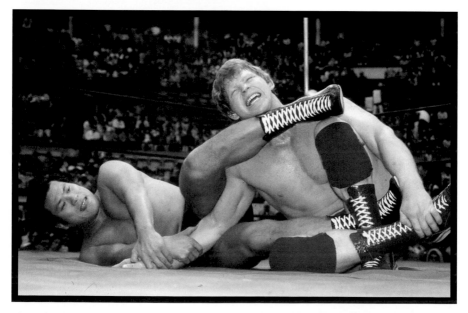

Antonio Inoki attempts to apply an armbar as Bob Backlund blocks by grape-vining Inoki's ankle.

PHOTO BY GEORGE NAPOLITANO

Kurt Angle catches Desmond Wolfe (Nigel McGuinness) in an ankle lock.

Calgary vs. Winnipeg: Chris Benoit hooks an abdominal stretch on Chris Jericho.

Eddie Guerrero: He could lie, cheat, and steal, but he was also a superior scientific wrestler.

A Legend and a Future Legend: Lou Thesz poses with Kurt Angle, the 2000 Cauliflower Alley Club Future Legend award winner, at the CAC reunion.

PHOTO BY GEORGE NAPOLITANO

Three of the Four Horsemen: Dean Malenko, Arn Anderson, and Chris Benoit.

PHOTO BY GEORGE NAPOLITANO

Billy Robinson posed at an Illinois house show in 1975.

PHOTO BY MIKE LANO

The Midnight Express ("Sweet" Stan and "Beautiful" Bobby, along with Jim Cornette) showing love for the NWA U.S. tag team belts.

PHOTO BY GEORGE NAPOLITANO

"Captain Redneck" Dick Murdoch.

PHOTO BY GEORGE NAPOLITANO

The feud between Shawn Michaels and Bret Hart was both professional and personal.

PHOTO BY GEORGE NAPOLITANO

The Great Muta getting prepared for battle.

"Cowboy" Bob Orton applies the pressure in a chinlock against Ricky "The Dragon" Steamboat.

Robert Gibson and Ricky Morton, The Rock 'n' Roll Express.

Face rearranging courtesy of Samoa Joe.   *Karl Gotch.*

Christopher Daniels uses the middle rope to choke out Charlie Haas.

Owen Hart was renowned for his high-flying aerial skills, but he was no slouch when it came to technical wrestling.

PHOTO COURTESY WWE

The in-ring rivalry between William Regal and Fit Finlay thrilled fans in both hemispheres.

PHOTO COURTESY WWE

Exhibiting form that would make Karl Gotch proud, Daniel Bryan hits a flawless German suplex on Kofi Kingston.

PHOTO COURTESY WWE

*AWA world champion
Curt Hennig.*

he'd hurdle the ropes into the ring and trip and fall on his face. He was also known for what later became a Lucha spot, where his opponent would sweep his leg as he held onto the ropes and he'd take an exaggerated bump on his neck."

Hennig held the AWA strap for a year before losing it to Jerry Lawler. He then left the AWA and joined the WWF, where he was given the moniker "Mr. Perfect." The WWF produced a series of vignettes showing Hennig competing in a variety of sports and games "perfectly," such as bowling a 300 game, throwing a touchdown pass to himself, putting a hole-in-one, and sinking three-pointers with ease. He was paired with "The Genius" Lanny Poffo and put on an undefeated streak, leading to a championship series with Hulk Hogan.

"Hogan knew Perfect would be big, that he had the talent, but he needed a mouth, a manager to give him that push," Poffo said. "Actually, Mr. Perfect wanted Bobby Heenan to be his manager, but Hulk insisted that I be his manager up until the end of the program and then he could go ahead and have Heenan. I don't blame Perfect for that because they were friends, plus Heenan is the greatest manager that ever lived. And because of that, I got four months of headliners, headlining Madison Square Garden with Hogan."

Despite smashing the WWF world title belt on *Saturday Night's Main Event*, "Mr. Perfect" proved to be just another foil for Hogan, but Hennig's wild, over-the-top bumps and selling made their matches — especially Hogan's "Hulking-up" comeback — particularly memorable. He won a tournament for the vacant Intercontinental title in May 1990 and took on Heenan as his manager. He lost the belt to "The Texas Tornado" Kerry Von Erich at SummerSlam 1990, but regained the title in February 1991. After Heenan retired, Hennig was briefly managed by "The Coach" John Tolos, but in June, Hennig suffered what was considered to be a career-ending back injury, exacerbated by years of risky and damaging bumps. Despite being in immense pain, Hennig dropped the IC belt to Bret Hart at SummerSlam 1991. The match earned four stars from Meltzer and was voted first runner-up in the Match of the Year category by readers of *Pro Wrestling Illustrated* (behind the dream match of Sting and Lex Luger versus the Steiner Brothers).

Hennig retired from in-ring competition and began collecting on a lucrative insurance policy from Lloyd's of London, but the insurance was cancelled when Lloyd's got wind that Hennig was considering a comeback. With his back and tailbone healed, Hennig returned to the ring at the 1992 Survivor Series, filling in for the Ultimate Warrior and teaming with Randy Savage to beat Ric Flair and Razor Ramon (his old tag partner Scott Hall). Hennig went on to beat Flair in a "loser-leaves-town" match in 1993, as Flair was headed back to World Championship Wrestling, but Hennig never enjoyed the sustained push he had before the injury. He wrestled on and off in a midcard role in the WWF, then jumped to WCW in 1997, where he became a member of the Four Horsemen. He ended up turning on Flair and the Horsemen and had a brief run as U.S. champion, but age and injuries prevented him from climbing higher on the card.

After a stint in the short-lived XWF, he returned to the WWF as a surprise entrant at the 2002 Royal Rumble but was released by the company after instigating an impromptu amateur wrestling match against

Brock Lesnar on a flight from England to the U.S. He had a brief run in NWA-TNA, but on February 10, 2003, he was found dead in a Tampa hotel. The cause of death was determined to be an overdose of cocaine. He was 44.

"There are a lot of guys who are good athletes who don't have charisma. There are a lot of guys who have charisma that aren't good athletes. To have everything come together at the same time, it'll make somebody great. And Curt Hennig was a great, great performer," Flair said in video package made by WWE for his induction into the WWE Hall of Fame in 2010.

TED DIBIASE

In act 2 of *As You Like It* by William Shakespeare, Jaques famously says, "All the world's a stage. And all the men and women merely players; they have their exits and their entrances, and one man in his time plays many parts." These words could have been written directly for Ted DiBiase.

Theodore Marvin DiBiase was born with the squared circle in his blood. While he was billed early on as the son of "Iron" Mike DiBiase, what few mentioned was he was actually Mike's adopted son, though he did have a biological connection to the ring through his mother, Helen Hild (Gladys Nevins). Hild was a star in her own right, wrestling for three decades, challenging the great Mildred Burke for the title on multiple occasions, and feuding later with the Fabulous Moolah. In 1954 Hild and singer Ted Willis welcomed baby Ted into the world, and four years later, when Hild married "Iron" Mike, DiBiase adopted the boy, giving him a famous last name . . . and large shoes to fill.

When Ted was only 15, his father suffered a fatal heart attack in the ring, leaving a grieving widow who, due to depression, was unable to continue to raise her son. Ted was sent to live with his grandparents. He excelled in athletics and received a football scholarship to West Texas State University, which — as it turned out — was the unofficial university of choice for pro wrestlers. Terry and Dory Funk Jr., Manny Fernandez, Bruiser Brody, Dusty Rhodes, Tito Santana, Stan Hansen, Kelly Kiniski, Tully Blanchard, Bobby Duncum, and Blackjack Mulligan all played football at West Texas State.

An injury sidelined Ted in his senior year, and he gradually lost interest in academics and eventually dropped out of school. He decided to get into the "family business," and he knew just where to turn.

"Ted was a (West Texas) A&M guy, like I was, and my brother, and Dusty, Tully, Brody. Ya had to be a tough guy there," said Terry Funk. "He came to Dory (Jr.) around '73 or '74. Dory was the one who started training him. I mean, I was there and all, I added the toughness.

"He was a great student because he wanted to be great. That's how Ted was, he wanted to be great for his father. It meant a lot to him to live up to the name, and boy, he did," Funk said.

DiBiase started as a referee in Amarillo but was soon off to Bill Watts's Mid-South Wrestling, where, within a few years, he took the Missouri championship from Dick Slater, only to lose it to Dick Murdoch (who also had connections to West Texas State, having played football there — at the very least, playing in an alumni game — without ever having attended the school). By 1978, DiBiase had gained a reputation as a brilliant technical wrestler as well as someone who could get over with the fans. It was inevitable that New York would come calling. In 1979, DiBiase joined the World Wide Wrestling Federation, billed as the company's inaugural North American champion. But after losing that belt to Pat Patterson — and facing Hulk Hogan in Hogan's Madison Square garden debut — DiBiase moved on.

As a new decade began, so did a new act in the play. DiBiase went to Georgia as a babyface, and once again got over with the crowd. He was so over with the fans that members of the TBS studio audience openly cried when he was viciously attacked by the Freebirds. The next few years saw DiBiase grow as a talent even more, gaining him a fan base across several NWA territories, including his old home of Mid-South. During these years he worked with NWA world champion Ric Flair in multiple territories and had a memorable feud with Paul Orndorff.

"Ted was good man. He could sell it. And he could take a hit and give one. But he could do it all, he was real good," Orndorff said.

DiBiase turned heel against fan favorite Junkyard Dog in 1982, and a new act opened. DiBiase picked up a gimmick of wearing a "loaded black glove" that he would have hidden in his trunks that enabled him to knock out his opponents with one punch, getting him unbelievable heat with the crowd. His star was also starting to rise in Japan, as DiBiase was able to keep up with the rigorous Japanese style athletically, showing versatility against a variety of opponents, be they Japanese or American. He captured the NWA United National championship in All Japan and became Stan Hansen's new tag team partner, replacing the venerable Bruiser Brody (another West Texas Stater). Yet, the biggest act of DiBiase's career was still about to play out upon the national stage of the World Wrestling Federation.

"The Million Dollar Man" took center stage June 1987 on an episode of *WWF Superstars*. The character was designed by the WWF as the character Vince McMahon would be if he were a wrestler (before the boss actually did enter the ring, of course). And it wasn't just an "on-camera" gimmick. DiBiase was told to actually live the lifestyle in public. He was given first-class travel everywhere he went, and plenty of cash to flash and show off. There were several vignettes where DiBiase would bribe, humiliate, and bully people. It was — if the reader will forgive the pun — a money gimmick, and it instantly made him the biggest heel in the business. The fact that DiBiase was a premier technician and one of the top pure workers in the game was just icing on the cake.

Investing so much money into the gimmick was a big gamble by the WWF and McMahon, and it was a testament to how respected and well thought of DiBiase was as a performer. But DiBiase was the perfect man for a very difficult period in the WWF. With Hulk Hogan looking to take time off and focus on moviemaking, the company needed a marketable villain to be used as a transition to its next babyface world champion, Randy Savage. DiBiase had the gimmick and the in-ring abilities to be the WWF's top heel and workhorse, and proved to be one of the company's most valuable players in the late 1980s. After his main-event angle of attempting to buy the WWF world title and subsequent feuds with Savage, Dusty Rhodes, and the Ultimate Warrior, DiBiase won tag team gold as one-half of Money Inc. (with Irwin R. Schyster, the former Mike Rotunda). He left the WWF in 1993 and went back to All Japan, where he suffered neck and back injuries that ended his wrestling career. He had stints as a manager and creative consultant in both the WWF and WCW (where he was revealed as the "financial backer" for the red-hot New World Order).

Not only did DiBiase live up to the DiBiase name, but he also passed it on to his sons, Mike, Ted Jr., and Brett, all of whom tried their hand in wrestling in the 2000s. In one more important act to the DiBiase play, the former "Million Dollar Man" became a Christian minister and motivational speaker with Heart of David Ministry.

THE RISE OF JAPAN, "STRONG STYLE," AND HYBRID FIGHTING

Japan has been one of the three largest wrestling markets since the 1950s and has proven to be extremely influential on the entire wrestling world because of its presentation of wrestling as a realistic athletic competition. Of course, there are Japanese promotions like DDT Pro-Wrestling and others that have put on wrestling shows featuring absurdist comedy (past DDT iron man champions have included a ladder and "The Beyond Wrestling Audience," for example) and Frontier Martial Arts, which showcased ultraviolent, bloody hardcore matches, but the pro wrestling tradition in Japan is based on realism and athleticism.

"The psychology was really different in Japan," said Joel Deaton, an American who worked for All Japan during the 1990s. "The fans in Japan are smart. They grow up on karate and judo, rugby, all those hard-contact sports. Sumo. They know pro wrestling. They respect the physicality of it. You have to be polished to hold a spot over there. You got to be tough, too."

That psychology originates from the godfather of Japanese *puroresu*, Rikidozan.

Born in Korea and beginning as a sumo wrestler, Rikidozan decided to try professional wrestling in 1951. Pro wrestling existed but was not well regarded in Japan in those post-war years, but that was soon to change. American wrestlers were brought over to play the heel and Rikidozan would beat them all, giving the people of Japan someone to cheer for, to look up to, to be able to defeat the mighty Americans. He gave a sense of national pride to a company still reeling from the physical and psychological effects of war and the atomic bomb. Plus, American servicemen still stationed in Japan following the war took to American-style pro wrestling, further growing the audience for the sport in Japan.

It wasn't just the Japanese fans who came to love and respect this outstanding performer. By 1957, no less than the great Lou Thesz agreed to give Rikidozan the rub by wrestling him to a 60-minute time-limit draw. The following year, Thesz dropped the newly established NWA international heavyweight title to Rikidozan, cementing a partnership between the NWA and Rikidozan's Japan Pro Wrestling Alliance. He faced Thesz many more times over the next few years and had great rivalries with such American stars as Freddie Blassie and the Destroyer (Dick Beyer). So popular were these men that the 1963 match between the Destroyer and Rikidozan set a record that still stands as the largest viewing audience in Japan's TV history; the match also ended in a 60-minute time-limit draw.

Perhaps Rikidozan's greatest contribution to professional wrestling in Japan was in the form of his two star pupils, two men who would carry the business on their shoulders for the next several decades: Kanji "Antonio" Inoki, and Shohei "Giant" Baba.

Rikidozan was murdered in December 1963 when he was stabbed during an altercation in a nightclub and died of peritonitis a week later. The Japan Pro-Wrestling Alliance continued on following his death, but a power struggle developed between Inoki and Baba. Inoki — having become a big follower of Karl Gotch — broke away and created New Japan Pro-Wrestling with the idea of presenting a more "shoot wrestling" style of matches. Baba regrouped and formed All Japan Pro Wrestling.

"The main difference between Inoki's New Japan and Giant Baba's All Japan was that New Japan was more of a *man's* company. Big TV production. Antonio Inoki superstar aura," said historian and journalist Fumi Saito. "Whereas Baba's All Japan operated more like a mom-and-pop company. The actual boss was Mrs. Baba, Motoko Baba. They never had children. All the boys were like their children."

Both New Japan and All Japan featured homegrown Japanese talent, though All Japan maintained stronger ties to most American territories and regularly brought in American, Mexican, and Canadian stars as *gaijin* (foreign) invaders. "Every tour, you had the Funks. You had Mil Máscaras. Harley Race. Billy Robinson. Nick Bockwinkel. You name it. By watching All Japan's TV show for a one-year period, you're probably watching the entire American territories," Saito said. "Guys from Dallas, guys from Florida, guys from Tennessee, the Sheik's guys from Detroit, the Bruiser's guys came, the Canadians. Gene Kiniski, Killer Kowalski, Don Leo Jonathan, and all their people. There was a very NWA mentality."

Inoki managed to forge relationships with Mike LeBell in Los Angeles, Don Owen in Portland, Eddie Graham in Florida, and some non-NWA affiliated promotions in Mexico and Montreal.

In 1976, Inoki took part in what could be his most famous (or infamous) match. It was a spectacle that began as an offhanded joke. In 1975, Muhammad Ali was talking to the president of the Japanese Amateur Wrestling Association when he remarked, "Isn't there any Oriental fighter who will challenge me? I'll give him $1 million if he wins." Ali made statements like this all the time and they were usually ignored by the American press. The Japanese press, on the other hand, ran with it, and soon, Inoki, along with his financial backers, declared he would accept Ali's challenge. He offered $6 million to "The Greatest" to come to Japan and face Inoki.

For Inoki, it was an opportunity to use the shoot wrestling skills he had perfected under Gotch to make a name for himself against the most recognized fighter worldwide. As for Ali, $6 million was hard to pass up for what most felt would be a simple exhibition. By March 1976 the contract was signed and Ali versus Inoki was scheduled for June 26 at Tokyo's Nippon Budokan hall.

The rules were changed and altered so much that this no longer seemed like a match between a boxer and a wrestler. In a sense, this match was the first large-stage mixed martial arts contest. However, in MMA, both participants and fans usually understand the rules. Not in this case. More than 40 years later, many of those involved in the bout still disagree about what the actual rules were, and any rules actually written out were never provided to the public. But none of that really mattered leading up to the fight. Inoki's status in Japan and Ali's status worldwide made this odd novelty match a huge public curiosity. More than 150 closed-circuit locations throughout the United States signed on to broadcast the fight one day later to compensate for the time difference in Japan.

Vince McMahon Sr. acquired the closed-circuit rights for Shea Stadium in New York and put on a card that would have the Ali-Inoki match as the main event, but also featured another boxer-versus-wrestler fight pitting Andre the Giant against pugilist Chuck Wepner. Wepner had faced Ali the previous year and would go on to be the inspiration for Sylvester Stallone's *Rocky*. McMahon, for his part, was able to sell more than 32,000 tickets.

As for the fight itself, it was a flop in every sense. For most of the 15 rounds, Inoki opted to remain in a crab-walk stance, kicking at Ali's legs. His strategy was that Ali couldn't knock him down if he never stood up. Ali landed more than 100 stiff kicks during the course of the fight. The match was declared a draw when the wrestling judge scored the fight 74–72 for Ali, the boxing judge scored it 72–68 for Inoki, and the referee (Gene LeBell) scored it 71–71.

Financially, though, the match was a success, with some reports claiming 1.4 billion viewers worldwide. The closed-circuit take in the United States alone was over two million, meaning that the fight grossed $20 million on closed-circuit buys alone (about $90 million adjusted for inflation). But the fight was an embarrassment to Ali and a snooze-fest for fans. For Inoki, however, it was a moral victory. He took Ali the distance.

Through this battle with Ali and other similar (though much lower-profile) "shoot-style" bouts against martial artists, Inoki developed "strong style," a hybrid pro wrestling style combining pro wrestling moves with martial arts techniques. Influenced by Johnny Valentine and his "I can convince you I'm real" ethos, Inoki's strong style featured realistic-looking stiff striking, though — like traditional pro wrestling — the outcomes of the matches were still predetermined. In December 1976, just six months after facing Ali, Inoki defeated Pakistani wrestler Akram Pahalwan in a "worked shoot," winning by referee stoppage after hooking Pahalwan with a double wristlock.

In time, other styles were added to the strong-style mix, including karate, judo, Muay Thai, and Sambo, incorporated with the catch style Inoki learned from Karl Gotch.

In 1984, a group of wrestlers who had grown frustrated with their booking in New Japan under Inoki broke out and created the Universal Wrestling Federation. The UWF was billed as a shoot-style wrestling promotion and was geared towards presenting an ultra-realistic in-ring product. Akira Maeda founded the group and was joined by Gran Hamada, Rusher Kimura, and — eventually — Yoshiaki Fujiwara, Nobuhiko Takada, and the original Tiger Mask, Satoru Sayama.

There were many who thought that the UWF was going to revolutionize wrestling. By presenting a completely shoot-style product, they predicted, it would expose the more stagey elements of pro wrestling, such as Irish whips, moves off the ropes, and the entire shine-heat-hope spot structure of the standard pro match.

The UWF was able to broker a short-lived deal with the WWF, and Maeda went on an extensive U.S tour with the new Goliath of American wrestling. The deal with the WWF ended when the UWF President, Hisashi Shinma, who had brokered the deal with the WWF, left and went to work for All Japan.

The UWF held its first event in April 1984. By 1985, problems were already developing between Maeda and Sayama; Sayama wanted more submission holds and Maeda wanted more striking. Not surprisingly, the bad blood spilled over into the ring, with Maeda shooting on Sayama and landing a deliberate low blow during a match. Sayama left the UWF a short time later and walked away from wrestling entirely. With the loss of Sayama and the inability to land a TV deal, the UWF folded in 1986.

But, though the UWF failed to live up to expectations, it had won over a fan base that yearned to see more realism in wrestling and began to appreciate the intricacies of the style. Maeda and the UWF defectors rejoined All Japan for an invasion storyline. But Maeda was still unable to play well with others. A 1986 match against Andre the Giant broke into a shoot that had to be ended by Inoki. And, in 1987, Maeda nailed Riki Choshu with a shoot kick to the face that broke his orbital bone. Maeda was suspended from New Japan and set out to reform the UWF, this time as the "Newborn UWF." Despite drawing more than 60,000 fans to the Tokyo Dome for an event in November 1989 (headlined by Maeda beating Olympic judoka Willy Wilhelm), the fledgling promotion ran aground in 1990.

Despite the failures of Maeda's UWF promotions, it had become apparent that there was a massive audience in Japan for a more realistic style. Both New Japan and All Japan began to feature strong-style and more realistic bouts. All Japan pushed the likes of Stan Hansen, Steve Williams, Terry Gordy, and Big Van Vader — massive power merchants who excelled in the stiff, hard-hitting style. New Japan featured Vader, Shinya Hashimoto, and Soviet freestyle gold medalist Salman Hashimikov.

New shoot-style promotions developed in the subsequent years. Maeda formed Fighting Network RINGS, which would run from 1991 through 2002; a revised RINGS reopened in 2008. Fujiwara ran Pro Wrestling Fujiwara Group (Fujiwara Gumi) from 1991 through 1996. In 1993, pro wrestlers Masakatsu Funaki and Minoru Suzuki founded Pancrase, a mixed martial arts promotion that merged the ancient Greek fighting sport of *pankration* with traditional professional wrestling.

Nobuhiko Takada formed the Union of Wrestling Forces International (UWFI) in yet another effort to get the UWF off the ground. Takada scored a big knockout win over Bob Backlund, but his boxer-versus-wrestler fight against Trevor Berbick failed to generate the excitement or box office of Inoki/Ali. Despite having the blessing of Lou Thesz, the UWFI ran out of steam quickly and closed in 1995. It did, however, go on to influence Pride Fighting Championships and the mixed martial arts movement that took hold in both Japan and in the U.S. in the 1990s. It's not too far-fetched to say that pro wrestling in Japan gave the world the blueprint for the multi-billion-dollar MMA industry.

THE TAG TEAM MASTERS

We have established that there is an art to professional wrestling. Tag team wrestling has a distinct art of its own.

The standard template for a singles wrestling match is fairly straight-forward. Babyface gets the shine (early advantage, demonstrating that the "good guy" is a better wrestler than the bad guy; if he isn't, why would the fans want to cheer for him, right?). The heel gets the cut-off, usually through nefarious means (firmly establishing him as the villain). The heel gets heat, administering a beating to the valiant babyface and jaw-jacking with the crowd. Sprinkle in a couple hope spots where the babyface rallies only to get cut off again. Then there's the comeback by the babyface, perhaps a few false finishes, and then it's time to take it home. Hit the showers, boys.

There are multiple variations to the formula, but that's pro wrestling in a nutshell. But tag team wrestling adds another pair of wrestlers to the mix, which allows some more opportunities for creativity. The babyfaces can use precision double-team attacks to dazzle the crowd and show teamwork and skill. The heels can use double-team moves to establish themselves as bullies (especially if they do it behind the referee's back as the babyface-in-peril's beleaguered partner frantically argues to the referee that his partner is being murdered behind him). And the heels can work over the babyface until the inevitable hot tag to the fresh partner, a moment guaranteed to pop the crowd if done correctly.

A great tag team isn't necessarily two outstanding singles wrestlers paired together. The great tandems have a certain chemistry and ability to communicate. These great teams might consist of complementary pairs, such as a technical wrestler and a powerhouse; a high-flyer and a mat-based wrestler; a veteran and a young up-and-comer. Sometimes both partners have the same strengths: a pair of powerhouses, a twosome of technicians, a duo of daredevils. In any case, when the right two wrestlers team up, the sum can sometimes be greater than the individual parts.

The where and when of the first tag team match are subject to debate. Some historians say the first tag team match was held in San Francisco in 1901, though other historians have rejected that claim, citing a lack of verifiable evidence. There was a four-man "tornado" match (where all four men were in the ring at the same time) that took place in Houston on October 2, 1936, featuring Whiskers Savage and accomplished weightlifter Heinrich "Milo" Steinborn against Tiger Daula and Fazul Mohammed. The spectacle didn't go over well with *Houston Chronicle* reporter Jimmie Lingan, who called it a "freak team match." Steinborn would later be the promoter in Orlando working with Eddie Graham.

In the following years, four-man tornado matches began to take root in other promotions, popping up in the Pacific Northwest, Georgia, Texas, Ohio, and Missouri. Somewhere along the way (exactly where and when has been lost to time), wrestlers were required to "relay" in and out of the ring by tagging one another, so that only two men were allowed in the ring at the same time, as their opponents waited on the apron. By 1944, the first tag team title was established. By 1953, tag matches had gone mainstream and were featured at Madison Square Garden.

Tag team bouts began as a novelty attraction, "gimmick matches" comparable to women's or midgets' matches. But some teams helped develop a very unique psychology, structure, and rhythm to tag team wrestling, firmly establishing a place for tag team wrestling on virtually every card from the mid-1950s to today. While there have been hundreds of successful tag team tandems, here are some of the teams that took tag wrestling from novelty spectacle to high art.

THE FABULOUS KANGAROOS

The Fabulous Kangaroos were so closely identified with tag team wrestling that they were often mistaken for the originators of the genre. In some territories, tag matches were also referred to as "Australian rules" bouts, and the Kangaroos — originally Al Costello and Roy Heffernan — hailed from the Land Down Under . . . and had the boomerangs and Australian bush hats to prove it. Costello (a native of Italy who immigrated to Australia as a child) had dabbled in boxing before finding success as a wrestler, earning the nickname "The Man of a Thousand Holds." Costello developed the concept of the Kangaroos, thinking an Australian-themed tag team would be a unique gimmick. He recruited a former training partner, a bodybuilder named Roy Heffernan, and the Fabulous Kangaroos made their debut on May 3, 1957, in Calgary. They eventually added manager and mouthpiece Wild Red Berry to the team, and success followed. Costello was the shooter; Heffernan was the showman; and Berry handled the promos. Costello and Heffernan collected titles throughout the U.S., Canada, and Japan, including a 409-day run as World Wide Wrestling Federation U.S. tag champions from 1960 to 1962.

In 1965, Heffernan returned home to Australia, breaking up the team. Costello reformed the Kangaroos with several partners, including Englishman Ray St. Clair, American Don Kent, and Welshman Tony Charles. Kent also carried the boomerang banner, forming versions of the Kangaroos with Bruno Bekkar and Johnny Heffernan (no relation to Roy).

The original Kangaroos were together for eight years, but there were versions of the team in action for more than 25 years, making the Kangaroos one of the most durable, influential, and successful tag teams in wrestling history.

THE BLOND BOMBERS

Earlier we established that a great tag team could be more than the sum of the individual parts, but what happens when the "individual parts" are widely considered to be the two best in-ring competitors of their era? In the case of Ray Stevens and Pat Patterson, you end up with a tag team for the ages.

Stevens is profiled in full elsewhere in this book, but his team with Patterson warrants separate mention. "Work-wise, we basically had the same style," Pat Patterson said in an interview for the book *The Pro Wrestling Hall of Fame: The Tag Teams*. "In the day, guys didn't take as many bumps as they do today. We were known for taking big bumps."

But the success of the Blond Bombers was more than just their willingness to fly around the ring for their opponents or take wild bumps through (or over) the ropes to the unprotected floor below. More importantly, they knew when to take those big bumps. A heel tandem, both Patterson and Stevens would sell early, then take control of the match with double-team brawling tactics. Patterson's explosive right hands and Stevens's stomps and kicks would bring opponents to the canvas, where the Bombers would work them over the front facelocks and knee drops until their opponent finally rallied or made the tag.

That's when they would truly shine, sailing all over the ring like rag dolls on a hurricane.

"I never saw them work live, but I watched them on tape and I thought Pat Patterson and Ray Stevens were the greatest," said Luke Williams, one-half of the Sheepherders/Bushwackers with Butch Miller. "Fucking incredible! They were in a class of their own. Timing, ring psychology, and bumps. Even when they were taking bumps, the people still want to fight them. It was 'Take that, you mother fucker!' The way they take the bump and get up and sell it and that, it was terrific."

Stevens and Patterson were packaged as the Blond Bombers by San Francisco promoter Roy Shire. In 1965, Stevens and Patterson beat the Destroyer and Billy Red Lyons to win the San Francisco version of the NWA tag title. They held that title twice and reunited to win the AWA world tag team title in September 1978. In 2006, they were inducted into the Professional Wrestling Hall of Fame (then based in Amsterdam, New York; currently based in Wichita Falls, Texas) as a tag team in 2006.

"Stevens and Pat Patterson were probably the greatest tag team of all time," said Kevin Sullivan, who teamed with Stevens in the San Francisco territory after the Bombers' run in that territory.

BOB ORTON JR. AND DICK SLATER

As a team, Bob Orton Jr. (also profiled elsewhere in this book) and Dick Slater are probably best remembered for an angle they did in 1983, when they attacked Ric Flair, piledriving him and collecting a bounty placed on Flair by Harley Race. The angle was a winner and a big storyline to lead into the first *Starrcade* event, but Slater and Orton were more than two hired goons. They had a real chemistry as a team. "They were fabulous together and became a legendary tag team," Gary Hart, the man who paired the two together in the Georgia territory, wrote in his autobiography.

Slater had been a standout collegiate wrestler and football player at the University of Tampa and was recruited to become a pro wrestler by Mike Graham. He was trained by some of the best in the game, including Jack Brisco, Bob Roop, and Bill Watts. But, despite his background as an accomplished grappler trained by some of the sport's top technicians, Slater adopted a roughneck style similar to that of Terry Funk. Orton was a second-generation wrestler, the son of former Missouri heavyweight champion Bob Orton Sr. Together, they were a pair of tough, versatile wrestlers with presence and expert ring awareness. Slater, in particular, was known for his hot temper and short fuse throughout his career. Somehow, Orton's deliberate and methodical approach and Slater's unpredictable aggression managed to balance each other out. They innovated tag team moves and, in many ways, set the table for heel teams like the Midnight Express and the Hart Foundation.

"Orton and Slater was a hell of a tag team," Greg Valentine told SLAM! Wrestling. "They never went up North, but they were great . . . (Orton) and Slater one time had the greatest tag team I'd ever seen."

THE MIDNIGHT EXPRESS

Under the management of James E. Cornette, the Midnight Express became one of the influential and acclaimed tag teams of the 1980s.

"Bobby (Eaton) and Dennis (Condrey). Those are Wrestlers' Wrestlers. That was the team," said Luke Williams. "They were just magic in the ring. They had great psychology and timing. They got over well in the South. Vince tried to re-create the Express up North when he tried to reopen the NWA and it didn't go."

Condrey and Eaton were recognized as solid hands in Jerry Jarrett's Tennessee territory, but Bill Watts paired them together and made them stars after bringing them to Louisiana in 1983. "Beautiful" Bobby and "Loverboy" Dennis were partnered with Cornette, and the two gelled immediately. The name "The Midnight Express" actually predated the team, as it was used previously by Condrey and partners Randy Rose and Norvell Austin, but that threesome never achieved the success as the Condrey/Eaton (and later Eaton/Stan Lane) pairings.

The Express relied on quick tags, innovative double-team maneuvers, and the constant distracting presence of Cornette to gain the upper hand on their opponents. While heels, they weren't brawlers or thugs, but a precision tandem. They got heat by being great wrestlers yet still resorting to cheating and hanging around with a loudmouth nuisance like Cornette.

Eaton and Condrey held the Mid-South tag title on two occasions. In 1984, their feud with the Rock 'n' Roll Express did huge business in Mid-South and would be a recurring feud throughout the 1980s (and far beyond on the independent circuit). They held the NWA tag team title (for Jim Crockett Promotions) in 1986 and feuded with the R 'n' R and the Road Warriors.

"Dennis and Bobby were both polished," said "Outlaw" Joel Deaton, who worked for Jim Crockett Promotions at the time as the masked Thunderfoot and teamed with Black Bart. "And Ricky and Robert were just natural opponents for them. You never got tired of seeing that. They could work and they could work with anybody. Same with the Rock 'n' Rolls."

When Condrey left JCP in March 1987, he was replaced by "Sweet" Stan Lane, who had previously been one-half of the Fabulous Ones (with Steve Keirn). Lane brought a new energy, and sex appeal, to the team. Though he was only a year younger than Condrey, he *looked* a good 10 years longer. Eaton and Lane recaptured the NWA world and U.S. tag titles and were named Tag Team of the Year by the *Wrestling Observer Newsletter* in 1986, 1987, and 1988, a period when tag team wrestling reached its high-water mark nationally.

In 1998, the WWF tried to re-create the Midnight Express with Bob Holly and Bart Gunn, but the team flopped hard, even with Cornette frantically waving the tennis racket in their corner.

THE ROCK 'N' ROLL EXPRESS

You simply can't mention the Midnight Express without talking about the Rock 'n' Roll Express, and vice versa. Ricky Morton and Robert Gibson were first paired together by Jerry Lawler in Memphis and positioned as a secondary babyface team behind local favorites the Fabulous Ones. With their MTV-inspired look and style, the Express won over fans and soon surpassed the Fabs as the most popular babyface team in the game.

The R 'n' R feuded with the Midnights on and off from 1984 through 1988 (and in various forms into the 1990s and 2000s on the independents). They held the NWA tag team title four times between 1985 and 1987. In 2019, they won that title for the fifth time, winning the belts in the relaunched NWA owned by Billy Corgan.

Morton's incredible ability to sell and Gibson's electrifying hot tags helped them become one of the most successful teams of their era, and their staying power has been remarkable. Among their many imitators was the Rockers, the team of Shawn Michaels and Marty Jannetty.

TULLY BLANCHARD AND ARN ANDERSON

Tully Blanchard was a second-generation wrestler, the son of wrestler and Southwest Championship Wrestling promoter Joe Blanchard.

"When I started wrestling, I knew I'm not going to be the biggest guy. I had to work and be better than the rest because I was the promoter's kid, and the promoter's kid didn't always get good treatment," Blanchard said when he was honored with the Cauliflower Alley Club's Iron Mike Award in 2017.

"Of all the wrestlers I've seen in 40-plus years, I've never seen as natural and athletic a heel (as Tully Blanchard)," Jim Ross said. "He was a Rembrandt on his chosen canvas."

Arn Anderson was a no-nonsense journeyman who got a break by being paired with Ole Anderson as his "nephew." In 1985, they (and Ole) came together as members of the Four Horsemen, a heel alliance with Ric Flair, along with their manager, J.J. Dillon. Blanchard was in a hot feud with Dusty Rhodes over the TV title and the Andersons were one of the territory's top tag teams, but in 1987 — after Ole was released by Jim Crockett Promotions — Blanchard and Anderson were paired as a tag team. The team was a natural. They defeated the Rock and Roll Express to win the NWA tag team title in September 1987, and held the belts for six months before dropping them to Barry Windham and Lex Luger. They regained the belts one month later (when Windham turned on Luger and joined the Horsemen) and held the belts until September 1988.

"There are some teams that the first time they got beat, the bubble's burst and the story's over," J.J. Dillon said in an interview for *The Pro Wrestling Hall of Fame: The Tag Teams.* "With Tully and Arn we had the ability to go out and get our butts kicked every night, come back on TV the next morning, tell lies, then the people would want to come back and see it again and maybe see a worse butt-kicking."

In the fall of 1988, Blanchard and Anderson decided to jump ship from the NWA to the WWF. It was a risky move; Tully and Arn were no-frills, boots-and-trunks rasslers from down South. The WWF was all about gimmicks. As it turned out, being superior wrestlers was a gimmick on its own. Tully and Arn were put with manager Bobby "The Brain" Heenan and christened "The Brainbusters." They won the WWF tag team title with a controversial best-of-three falls match against Demolition in July 1989, but lost the belts back to Demolition a few months later.

The title change was the beginning of the end for the team. The NWA — now under the ownership of Ted Turner and transitioning into World Championship Wrestling — made a big-money offer for the Horsemen to return, but when Blanchard failed a drug test and was fired by the WWF, WCW withdrew the offer. Anderson eventually returned to WCW. Blanchard made a stop in the AWA, ECW, and a handful of indie appearances before retiring in 2007 and eventually becoming a minister. They wrestled their last match as a tag team on November 5, 1989.

Despite only teaming for slightly more than two years, Anderson and Blanchard became the first team ever to win the NWA and WWF tag titles, were voted Tag Team of the Year of 1989 by readers of *Pro Wrestling Illustrated*, and are still widely regarded to be one of wrestling's top teams of all time.

THE BRITISH BULLDOGS

Cousins Tom Billington and David Smith discovered pro wrestling as an alternative to the arduous labor of the coal mines in their native Lancashire, England. Billington — later known as the Dynamite Kid, given that name by promoter Max Crabtree — was trained by Ted Betley and made his debut in December 1975. "Young David" made his debut two years later at the age of 15.

The Dynamite Kid was invited to Stu Hart's Stampede promotion in Alberta in 1978 after being discovered by Bruce Hart. The elder Hart was reluctant to take a chance on the five-foot-eight, 170-pound Kid, but eventually succumbed to Bruce's persuasion. Dynamite's tireless work ethic and athleticism got him over in Stampede, and in 1981, Davey Boy was invited in to Calgary as well. Dynamite and Davey Boy didn't become a tag team until January 1, 1984, when they teamed up to face Isamu Teranishi and Kuniaki Kobayashi at Korakuen Hall in Tokyo. They would team together almost exclusively until 1990.

The team developed a stiff style of jarring double-team moves that combined Dynamite's intensity and crisp delivery with Smith's raw power. In 1984, Vince McMahon acquired the Stampede Wrestling promotion as part of his expansion throughout the U.S. and Canada. He offered Dynamite and Smith a deal where they would compete for the WWF while still working with All Japan (having made an abrupt jump from NJPW to AJPW in late 1984).

The WWF christened them the British Bulldogs and, in a featured match at *WrestleMania* 2 at the Rosemont Horizon in Chicago, the Bulldogs (with countryman Ozzy Osbourne in their corner) defeated Greg Valentine and Brutus Beefcake to win the WWF tag title.

With their unique combination of British catch-as-catch-can technique and stiff and athletic Japanese style, the Bulldogs were unlike any other team in the WWF during the era. "Their hard wrestling style didn't fit in with a lot of the WWF teams at the time, whereas the Japanese wrestlers and style made them seem a lot more special," *Wrestling Observer Newsletter* publisher Dave Meltzer said. "I think their impact was strong among hardcore fans and a lot of people who grew up to be top wrestlers. It's funny, because at the time, the Road Warriors were the kings of tag teams and everyone wanted to be like them . . . but long-term, it was the Bulldogs and Midnight Express who popularized the big-move style that the next generation of wrestlers studied."

The Bulldogs left the WWF in late 1988 after Dynamite Kid was involved in a backstage skirmish with Jacques Rougeau. They returned to Stampede Wrestling, which was on its last legs, and made some tours of AJPW, but when Davey Boy Smith returned to the WWF with a big singles push in 1990, it proved to be the final nail in the team's coffin. Dynamite Kid wrestled on and off until 1996; he spent the last years of his life confined to a wheelchair and died on December 5, 2018 (his 60th birthday). Smith died of a heart attack on May 18, 2002.

PART 5:
The "Attitude Era" and the Rise of Extreme Wrestling

A large component of Vince McMahon's success in the 1980s came from marketing his vision of sports entertainment to kids. Hulk Hogan was basically a comic book character — in fact, he was the star of his own animated series, *Hulk Hogan's Rock 'n' Wrestling* in 1985–86. The LJN eight-inch action figures were as ubiquitous as Star Wars or G.I. Joe figures. WWF matches, by and large, were short, basic, and easy-to-understand battles between good and evil.

The NWA tried to present itself as an alternative to the WWF's three-ring circus with an emphasis on pure wrestling and old-fashioned storytelling, but by the early 1990s, Ted Turner's management team was trying to replicate the WWF's financial success with cartoonish wrestlers, gimmicky storylines, and celebrity endorsements.

The kids who got hooked on wrestling with the first *WrestleMania*s were headed to college. They had no time for that "childish" pro wrestling. They wanted an alternative.

"Alternative" was the buzzword of the 1990s. In a paradoxical twist, "alternative music" (the kind of non-mainstream alt-rock played on college music stations) became a genre in itself, and actually became the dominant musical genre of the decade — so much for being "alternative." *Twin Peaks* changed the standards of standard nighttime television programming. The internet was becoming more and more entrenched and changing the way people interacted and the information and content that was available.

Pro wrestling wasn't immune to the changes that were rapidly occurring within society. In August 1994, Shane Douglas was slated to win a tournament for the vacant NWA world title in Philadelphia, as the

NWA had parted from Ted Turner's World Championship Wrestling the previous year. Douglas won the title belt but then denounced the title and said he refused to be the champion of a "dead organization" and declared himself the first Extreme Championship Wrestling "world" champion.

Promoter Paul Heyman, who had been the mastermind of the swerve that basically buried the remaining NWA-affiliated promoters and stole the world title credibility of the tournament and NWA name for himself, basically said he did so because NWA wrestling wasn't cool in the 1990s.

"The National Wrestling Alliance was old-school when old-school wasn't hip anymore," Heyman said in a 1998 online chat. "We wanted to set our mark, we wanted to breakaway from the pack, we wanted to let the world know that we weren't just some independent promotion."

ECW established itself as an alternative, featuring bloody hardcore matches, risqué storylines, catfights between scantily clad valets, copious amounts of swearing, and a "let's give the fans something they've never seen before" ethos that made the promotion a cult phenomenon. By 1997, the WWF had taken note, with ECW stars Heyman, the Sandman, Tommy Dreamer, Sabu, Rob Van Dam, and others "invading" a WWE *Raw* broadcast at the Manhattan Center in New York. Before long, WWE began pushing boundaries with increasingly risqué storylines and hardcore matches. McMahon dubbed it the start of the WWF's "Attitude Era."

In addition to blood and babes, the 1990s also saw an increased emphasis on workrate. Wrestlers traditionally considered "too small" to push worked their way into the spotlight. While wrestlers like Sandman, Cactus Jack, Sabu, and — later — Steve Austin and the Rock — were taking things to the extreme, a new breed of wrestlers was also rising to the forefront.

WILLIAM REGAL

"A Wrestlers' Wrestler and a man's man."

That's how Rob Van Dam described William Regal, the man he defeated to win the WWE Intercontinental title at *WrestleMania* X8 in Toronto.

"He's s a wrestler all the way through, not just on the outer skin but through his organs, through his bones," Van Dam said. "The man came up by being the man in the ring who challenged people from the crowd to come last with him to make money in circuses. He's a tough guy. He's one of the last guys that somebody should pick a fight with. He goes by the old-school rules of if somebody needs a headbutt, he's not afraid to do it."

Darren Matthews was born on May 10, 1968, in the village of Codsall Wood in Staffordshire, England. His parents split when he was seven years old, and he stayed with his father. When his father was out at work, Darren was watched by his grandfather, Bill Matthews, who had wrestled and boxed at a local pub in the 1920s and 1930s. Darren was enraptured by his grandad's stories, and by the time he was a teenager, he knew what he wanted to do with his life.

"I remember one of my last days at Codsall High, when I was sent to see the careers officer," he wrote in his 2005 autobiography, *Walking a Golden Mile*. "'What are you going to do?' he asked me. 'Are you going to get a trade?' 'No,' I said. 'I'm going to be a wrestler.' He threw me out of the office and told me to come back when I wanted to talk some sense. I expect he's still there today."

Matthews's father took his son to the matches at Wolverhampton Civic Hall, where he watched Giant Haystacks, Big Daddy, Mick McManus, "Cyanide" Sid Cooper, and Kendo Nagasaki with his autograph book in his back pocket. By the time he was 15, he was taking the bus to the arena himself and headed farther from home to catch independent cards. He studied the wrestlers — the technicians, the gimmick attractions, the personalities — and he paid particular attention to the heels.

"It wasn't long before I realized there was a great deal more to this wrestling caper than what you saw on Saturday afternoons on World of Sport," he wrote. "Some were just entertainers. Others were very skilled wrestlers. But the ones who were both, who had the whole package, were the ones to emulate. I began to watch the wrestlers who made me believe that what they were doing in the ring was real. As far as that goes, England has the best wrestlers in the world — or did in those days, at any rate. I was determined to learn that really serious style. I wanted to be a wrestler whose matches were completely believable."

He began teaching himself how to bump by watching the way wrestlers fell and going home and practicing on the lawn and on a sheet of plywood. "I was tall enough to be a wrestler, but there was a problem:

William Regal hooks CM Punk with a three-quarter nelson.

PHOTO BY GEORGE NAPOLITANO

I had no athletic ability whatsoever," he wrote. "I'd never done any sports, watched any or cared about them, for that matter. At school I'd get out of them any way I could. So pretty early on I recognized I couldn't be a high-flying wrestler, even if it was my favourite style to watch. I just didn't have the ability for it. When I tried to fly I looked like a very sad sack indeed. I'd never be a performer like Rocco in the past or Eddie Guerrero and Chris Benoit today. That's why I decided I had to concentrate on mat wrestling and entertaining. Making my matches look more believable and fluid became my obsession."

Regal has said he was influenced by Terry Rudge, Pete Roberts, Johnny Saint, and Sid Cooper. Rudge's aggressive offense and wide stance, Cooper's body language and facial expressions, Roberts's unique counters, and Saint's sense of showmanship can all be seen reflected in Regal's wrestling style.

He mustered up the courage to approach promoter Bobby Baron, who promoted matches in the beachside holiday town of Blackpool, and said he wanted to be a wrestler. Baron humored the kid and gave the 15-year-old self-taught aspiring wrestler a match against the six-foot-six Magnificent Maurice. Maurice manhandled Matthews, but didn't injure him. When the match was over — though he had lost — Matthews was even more convinced that wrestling was his destiny.

Matthews began training under Marty Jones and started wrestling open challenges against audience members on the English carnival circuit, using hooking skills he had learned to submit all comers. He adopted the name Steven Regal and began touring the country, teaming with Robbie Brookside as the Golden Boys. He traveled throughout Europe, South Africa, and the Middle East and received a tryout with the WWF in 1991, but ended up signing with WCW after making several appearances on a WCW tour of the U.K.

As Lord Steven Regal, he was presented as the stereotypical British upper-crust snob, claiming to be a descendant of William the Conqueror, a far cry from his real-life working-class background. Regal was slotted as a midcard heel, but his presence, unique grappling style, body positioning, and exaggerated facial expressions made him a compelling character, even without a major push. In September 1993, he won his first American title, beating Ricky Steamboat for the WCW TV title. He would hold that title four times between 1993 and 1997. He also formed tag teams with Jean-Paul Lévesque (the man who would become Triple H in the WWF), "Earl" Robert (formerly known as Beautiful Bobby) Eaton, and "Squire" David Taylor.

In February 1998, Regal was fed to Bill Goldberg, a promising but very green rookie that WCW was pushing as an unbeatable monster. Instead of doing a typical squash job, Regal took down Goldberg with an overhead neck cravat, landed a stiff kick to the back, and — instead of begging off when Goldberg squared up on him — came out firing with European uppercuts, armbars, and go-behinds. The inexperienced Goldberg looked lost and foolish as Regal kept forcing him to wrestle. After a five-minute match, Regal eventually ate the pinfall after a jackhammer — but he made Goldberg work to earn the win. WCW executives weren't amused, and Regal was fired from the company.

Regal later said that the agents had asked him to have a competitive six-minute match and maintains that he didn't set out to make Goldberg look bad. However, Regal had already been on thin ice in WCW after having been arrested for being intoxicated on an airplane a few months earlier. The Goldberg match proved to be the last straw.

Regal appeared in the WWF in mid-1998 and was given a hokey gimmick as a flannel-clad "Man's Man," the exact opposite of his aristocratic character in WCW. The gimmick didn't get over, and Regal's problems with drugs and alcohol worsened. He was sent to rehab and eventually released by the WWF in April 1999. He returned to WCW later that year, re-forming his Blue Bloods tag team with Taylor, but left the company after losing a career-versus-career match against Jim Duggan in February 2000.

He returned to the WWF and reported to Memphis Championship Wrestling, the developmental territory for the WWF. Given his issues with injuries, health, and addiction, many wondered whether Regal's time on the national stage was finished. But on May 25, 2000, Regal answered his critics with a show-stealing match against Chris Benoit at the third annual Brian Pillman Memorial Show in Cincinnati. He was brought up to the main roster that fall, under the name William Regal, and defeated Al Snow to win the European title in October 2000.

Regal made the most of his opportunity with WWE, showcasing more personality and comedy chops than ever before, and showing more passion and dedication to his physical appearance. "A wrestler or a clown or a comedian, I've ended up becoming a mixture of all three," Regal later wrote.

Van Dam said he appreciated working with Regal, who had a very different style from many other wrestlers of the era. "I remember it being somewhat challenging, but he was so good and I didn't suck, either, so we were able to work through it and I was able to learn a lot," Van Dam said regarding his acrobatic style against Regal's submission style. "There's certain things he would do — like, just working a top wristlock over my head when most people were doing it underneath. During a match, he's doing it, he's got me in a move. So I have to adjust to that. The results were some stuff that was different from what I was doing. To try to reverse it from there I might jump up and throw some headscissors on him, things like that. It was adding to my repertoire and my knowledge of different ways to tell a story."

"Regal would shield his body in a certain way and you wouldn't know that he has two fingers in somebody's mouth or sticking a thumb in their eye. It was so brilliant the way he did it," said former WWE referee Jimmy Korderas. "He looks so intimidating doing it, too."

In WWE, Regal had runs as WWF commissioner (in storyline), *Raw* general manager, two runs as Intercontinental champion, four runs as European champion, and four tag title reigns (with Lance Storm, Eugene, and Tajiri). In 2008, he received a major push, winning the 2008 King of the Ring tournament and starting a feud with world champion CM Punk, but the push was dropped after he was suspended for violating the company's Wellness Policy.

He quietly retired from wrestling 2013 and settled into a role as general manager of NXT. In 2018, he was officially named WWE director of talent development and head of global recruiting. He became a mentor to many of WWE's developmental talents.

"Since I was trying to switch to a less risky style, Regal was the perfect teacher for me," Daniel Bryan wrote in his autobiography, *Yes: My Improbable Journey to the Main Event of WrestleMania*. "He would go into detail explaining the finer points of basic holds, and why certain counters make sense and others don't, given the intuitive visual intelligence people have about the human body. He opened up a whole new world of wrestlers like Johnny Saint and Mark 'Rollerball' Rocco, who were great wrestlers, and the way Regal thought and talked about wrestling transformed the way I thought and talked about it."

"You often get a lot of people who have come through the business and they've done all the miles on the road and been looked after and trained by others, but some of them get sour and walk away and they don't give back," said Fit Finlay, one of Regal's top in-ring rivals throughout his career, in an interview on WWE.com "Regal is still here. He still gets in the ring, still trains guys. He tries to help them all out and give them advice. To give back is just the right thing to do and he's doing well. Everybody will benefit by having Regal around. There's not many of him left. He's well-schooled and he's passing it on, which is a great admirable thing."

MITSUHARU MISAWA

"Misawa was arguably the best in-ring performer in the world in his prime . . . In addition to (being) a physical, fundamentally sound athlete, timing and toughness were two of his greatest attributes. Great timing is a gift that largely can't be taught. It's like ring psychology. Some of it can be taught but mostly it must be a learned trait and some people are in the business for years and never learn great timing or main event level ring psychology. Toughness is another trait that can be nurtured but generally can't be taught. Misawa was naturally tough and it showed. And his fans loved him for it. They also loved his passion and the emotional ride on which he would take them. That's what pro wrestling is, selling emotion."

—Jim Ross, in an article on his website
following Misawa's death in 2009.

A five-time All Japan Triple Crown champion and three-time Pro Wrestling NOAH champion, Mitsuharu Misawa was one of the finest wrestlers in the world in the 1990s and early 2000s. His matches against longtime rival Toshiaki Kawada were feverishly exchanged by tape traders in the days before the internet and YouTube. His Emerald Flowsion side suplex, forearm strikes, suicide elbow, rolling elbow, and tiger suplex were widely emulated throughout Japan, the U.S., and all over the world.

When he left All Japan after a falling out with Motoko Baba, virtually the entire roster walked out of the company with him. He named his new company Pro Wrestling NOAH, and he was Noah himself, captaining his crew through the storm and into a new beginning.

Born June 18, 1962, he grew up in the city of Koshigaya. His parents divorced when he was young. Pro wrestling — All Japan in particular — gave him respite from the realities of a grim home life. By the time he was 12 years old, Misawa had set his mind to becoming a pro wrestler. He enrolled in high school at the Ashikaga Institute of Technology, where he dormed with Kawada, who was a year younger. The two formed a friendship and a relationship that would last their lifetimes. "Misawa gave his school uniform — the pants, the blue blazer — to Kawada when he graduated," said historian and journalist Fumi Saito.

In 1980, Misawa won the national high school wrestling championship at the 187-pound weight class. He also placed fifth in the freestyle World Championships. In March 1981, he joined the All Japan Pro Wrestling training camp, where he was trained by Kazuharu Sonoda and Akihisa Takachiho, with additional training from Giant Baba, the Destroyer, Dory Funk Jr., and Lou Thesz.

"Misawa had Mr. and Mrs. Baba's blessing right away," Saito said. "They saw this guy was talented. He was going to be the guy after Jumbo Tsuruta."

Misawa wrestled his first pro match in August 1981. Despite his amateur credentials, Baba kept him in preliminary matches doing job duty as he continued to develop as a pro. It wasn't until April 1983 that Misawa received a bit of a push, making it to the finals of the Lou Thesz Cup tournament, but lost to Shiro Koshinaka in a match refereed by Thesz.

Koshinaka and Misawa were both sent for a tour of Mexico to become familiar with the Lucha Libre style and continue to develop. In April 1984, Misawa earned an NWA world middleweight title match against El Satánico at the Arena México. Impressed with his development and aerial abilities, Baba brought Misawa back to Japan and gave him the gimmick of Tiger Mask, a masked character based on a manga series. The character had previously been portrayed by Satoru Sayama in New Japan. Baba had bought the rights to the character and handpicked Misawa to be his resident superhero.

Tiger Mask II received a strong push and Baba brought in a string of top junior heavyweights to face him, including the Dynamite Kid, Kuniaki

Kobayashi, and Chavo Guerrero. In August 1985, he defeated Kobayashi to win the NWA international junior heavyweight title. However, the high-flying style was causing considerable damage to Misawa's knees, forcing him vacate the title in 1986.

Misawa moved into the heavyweight division, where he could alter his style to better protect his knees. With Baba, he toured the U.S. in 1986, competing in the inaugural Crockett Cup tag team tournament (he and Baba lost to Magnum T.A. and Ron Garvin in the quarterfinals) and the AWA WrestleRock supercard, where he scored a win over Buck Zumhofe. Over the next few years, he received shots at NWA world champions Ric Flair and Ricky Steamboat and AWA world champion Curt Hennig, and he wrestled Bret Hart to a time-limit draw at a joint WWF/AJPW/NJPW card in 1990.

When Genichiro Tenryu led an exodus of talent out of All Japan to form the short-lived Super World of Sports promotion, Baba turned to Misawa to take over and fill the void. Following a tag team match, Misawa asked his tag partner, Kawada, to help him remove his Tiger Mask hood. He was symbolically stepping out of the role and assuming his own identity. He issued a challenge to Tsuruta and, on June 8, 1990, Misawa defeated Tsuruta at Nippon Budokan.

According to *Wrestling Observer Newsletter* publisher Dave Meltzer, Baba decided on Misawa going over in that match at the spur of the moment.

"(Tsuruta) was shocked when Giant Baba asked him a few hours before their match to lose in a Budokan Hall main event to Misawa," Meltzer wrote. "That wasn't how wrestling in Japan worked at that time, but as history has shown pretty clearly, Baba's instincts in seeing the audience reaction with loud 'Misawa' chants coming out of nowhere every few minutes in the hour before the show started in the building, as well as in the hours before outside the ring in the giant line to get in the lone exit, sensed it was the right time to do the unexpected. . . . Baba was sitting at the concession stand near the entrance of the building, seeing the huge business for Misawa merchandise almost out of nowhere, hearing the buzz of the crowd, and sent the message to Tsuruta, in the dressing room."

With that win, Misawa was anointed as the top new star in All Japan. Misawa went in pursuit of the Triple Crown title, finally defeating Stan

Hansen for that championship in August 1992. Misawa's first reign would last just short of two years. He held the Triple Crown title a total of five times through 1999. During that time, he was voted Most Outstanding Wrestler (1997 and 1999) and Wrestler of the Year (1995, 1997, 1999) by the *Wrestling Observer*. His battles with Kawada, Kenta Kobashi, Jun Akiyama, and Akira Taue became the stuff of legends in the wrestling world.

"Misawa is an absolutely incredible athlete. He could do things that were just incredible. I loved working with him," said "Outlaw" Joel Deaton. "He made you work hard but that's the way I always worked anyway. I really have a lot of respect for Misawa as a person and as a fabulous wrestler. He was a polished pro!"

Perhaps sensing his failing health, Baba put Misawa in charge of booking in 1998. When Baba succumbed to renal cancer the following year, his widow, Motoko, assumed control of All Japan. Motoko was not popular with the crew and was often called "The Dragon Lady" behind her back. Misawa clashed with Motoko, with Misawa wanting to modernize the style of the promotion and Motoko resisting, as well as disagreements about the allocation of merchandise money and compensation. In June 1990, he — along with the entire locker room except for Kawada and Masanobu Fuchi — announced they were leaving All Japan to form Pro Wrestling NOAH. Misawa worked to find balance between being a businessman and NOAH's top star. He won a tournament to become the first NOAH champion in April 2001, but dropped the belt to Jun Akiyama a few months later. He had a second title run in late 2002, and his third — and final — GHC reign lasted from December 2006 through March 2008, when he lost the belt to Takeshi Morishima.

"Misawa found himself in the exhausting position of being company president, booker, and the top wrestler in the world, all at the same time," Meltzer wrote. "His career at the top had survived multiple injuries that would have crippled most humans and ended the careers of most wrestlers. He worked through them, and rarely missed a match, because of the mentality instilled in him to be tough and never complain. He could not go all out every night, but remained as good a big show wrestler as there was. He had learned how to work believable enough to bring people into his matches and have them believe the roller coaster rides were really the most exciting athletic competitions around, done well enough that they overcame his own lack of facial expressions, usually the death knell for a successful drawing card. He regularly took psychotic bumps, most notably back suplexes where he and his partners in crime would be dropped on their heads. His neck, knees and back ached all the time. He relied on chiropractic help and acupuncture therapy but never used traditional medical treatment, nor in recent years did he take time off from the ring."

Tragically, Misawa died in the ring on June 13, 2009. He had been wrestling a tag team match with Go Shiozaki against Akitoshi Saito and Bison Smith when he landed on his neck during a high-angle suplex from Saito. It was one of his signature bumps, a frightening-looking fall that he had done countless times throughout his career. But this time he didn't get back up.

"Misawa just laid there. He immediately told ref Shuichi Nishinaga, 'I can't move,' and then passed out," Meltzer reported. NOAH did not have a doctor on hand and made an announcement asking if there were any doctors in the audience. A spectator answered the call and began to perform CPR, then tried to restart Misawa's hart with a defibrillator, to no avail. The injury was reported to be a cervical cord transection — basically, an internal decapitation. He died at the age of 46, five days before his 47th birthday.

Misawa headlined Budokan Hall a record-setting 69 times during his career. Twenty-four of his matches were rated five stars by Meltzer (an additional match versus Kawada in June 1994 received a six-star rating). While the Rock, Steve Austin, Triple H, Goldberg, and Sting were bigger stars worldwide, Misawa was universally regarded to be the finest all-around wrestler of the late 1990s and early 2000s.

"Vader once described Misawa as 'the ace quarterback and locker room leader,' and I think that's the perfect description," Saito said.

EDDIE GUERRERO

It would have been nearly impossible to predict the success achieved by Eddie Guerrero, a five-foot-eight Latino cruiserweight schooled in the Lucha Libre style who became the WWE world champion and one of the most beloved and influential stars of his generation. His success and remarkable legacy are a true testament to his talent as a wrestler and a storyteller.

Eduardo Gory Guerrero Llanes was born in El Paso, Texas, on October 9, 1967. He was born into the Guerrero wrestling family, which included his father (wrestler and promoter Gory Guerrero) and older brothers (Chavo Sr., Mando, and Hector). His brothers all broke into the business during the 1970s, and Eddie grew up watching them in action at the El Paso County Coliseum. Occasionally, Gory would allow young Eddie to wrestle his little nephew, Chavo Jr., in the ring during the intermission of these cards.

Eddie graduated high school and attended college at the University of Mexico and New Mexico Highlands University, where he wrestled collegiately, before training for the pros. He wrestled his first official match in September 1986, competing under a mask as Máscara Mágica in Mexico's Consejo Mundial de Lucha Libre. He also made a handful of appearances in WCW, wrestling in prelims and dark matches. In 1992, he moved to the rival Asistencia Asesoría y Adminstración, teaming with fellow second-generation *luchador* El Hijo del Santo, reprising the famous "Atomic Pair" team of their fathers, Gory Guerrero and El Santo.

Eddie turned on El Hijo Del Santo and formed La Pareja del Terror ("The Pair of Terror") with Art Barr. Guerrero and Barr generated massive heat throughout Mexico and headlines throughout the wrestling world. The duo became the cornerstone of the Los Gringos Locos stable. Guerrero and Barr were voted Tag Team of the Year in the 1994 *Wrestling Observer Newsletter* awards, despite not being seen on American television, save for their five-star match at the AAA When Worlds Collide pay-per-view, where they lost a mask-versus-hair grudge match to El Hijo de Santo and Octagon.

Following that run, Guerrero moved to New Japan, where he wrestled as Black Tiger, a character previously portrayed by British star Mark "Rollerball" Rocco. As Black Tiger, Guerrero won the 1996 Best of the Super Juniors tournament in a field that included Jushin Liger, Dean Malenko, Shinjiro Otani, and "Mr. J.L." Jerry Lynn.

Guerrero's success in Mexico and Japan caught the eye of ECW promoter Paul Heyman, who looked to re-form La Pareja del Terror in Philadelphia. However, Barr died on November 23, 1994, from what has been reported as a drug-related heart attack. Guerrero went on to ECW as a single act and won the TV title in his first match with the company, defeating 2 Cold Scorpio. Guerrero had noteworthy rivalries with both Scorpio and Dean Malenko, matches which injected a massive dose of technical wrestling wizardry on cards that were otherwise stacked with brawling and bloody hardcore matches.

In late 1995, Guerrero signed with WCW along with Malenko and Chris Benoit. He defeated Diamond Dallas Page in the finals of a tournament to win the vacant U.S. title at *Starrcade* 1996. Guerrero's Lucha Libre style of quick counters and reversals, flips, and crisp aerial attacks made him stand out in a promotion that was largely built around older, slower wrestlers in their 40s, but though he was amassing a vocal fan following, his head continually butted up against WCW's glass ceiling. He had a pair of cruiserweight title reigns, had highly-regarded matches against Malenko, Rey Mysterio, and Chris Jericho, and even formed his own stable, the Latino World Order, a take-off of the massively pushed New World Order, yet he never gained traction in WCW, where Vince Russo — a man who famously said, "I'm an American, and I don't give a (expletive) about Japanese and Mexican wrestlers" — was one of the bookers.

In January 2000, Guerrero — along with Malenko, Benoit, and Perry Saturn — requested and received their releases from WCW. The four, dubbed the Radicalz, debuted on WWE *Raw* on January 31, and were pushed as new babyfaces coming into the company. But in his debut match with WWE, Guerrero dislocated his elbow on a frog splash, which put him on the sidelines for several weeks.

Upon his return from injury, Guerrero was placed in a storyline with Chyna as his love interest, his "mamacita." The unlikely pairing was a hit and showcased Guerrero's talent for comedy. The angle saw Guerrero "invade" the Playboy Mansion to protest Chyna appearing in the magazine and ended when Guerrero was caught cheating with a couple of the Godfather's ladies of the night.

However, Guerrero's body was giving him problems. The in-ring pains, amplified by an injury from a car accident in 1999, caused Guerrero to become dependent on painkillers. He went to rehab, but while out, he was arrested for drunk driving and released from his WWE contract. Guerrero had to rebuild his career, his body, and his reputation.

Guerrero began a tour of the indies, including appearances in Ring of Honor, still a relatively small promotion at the time. He also worked for World Wrestling All-Stars out of Australia, and in less than two years he was welcomed back to the big time, settling in on WWE SmackDown.

Referee Jimmy Korderas, who officiated many of Guerrero's WWE matches, said Eddie was a master of improv and calling audibles in the ring.

"Obviously, the outline and the structure (of the match) were there, but a lot of times, he just decided to do something on the fly," Korderas said. "There was a tag match, Eddie and Chavo against Shelton Benjamin and Charlie Haas. In the middle of the match, in the corner Eddie was standing in, the bolt that holds the turnbuckle in the corner was coming loose. It was literally halfway off. The ring announcer, Tony Chimel, went to go tighten it real quick with a wrench and Eddie said to him, 'Tony, give me the wrench.' I'm reffing the match so I have no idea this is going on. They bring Shelton over to the corner and I heard Eddie say, 'Chavo, take a ref.' So Chavo draws me away. So they do a spot with this wrench where they kept hitting the guy with the wrench back and forth. The crowd was loving it. I wasn't seeing any of it. At the end of this entire improv spot, they end up with Charlie being the one to take the wrench out of his hand and go, 'Hey ref, look!' And then I end up giving him crap for having a wrench."

In 2004, Guerrero reached the top of the mountain and became the WWE champion by defeating Brock Lesner. He successfully defended the crown against Kurt Angle at *WrestleMania* XX. In a moment of pure joy, he joined his longtime friend Chris Benoit in the ring that night, after Benoit had won the world championship (a title that had been the successor to the NWA world title), celebrating amidst falling confetti. The new guard had taken over WWE.

Guerrero died of heart failure on November 13, 2005. He was 38 years old.

DEAN MALENKO

When the topic of "Wrestlers' Wrestlers" of the Monday Night Wars era arises, one name always seems to come up in the conversation.

"I think Dean Malenko fits in that category," said Chris Jericho. "I think Dean is one of the best actual technical wrestlers ever. Backstage, Dean is one of the funniest guys you'll ever meet, but in the ring he's always the straight man. He's very methodical, very practical as a personality."

"'The Man of 1,000 Holds' Dean Malenko. Yeah, he's a Wrestlers' Wrestler," said Kevin Sullivan. "He learned from Karl Gotch and his father (Boris Malenko). He's another one of these second-generation wrestlers. He's done very well for himself. He was one of the really integral members of ECW at the time when they were drawing."

"Dean was great. Very talented. He and his brother, Joe, were in the middle (of the card) in All Japan when I was there. If you put them out there with people who could work their style, you'll never see a better match. In tag or in singles, man, it was a fun match to watch," said Joel Deaton.

In an era of the bigger-than-life personalities like New World Order, "Stone Cold" Steve Austin, and the Rock, Dean Malenko was an old-school alternative. He wasn't a particularly great promo man by the standards of the time (though he could exude intensity like few others, earning him another of his nicknames, "The Iceman"). He wasn't an enormous physical specimen, billed at five-foot-eleven but actually standing about five-foot-eight. In terms of ring gear, he wouldn't have looked out of place in the 1950s . . . or the 1920s. But boy, he could wrestle, and he could hold his own against anyone.

Dean Simon was born on August 4, 1960, the son of wrestler Boris Malenko. He trained under his father, Gotch, and his older brother,

Joe, and made his pro debut in Florida in 1979. By the early 1980s, the Malenko brothers were landing tours of Japan, ultimately settling in as a tag team in All Japan Pro Wrestling. Joe (who had wrestled under the name Karl Gotch Jr. early in his career) and Dean won over the Japanese fans with their aggressive, realistic grappling style, but they never received a major push in All Japan.

"It was the style — the many holds and reversals they could put on you that nobody else could do. That was different. It caught the eye. And it's a great style. Not many guys can do that shit," Deaton said. "Joey and Dean were probably the best tag team in their style. But when you took them out of their style, they didn't hit you like they did otherwise. They're not as comfortable, not as versatile. But guys like that don't need to get out of that style because that's what got them over to begin with."

In 1992, the brothers made an appearance in World Championship Wrestling, participating in the NWA tag team title tournament, losing an opening round match to Ricky Steamboat and Nikita Koloff. It marked the Malenkos' debut on the national stage in the U.S.

In 1994, following WCW's withdrawal from the National Wrestling Alliance, the Philadelphia-based Eastern Championship Wrestling hosted a tournament to crown a new NWA "world" champion. Malenko was booked in the tournament, beating Osamu Nishimura in the opener before falling to the eventual tournament winner, Shane Douglas, in the semifinals. The tournament proved to be the birth of Extreme Championship Wrestling, as Douglas pulled a shoot (at the behest of ECW owners Paul Heyman and Tod Gordon), rejected the NWA title, called the NWA "a dead organization," and declared himself ECW champion. Heyman, who had been impressed with Malenko's work in the tournament, made Malenko a cornerstone of his rebranded ECW, dubbing him "The Shooter."

While ECW was known for its extreme violence and blood (and, eventually, barely clothed valets), Malenko provided the company with pure wrestling virtuosity. He defeated 2 Cold Scorpio to become ECW TV champion, then won the ECW tag title with Chris Benoit. In the summer of 1995, Malenko feuded with Eddie Guerrero over the TV title. Their innovative matches featured Guerrero's Lucha Libre–inspired takedowns and reversals and Malenko's catch-as-catch-can submission grappling, and elicited standing ovations from the ECW faithful and was voted Feud of the Year by readers of the *Wrestling Observer*. WCW, looking to strengthen its cruiserweight division to compete with the WWF, and looking to curb ECW's growth as a competitor, signed Malenko, Guerrero, and Benoit based on the strength of their matches in ECW.

Malenko debuted in WCW in September 1995, where he was billed as "The Man of 1,000 Holds." He went on to hold the WCW cruiserweight title four times, having memorable feuds with Jericho, Guerrero, and Rey Mysterio.

In his autobiography, *Yes: My Improbable Journey to the Main Event of WrestleMania*, Daniel Bryan wrote about how seeing Malenko wrestle Mysterio on TV changed his life.

"Dean Malenko was the one who appealed to me most," Bryan wrote. "In 1996, at WCW's Great American Bash (the first WCW pay-per-view I ever ordered), Dean wrestled a debuting Rey Mysterio Jr. for the cruiserweight championship in the match that convinced me there was no excuse for me not to follow my dream. Both men were shorter than me, but between Dean's aggressive mat wrestling and Rey being the most spectacular high flyer I had ever seen, not a single person watching would have noticed. They transcended the preconceived notion that most people had (myself included) that wrestlers had to be big."

In 1997, Malenko was named number one in *Pro Wrestling Illustrated*'s annual PWI 500 ranking of the top 500 wrestlers in the world. It was a stunning choice, as Malenko was a midcard competitor in WCW, and nowhere near as well-known as the main-eventers of WCW or the WWF. It turned out, Malenko just happened to be the right person at the right time.

"This is not intended to be disparaging, but Dean Malenko was selected number one in the PWI 500 in 1997 more or less by default," said *PWI* publisher Stu Saks. "Most of the top-level stars, including Bret Hart, the Undertaker, Hulk Hogan, Shawn Michaels, and Steve Austin, had major blemishes on their record, be it a lack of activity or coming up short against lesser opponents. There really wasn't a valid reason for not giving the top spot to Mitsuharu Misawa, who started a run of 466 days with the All Japan Triple Crown title with a win over Kenta Kobashi in January 1997. But that's looking at things from a 21st-century perspective. In 1997, only a small segment of our readership was familiar with Japanese wrestling. We could have — and probably should have — made Misawa number one, but we can't re-write history. With no obvious choice, we chose to make the selection based on wrestling ability alone. Over time, the selection of Malenko in 1997 has become a punchline for people who love to denigrate the 500. That's unfortunate because Malenko really did have a great year in WCW, winning the U.S. title from Eddy Guerrero and the cruiserweight title from Rey Mysterio Jr. and Ultimo Guerrero. And he is, quite arguably, the best pure wrestler around."

In 1998, Malenko had a run as a member of the Four Horsemen (with Benoit, Ric Flair, and former NFL star Steve McMichael, with Arn Anderson as their manager) and had a two-week reign as tag champion with Benoit, but WCW creative never fully got behind the new Horsemen, and the group split apart within eight months.

In January 2000, Malenko left WCW for the WWF along with Benoit, Guerrero, and Perry Saturn, as all four men had grown frustrated with the bad booking and poor morale of WCW. Dubbed the Radicalz, the four were an injection of workrate and adrenaline into the WWF, and their defection proved to be one of the final nails in the coffin of WCW. Though he didn't enjoy the success of Benoit or Guerrero (who both went on to world title reigns), Malenko did capture the WWF light heavyweight title twice. Ironically, Malenko — who had been dogged as having little charisma and no personality for most of his career — added more showmanship to his game, including a storyline where he acted like a pervert around Lita and Ivory, leading to a series of entertaining intergender matches.

Malenko quietly retired from the ring in 2001, settling into a role as a road agent. He remained with WWE until 2019, when he joined All Elite Wrestling as a senior producer.

TOSHIAKI KAWADA

The rivalry between Mitsuharu Misawa and Toshiaki Kawada — high school classmates who joined All Japan Pro Wrestling in 1981 and 1982, respectively — proved to be one of the most influential wrestling feuds ever to grace the ring. While both Misawa and Kawada were all-time greats and first-ballot Hall-of-Famers, they managed to push each other to new heights, each match adding a new chapter to a feud for the ages.

In 1994, Kawada was voted winner of the Lou Thesz/Ric Flair Wrestler of the Year award by the *Wrestling Observer Newsletter*. In 1995, the award went to Misawa, who won it again in 1997 and 1999. It's entirely possible that neither man might have achieved such success without having the other as his opponent.

Toshiaki Kawada was born on December 8, 1963, in Tochigi, Japan. He excelled in wrestling in high school, winning a national championship his senior year (ironically enough, beating Keiichi Yamada in the tournament finals; Yamada would go on to a HOF-worthy pro career himself as Jushin "Thunder" Liger).

After graduation, Misawa convinced Kawada to join him at the All Japan dojo, talking him out of signing with rival New Japan Pro-Wrestling. After their initial training, Misawa was sent to Mexico for seasoning while Kawada was sent to North America, making stops in San Antonio, Stu Hart's Stampede Wrestling in Calgary, and in Montreal for promoter Frank Valois. When both men returned to AJPW, Misawa dazzled the matchmakers and fans with his newly learned Lucha Libre skills. Misawa got the push, receiving the mask and the established character of Tiger Mask, a character that had been popularized by Satoru Sayama and was already one of the most popular gimmicks in Japan.

If Misawa had the sizzle, Kawada had the steak. Kawada was a barrel-chested fireplug of a man with a methodical and stiff offense. While Misawa (as Tiger Mask) went on to high-profile bouts, Kawada was slotted in the undercard, winning the All-Asian tag title with Samson Fuyuki three times.

In 1989, AJPW was thrown into an upheaval when Genichiro Tenryu defected and created his own promotion, Super World of Sports. "(Giant) Baba had a lot of guys there. When that billionaire guy that owned the eyeglass company or whatever it was (Hachiro Tanaka, an executive with eyeglass manufacturer Megane Super), he paid Tenryu all that money to start the SWS," said Joel Deaton who was working for All Japan at the time. "So Tenryu left and took about seven or eight guys from Baba's crew with him (including the Great Kabuki and Yoshiaki Yatsu), so a lot of those middle and upper-middle positions opened up. That's where Misawa, Kawada, (Kenta) Kobashi — that's when they started their rise."

Kawada and Misawa (now unmasked and competing under his own name; Kawada symbolically helped him remove this mask) became the young lions positioned against Jumbo Tsuruta and the established top stars of the company. Misawa, Kawada, Kobashi, and Akira Taue became known as "The Four Pillars of Heaven," laying the new corner-stone for All Japan. In August 1992, Misawa beat Stan Hansen to win the AJPW Triple Crown title. Fittingly, Kawada soon became the top contender for the title by virtue of a win over Taue in a number-one contender's bout. And, just as fittingly, Kawada came up just a little bit short, losing to the more charismatic Misawa in a match that earned *six stars* on Dave Meltzer's five-star scale. It wasn't until October 22, 1994, that Kawada finally captured the Triple Crown title, beating "Dr. Death" Steve Williams.

But while Misawa had a long-lasting title reign, Kawada only had one successful title defense (a 60-minute draw against Kenta Kobashi) before he dropped the title to Stan Hansen. When Misawa beat Hansen to regain the belt, Kawada once again found himself playing second fiddle to his high school classmate.

Misawa turned back Kawada's challenge yet again in July 1995, but Kawada kept battling his way back into title contention by scoring pin-falls over Misawa in tag team bouts. Kawada scored a non-title singles win over Misawa in the 1997 Champion Carnival tournament, but when the title was on the line, Misawa always managed to come out on top.

Finally, on May 1, 1998, Kawada finally defeated Misawa to win the Triple Crown title in front of an announced crowd of 58,300 fans at the Tokyo Dome . . . only to lose the belt to Kobashi in his first title defense one month later. To add insult to injury, Misawa would go on to beat Kobashi for the belt. On January 22, 1999, Kawada again defeated Misawa to win the title for the third time, but he suffered a broken hand in the match (when he cracked his elbow on Misawa's head during a spinning backfist seven minutes into the match) and was forced to vacate the title. Giant Baba, who was forced to miss this tour and watched the match from his hospital bed, called it the greatest match he had ever seen. Baba died one week later of renal cancer.

Kawada faced Misawa once more for the Triple Crown in July 1999, a match won by Misawa. It would prove to be the final chapter in their epic series, as Misawa — along with a contingent of AJPW wrestlers — would leave the company and establish Pro Wrestling NOAH following the death of AJPW founder Giant Baba. Kawada remained with All Japan and went on to hold the Triple Crown on two more occasions, but the company had become a shell of its former self following the mass defection.

Kawada worked as a freelancer for several Japanese promotions before returning to All Japan. He quietly retired in 2010.

The Misawa/Kawada rivalry can be compared to the boxing rivalry between Muhammad Ali and Joe Frazier. Kawada found himself in the Frazier role: a quiet, methodical, workhorse pitted against a handsome, flashy, showman. Their careers were intrinsically intertwined. Misawa got the glory, but Kawada's stiff kicks, believable and methodical ring style, and intensity ultimately influenced such wrestlers as Daniel Bryan and Samoa Joe.

OWEN HART

*"Owen learned very early that not everyone can be the
same. He could wrestle the same style as Bret and some
might even say a little better. He was actually a very
funny guy and he could translate that to the ring as well.
He understood that if he was going to stand out from Bret,
he had to do different things. He could have just gone
down the same road and people would have said, 'There's
Bret's little brother, the clone.'"*

—Former WWE referee Jimmy Korderas.

Owen Hart was born in Calgary, Alberta, on May 7, 1965, the last of Stu
and Helen Hart's 12 children. Though he made several early attempts
to forge his own path outside of wrestling, he was ultimately unable to
avoid the pull of the family business.

Stu Hart had developed the Calgary territory, establishing Klondike
Wrestling with partner Al Oeming in 1948. Klondike would become
Big Time Wrestling and — following Oeming's retirement — Wildcat
Wrestling and eventually Stampede Wrestling. Owen's older brothers,
Smith, Bruce, Keith, Wayne, Dean, and Bret, all started their careers in
Stampede, training in the legendary Hart family "Dungeon," where Stu
gleefully stretched students and aspiring wrestlers who thought they had
what it took to make it in wrestling.

Owen wrestled on the amateur mats in high school and made his pro
debut while he was attending university in 1983. Thanks to his family
connections and his athletic promise, Owen landed early bookings in

England for promoter Max Crabtree and was exposed to the British catch-as-catch can style during his formative years as a pro.

Owen made Stampede his home base, winning the Stampede international tag team title with Ben Bassarab in 1986. He was voted Rookie of the Year by readers of *Pro Wrestling Illustrated* in 1987, and fans wondered when Bret Hart's little brother would make his inevitable WWF debut. But before making his way to Stamford, Owen headed off to the Land of the Rising Sun for tours of New Japan Pro-Wrestling. While in New Japan, Owen faced some of the country's top junior heavyweights and high-flyers, including Jushin Liger and Hiroshi Hase, whom he defeated to win the IWGP junior heavyweight title in 1988.

While his father and brothers had practiced a ground-based mat wrestling style, Owen added flips, forward somersaults off the top rope, daredevil dives to the floor, and snap dropkicks to his repertoire. He developed a style thoroughly his own and was voted Best Flying Wrestler by readers of the *Wrestling Observer Newsletter* in 1987 and 1988.

Owen signed with the WWE in the summer of 1988, but rather than be paired up with his brother, Bret, and brother-in-law Jim Neidhart in the tag team the Hart Foundation, Vince McMahon opted to put Owen under a mask and give him the persona of the Blue Blazer, a high-flying superhero in the vein of Liger and Mil Máscaras. While the Blazer was an exciting character who was popular with the fans, he was firmly slotted in the midcard. At five-foot-ten and a billed weight of 228 pounds, Owen was considered too small to be a headliner. Following a *WrestleMania* V loss to "Mr. Perfect" Curt Hennig — a match that could have been an absolute show-stealer but was booked as a showcase match for Hennig more than a competitive bout — Owen left the WWF. He returned to Stampede and then, when Stampede closed its doors in 1989, he made tours of Mexico (where he lost the Blazer mask to El Canek in the mask-versus-mask match), New Japan, and Germany's Catch Wrestling Association. He had a handful of matches in WCW in 1991, then re-signed with the WWF, where he was paired with Neidhart as the New Foundation and then Koko B. Ware as High Energy.

"Owen was already polished because of his background and his family, wrestling down in the basement of the Hart house with Stu," said Koko Ware. "We were put together right after he and Jim Neidhart split up.

Bobby Heenan was the one who put us together. He said, 'We're not doing anything with Koko. Let's pair him up with Owen.' We became High Energy. We got Jimmy Hart to come up with a theme song, got the matching gear. Our styles worked together. We were the WWF's very first ebony-and-ivory tag team. We really got over. The fans wanted to see us win the world tag team title, but just like that, they split us up. Owen went his way in a program with Bret, and I went my way. The WWF missed the boat on that one. High Energy could have had a long run."

But the end of High Energy marked the start of Owen's singles career. In 1993, he and his brothers Bruce and Keith were drawn into Bret's feud with Jerry Lawler, who had made disparaging comments about Stu, Helen, and the entire Hart family. During a 1993 Survivor Series bout between the Hart brothers and Shawn Michaels (subbing for Lawler, who was taken off WWF TV following allegations of sexual misconduct that were later dropped) and Lawler's masked "knights" (Greg Valentine, Barry Horowitz, and Jeff Gaylord), Bret and Owen had an "accidental collision," causing Owen to be pinned. The seeds of the Hart family feud were sown. Owen's heel turn officially came two months later, when he attacked Bret after a tag loss to the Quebecers.

In a masterful bit of storytelling, Owen scored an upset win over his brother in the opening match of *WrestleMania* X at Madison Square Garden, but Bret went on to defeat Yokozuna for the WWF world title later in the night. Owen's moment of glory was eclipsed by his brother's title win, causing him to become more bitter and hungry for revenge. It also positioned Own as the top contender to the world title. The feud between the brothers Hart was voted Feud of the Year for 1994 by *PWI* readers.

Following the feud with Bret, Owen had WWF tag title runs with Yokozuna and Davey Boy Smith. In 1997, he was part of the Hart Foundation reunion with Bret, Smith, Neidhart, and fellow Stampede alumnus Brian Pillman. He beat Rocky Maivia to win the Intercontinental title in 1997. Though Owen had a sterling reputation as a worker, accidents can happen in wrestling, and an accident happened at SummerSlam 1997 when Owen slipped during a piledriver, dropping Steve Austin on his head and fracturing his neck. It was a rare mistake for Owen, who had always prided himself on taking care of his opponents.

When Bret left the WWF and signed with WCW, Owen opted to remain with the WWF, where he was slotted into a natural feud against Bret's arch-enemy, Shawn Michaels. As "The Black Hart," Owen was white-hot for a short period, but with Michaels and Triple H in management's ear, Owen's main-event push proved to be brief. After a heel turn, he joined the Nation of Domination faction, then formed a tag team with Jeff Jarrett.

In late 1998, Owen did an angle where he "left" the WWF, only for the Blue Blazer to return. This time around, the Blazer was presented as a pure comedy act, making pratfalls and preaching to kids to "take your vitamins, say your prayers, and drink your milk," a hokey take-off of Hulk Hogan's routine from the 1980s. The gimmick was Owen at his playful, comical best.

On May 23, 1999, Owen died in a tragedy that still resonates throughout the wrestling world, when he accidentally triggered a quick-release harness on a mechanism lowering him from the roof of the Kemper Arena in Kansas City, Missouri. Owen fell an estimated 78 feet, landing chest-first on the ring ropes and barely missing referee Korderas, who said he heard Hart calling out to him to move, which likely saved his life. He was pronounced dead from blunt force trauma at Truman Medical Center. Owen had been uneasy about performing the stunt entrance, which was to see him get "stuck" about five feet above the ring in a comedy bit. He was 34 years old.

LANCE STORM

Throughout most of his wrestling career, Lance Storm was the straight man surrounded by assorted extreme Attitude Era weirdness. Whether he was covering up a scantily clad Dawn Marie in ECW, leading a motley crew Team Canada in WCW, or doing a gimmick as a "charismatically challenged" midcarder in WWE, Storm was a versatile and consistent hand from bell to bell regardless of storyline.

Born Lance Evers in Sarnia, Ontario, in 1969, he grew up in North Bay and left his studies at Wilfrid Laurier University to enroll in the Hart Brothers Wrestling Academy in Calgary. There, he trained under Ed Langley and met another young trainee by the name of Chris Irvine, better known today as Chris Jericho.

"He's a Wrestlers' Wrestler, but Lance is very acrobatic as well, so he does more than just work on the mat, which to me is what I think of as a Wrestlers' Wrestler," Jericho said. "It's weird. Lance has a little more of a personality than you'd ever see on TV. He has a very quirky sense of humor, a little anal-retentive. Even that 'If I can be serious for a minute' (promo catchphrase). Obviously, he was in on the joke, but the way he plays it, he's not. So if a Wrestlers' Wrestler's personality makes up 10 percent of his performance, I'd say Lance's personality made up 20 percent."

That personality came across as a dry, deadpan sense of humor. As Jericho said, the best example of Storm's wit was his trademark shtick to start each of his promos. A stone-faced Storm would take the mic and begin his spiel with "If I could be serious for a minute . . ." The character of Lance Storm was *always* serious. By reminding the audience that he was there to — once again — be a stick-in-the-mud instead of partaking in the frequently silly, often risqué antics others enjoyed, he garnered heat, a challenge for any technician of Storm's caliber.

After cutting his teeth in Calgary and completing a few international tours of Japan and Europe (occasionally teaming with Jericho as Sudden Impact), Storm wound up in Jim Cornette's Smoky Mountain Wrestling in 1994. Cornette decided to push Storm and Jericho right out of the gate as the Thrillseekers, the heir apparent to his top tandem, the Rock 'n' Roll Express. That plan went out the window when Jericho broke his arm on August 5, 1994, as he was practicing a 450 splash prior to the start of SMW's big Night of Legends event. Jericho still wrestled that night as the Thrillseekers defeated the Heavenly Bodies (Jimmy Del Ray and Tom Prichard), but then took time off to recover, which slammed the brakes on the Seekers' push.

When SMW folded, Storm went on to Japan's WAR, where he shared the ring with the likes of Jushin Liger and Último Dragón. In 1997, Storm was invited to ECW thanks to a referral from Jericho. After a brief babyface run, Storm hit his stride as a heel managed by the sultry Dawn Marie. He held the ECW tag team title three times, once with Shane Douglas and twice with his Justin Credible, a former student of his back in Calgary when he assisted at the Hart academy.

"I met Lance in '96 in the hotel room," said Rob Van Dam. "Back then, Paul (Heyman) would put us up with two in a room. That's how I would meet some of the guys. 'Oh, hey. I'm in the bed next to you for tonight. What's your name?' And I thought right off the bat, what the hell is this guy doing in ECW? Because we were extreme and everybody's doing drugs in the back and in the ring and on the way to the ring. And we're violent and we're bloody and we're hardcore. And he wasn't like that at all. I didn't understand why he was there. And maybe I didn't even expect him to last. But I was pretty young, also, so my perspective was not as educated as it is now, obviously. And I learned that the crowd really took to him because his technical skills were so above par that that made him extreme compared to the status quo."

In May 2000, Storm jumped to WCW and received the biggest push of his career, winning the U.S., cruiserweight, and hardcore championships simultaneously that summer. Storm became the leader of the Team Canada faction (which included, at various times, Bret Hart, Carl

Ouellet, Jacques Rougeau, and noted "Canadians" Jim Duggan, Mike Awesome, Major Gunns, and Elix Skipper) and solidified himself as one of the company's upper-midcard heels.

Storm remained with WCW until the bitter end. WCW closed its doors in April 2000, and Storm's contract was picked up by the WWF. On May 28, 2001, Storm made history by becoming the first WCW competitor to "invade" WWF programming, doing a run-in to attack Perry Saturn on a *Monday Night Raw* event held in Calgary.

On July 23, 2001, Storm defeated Albert to win the WWF Intercontinental title in Buffalo, New York. Storm's IC title reign lasted less than one month, as he dropped the belt to Edge at SummerSlam 2001. A major singles push never materialized. He held the WWF tag team title as a member of the Un-Americans (with Christian, Test, and William Regal), a gimmick that got easy heat in the aftermath of the terrorist attacks of 9/11. He and Christian won the tag belts from Edge and Hulk Hogan in July 2002. But the Un-Americans faction didn't have legs. By 2003, Storm was struggling on the lower midcard, and his standing wasn't helped by a June 2003 segment where Steve Austin encouraged the fans to chant "boring" at Storm.

Subsequent attempts to make Storm less "boring" all fizzled out. In April 2004, Storm announced his retirement. In 2019, he rejoined WWE as a backstage producer, but he was furloughed a few months later when WWE released staff during the COVID-19 pandemic.

MANAMI TOYOTA

In his 2002 book *Top 100 Pro Wrestlers of All Time*, John F. Molinaro refers to Manami Toyota as "the Ric Flair of women's wrestling, arguably the greatest female pro wrestler of all time."

"Manami Toyota is maybe the most influential Joshi star in women's wrestling," Sara Del Rey said in a 2011 interview with *Diva Dirt*. "She was one of the first women I saw doing things equally spectacular as the guys. . . . She presented herself with style, grace and a feminine beauty, but you also knew she could downright kick your butt. She is the perfect combination of everything people love about the sport and she appeals to everyone. There are a million reasons why she is considered the best and none can be argued because she is."

Toyota took the art of women's wrestling to new heights in the 1990s and ultimately played a pivotal role in changing expectations not only for women in wrestling but for men too. She was both a master technician and a high-flyer, dazzling fans with her moonsaults, suicide dives, and diving headbutts off the top rope. Toyota was a part of 24 matches that received a five-star rating from *Wrestling Observer* publisher Dave Meltzer over the course of her career, according to Meltzer himself (the number varies with different online sources).

"Toyota, to this day, is the most impressive woman wrestler I would say in history," Meltzer said. "There were women with more charisma, but the key to her is how hard she would work and the variety of things she could do, from unique suplexes with great bridges, to her escapes from pins, to her high flying, particularly repeated dropkicks, and some of the most incredible stamina ever, going 60 minutes at times without ever slowing down. Her body of work is as impressive as any wrestler in history, as is her durability, because in her heyday she was working 250 or more matches a year. Having seen her at spot shows, she never took it easy or rested on her laurels. She was a natural, world class at 18 or 19, and remained great for decades."

Born March 2, 1971, she began wrestling at the age of 16, making her debut in August 1987. She quickly began to stand out from her peers for her pacing, the depth of her moveset, and her incredible sense of timing, making last-minute kick-outs from pin attempts that kept fans on the edges of their seats. All Japan Women named her its Rookie of the Year in 1988.

Toyota had a lengthy feud with Toshiyo Yamada, which culminated in a hair-versus-hair match in August 1992. Toyota won the match, but the storyline was that she had earned so much respect for her opponent that she did not want Yamada to have to lose her hair. Toyota had to be restrained, while Yamada did the honorable thing and adhered to the stipulations of the match, having her hair sheared off. That experience brought the two enemies together, and Toyota and Yamada began teaming, beating Aja Kong and Bison Kimura for the WWWA tag title in March 1992.

On April 11, 1993, Toyota and Yamada lost the tag belts to Dynamite Kansai and Mayumi Ozaki in a best-of-three falls match that would be voted Match of the Year by readers of the *Wrestling Observer Newsletter*, the first time a women's match would earn that distinction in the history of the *Observer* awards since they were instituted in 1980. Two years later, she won the same award for a 60-minute draw against Kyoko Inoue in 1995. Toyota was also named Most Outstanding Wrestler of the Year for 1995, an award given based on workrate. It was the first — and only — time that award was given to a woman, as Toyota beat out the likes of Eddie Guerrero, Rey Mysterio, and Chris Benoit.

On March 26, 1995, Toyota arrived at the pinnacle of AJW, beating Aja Kong to win the WWWA championship in Yokohama. She lost the belt back to Kong three months later. On December 4, 1995, she won the title for a second time, beating Kansai in Tokyo. Her second WWWA title reign lasted a year, until it was ended by Inoue in a rematch of their classic 60-minute draw, which unified Inoue's All Pacific and IWA titles with the WWWA title.

Fans were treated to a dream match between two of the best female wrestlers of all time on November 28, 1998, when Toyota faced former Crush Gal Chigusa Nagayo, a match Nagayo won.

Toyota moved on to the GAEA promotion in 2002, rekindling classic rivalries with Yamada and Kansai and winning the GAEA title in October 2002. In 2007, she took a sabbatical from the ring after a tribute show held in her honor, where she wrestled in every match on the card.

In 2010, Toyota made her first appearance in the United States with a tour of the CHIKARA promotion. She defeated Daizee Haze in a singles bout in Baltimore, Maryland, then teamed with CHIKARA founder Mike Quackenbush to beat Claudio Castagnoli and Sara Del Rey, making Del Rey submit. She returned to CHIKARA in 2011 to compete in the annual King of Trios Tournament, teaming with Mike Quackenbush and Jigsaw. She made subsequent returns to the company in December 2011 and September 2012.

"There are a lot of things about Manami that I find inspirational," Quackenbush said. "Her work ethic, her pride in the craft maybe most of all. It's one thing to perceive that by studying her and watching her arc. You can't miss that. But then to team with her and feel the energy she brings to the work, that's of a different magnitude altogether. It was like, we couldn't conjure a challenge big enough for her. How does that not inspire you to work harder? If we weren't on opposite sides of the globe, I'd want to be around that energy every day, as much as I possibly could. She makes me want to be a better wrestler."

In 2017, Toyota announced her retirement after 30 years in the ring. A retirement event was held on November 3 where Toyota wrestled a series of one-minute time-limit exhibition mini-matches, ending with 12 wins, 29 draws, and 10 losses against a variety of opponents. It was a rare opportunity for different wrestlers to share the ring one on one (or two on one, as she wrestled two handicap matches during the series, a sign of her willingness to put several women over on the way out. Some of her opponents included luminaries such as Bull Nakano and Ayako Hamada. Her final bout was a symbolic passing of the torch where she lost to Tsukasa Fujimoto in a five-minute match.

JERRY LYNN

Despite managing to capture championship gold almost everywhere he went, Jerry Lynn is still widely regarded as one of the most underrated — and polite — grapplers of his era.

"He's the nicest man in professional wrestling. Too nice, actually, for professional wrestling," said Brodie Lee, formerly known as Luke Harper. "We wrestled in ROH for the championship he had and, in the middle of the match, he picked me up and gave me a TKO. Fast-forward to five years later at WWE in Minnesota and he finds me ringside and apologizes for picking me up, and says that it didn't make sense due to the size differential." (Harper stands 6'5" and weighed about 260 pounds at the time, while Lynn was closer to 5'10" and a billed 220 pounds).

Born in Minneapolis in 1963, he made his pro debut in 1988. By 1990, he was challenging for the AWA World title. The following year, his matches with fellow Minneapolis native The Lightning King (Sean "X-Pac" Waltman) were thrilling international audiences as the Texas-based Global Wrestling Federation aired on ESPN. Following stints in Mexico and Japan, Lynn wound up in World Championship Wrestling, where he became a vital part of the company's fledgling cruiserweight division.

In an effort to capitalize on the popularity of Japanese sensation Jushin Liger, whose 1991–92 series with Brian Pillman put the light heavyweight division on the map, Lynn was put under a mask and re-named "Mr. J.L.," an apparent ploy to fool fans into thinking Liger was moonlighting in WCW.

Despite a series of critically acclaimed matches against Chris Benoit, Dean Malenko, Eddie Guerrero, and others, Lynn remained mired in lower midcard bouts and never had a run as cruiserweight champion. He was released from WCW in July 1997, fired while at home recuperating from an injury.

Lynn moved to Extreme Championship Wrestling and was slotted into a feud with Justin Credible for several months. However, his hard work and sterling reputation finally resulted in a push in 1999 when he worked a series of show-stealing matches against Rob Van Dam for the ECW TV title. Since RVD's nickname was "The Whole F'n Show," Lynn dubbed himself "The New F'n Show."

"Jerry did everything well. I loved working with him," Rob Van Dam said. "As soon as we started working together we had this amazing chemistry but we really weren't friends. Like, I barely knew him before that. So it was all organic. Everything came out as a combination of what we both offered. He had his old-school fundamentals, which was great because if I had an idea, he would check me on it without even thinking on it. It was important to him that, looking ahead into the match, things were going to happen a certain way to make the most sense according to him and his values. And that's great. I respected that. And he was very physically gifted. Our matches were very physical and competitive. But we were also trying to out-think each other. And he could definitely hang with me in both ways."

On October 1, 2000, Lynn defeated Justin Credible to win the ECW World championship.

After ECW closed its doors in 2001, Lynn jumped to the WWF where he defeated Crash Holly for the light heavyweight title in his TV debut. He held that title for one month and was released by the WWF in February 2002.

He found a new home in Total Nonstop Action, the NWA-affiliated new promotion established by Jerry and Jeff Jarrett, and became the cornerstone of the company's innovative X Division, a showcase division that showcased high spots and prized work rate. It was a tailor-made fit and Lynn went on to hold the X Division title twice. He also won the NWA-TNA tag team with a young A.J. Styles.

Lynn won the prestigious ECWA Super 8 tournament in 2007 and moved on to Ring of Honor in 2008. He defeated Nigel McGuinness to win the ROH heavyweight title at Supercard of Honor IV on April 3, 2009, holding that title for two months and earning the Comeback of the Year award from the readers of *Pro Wrestling Illustrated*.

"He did everything well and moved in his own way, and had a certain snap on his moves while being deceptively athletic," Brodie Lee said. "He was an absolute pleasure to know and to work with."

Lynn spent the next few years on independents, with a brief return to TNA in 2013 that included a rematch against his old rival Van Dam at One Night Only: X-Travaganza. He wrestled his retirement match on March 23, 2013, at the Minneapolis Convention Center, winning a four-way bout over Waltman, JB Trask, and Horace the Psychopath. Following his retirement from in-ring competition, he worked as a backstage agent and producer with ROH. He joined All Elite Wrestling as a producer and coach in 2019.

DOING THE JOB: THE THANKLESS — AND VITAL — ROLE OF ENHANCEMENT TALENT

In the 1950s, the advent of television helped push the popularity of wrestling to new heights. The boob tube brought the ring wars right into living rooms across America, which was a wonderful new way to get more eyes on the product. Wrestlers were becoming regional celebrities, and Gorgeous George became a national sensation.

But television also presented a new challenge. The territories were still relying on event attendance to make money. But if fans could watch the matches for free from the comfort of home, why would any but the most diehard of fans fork over money to see the matches in person?

It quickly became apparent that marquee matches couldn't be given away on free TV without killing the house. However, if presented wisely, the charismatic top stars could still be featured on television to attract eyeballs and compel TV viewers to buy a ticket to see their favorite "TV rasslers" in person. The concept of "enhancement talent" and "squash matches" was born.

They go by many names. "Job guys" or "jobbers" (or, thanks to The Rock, "jabronis").

"Prelim bums." Bobby Heenan used to call them "ham-and-eggers." They were largely anonymous wrestlers whose job was to go on TV, take a beating, and make their opponent look like a superstar for the TV audience. Some were weekend warriors, guys who had a full-time job but liked to moonlight as a wrestler for a few extra dollars or for the thrill of it. Others were veterans who were past their prime, still clinging to their wrestling career long after the matchmakers had any plans to push them. But a good job guy could be an invaluable resource. They could take a beating and sell their asses off for their opponent and give them credibility to fans and TV viewers at home. Veteran job guys could call spots through the match, help walking greenhorns through the bout and protecting them, covering any blown spots or missteps.

Barry Hardy worked as enhancement talent for the WWF regularly through the late 1980s and 1990s, both as a singles competitor and in tag teams with partner Duane Gill (who would later receive a small push as Gillberg, a parody of Bill Goldberg). Hardy outlined the essential responsibilities needed to be "a good jobber."

"Create your own image. Get in the gym, tan, and make your body look like you belong in the ring, but don't outshine the star," Hardy said. "Come out immediately working the crowd. Let them know who's the heel and who's the baby without a doubt in their mind. Know your opponent's style and moves so you can set them up and make them look their best. Sell your ass off so they know you're giving 110 percent. Know where you are when you're in the ring to set up the next move for the star. When doing TV, know where the hard cam is and keep your eye on the handheld ones as well. And, most importantly, remember you're there to get your opponent over. If you have a great working attitude and do a great job, you both end up getting over and you win something you can't buy — your opponent's respect. Now you have become a star in the eyes of that superstar and in all the agents' eyes because you know your job in the ring and your place in that promotion.

"Gill and I called most of our matches for the stars back in the day. They had enough on their minds from doing interviews all day. There was a lot of friction back then. We were recording three weeks of TV per taping, and multiple different shows, so we made it easy for our opponents by calling the match. The guys started telling the agents they wanted Hardy and Gill as soon as they entered the building. That's how we were able to work three times a night with our different gimmicks (including wearing hoods as the Lords of Darkness and the Executioners). We had a lot of locker room respect and we became one of the boys," Hardy said.

As wrestling programming went national in the mid-1980s, jobbers became almost as recognizable as their more winning opponents. Some — like "Iron" Mike Sharpe, Johnnie Rodz, and Frankie Williams — developed something of a cult following. S.D. Jones actually had an LJC action figure in his likeness, though his highest-profile match was a 22-second squash against King Kong Bundy at the first *WrestleMania*.

As a 12-year-old boy, George South used to hang around the Park Center in Charlotte, North Carolina, before the matches and offer to help carry the wrestlers' bags as they arrived at the arena. In a 2010 interview with *Charlotte Magazine*, he recounted his first day of training.

"I got to this old building. It looked like something out of a scary movie," South said. "The windows were broken out of it. I opened the door and it fell off the hinges. They had an old ring set up like a Rocky movie and there was a big Samoan, an old guy, and a midget. They beat the crap out of me, tore my clothes, and left me over in the corner with my britches split. I was pulling myself up when I saw the midget coming . . . he kicked me as hard as he could right in the stomach. For some stupid reason the next day I came back. A week later I had a match."

Years later, as a reward for his service with Jim Crockett Promotions, South received a nationally televised match in 1988 against NWA world champion Ric Flair, a fan of South's work. Instead of being a one-sided squash, Flair approached South backstage and said, "Today you're Ricky Steamboat." Flair sold for South and the two had a back-and-forth match with near falls before Flair finally earned the win. "The biggest compliment I get is when people say, 'For a moment, I thought you were going to win,'" South said.

In 2002, Bob Evans faced Aaron Stevens (later known as Damien Sandow) in a dark-match tryout for Stevens. "I was running late from my regular job to get to TV and when I got to TV, (agent) Tony Garea didn't even know I was booked. Kevin Kelly booked me and forgot to tell Tony Garea. So they had sent all the extras to do some big bar scene where they were going to get beat up by the APA and Aaron was around and I was around, so Garea said 'Well, you might as well wrestle Aaron.' Aaron was super nervous. And I knew how talented the kid was. I felt like my time as an extra was kind of wrapping up so I didn't have a lot of pressure on me. I was 30 and my goals were changing in wrestling. I was opening my wrestling school and I didn't want to be a national star. I said, 'This is more about you than me so let's just go out and have a good match.' I remember the first spot we did he whiffed real bad with a dropkick and I took a bump anyway. They booed us but we managed to get it back and have a good match, and five or six minutes later Aaron thanked me and said 'I really appreciate you getting me through that.'"

Stevens received a WWE developmental deal and went on to debut in WWE in 2006.

"My trainer, Jeff Costa, trained me to be a carpenter," Evans said. "I was carrying people a year and a half into wrestling . . . And it can be an ego blow, too, if you're carrying those guys every night and you know you're a better wrestler, but you have to get them over. It's like getting shot in a movie. You can't be an actor and be mad that you're the one who gets shot in a movie."

Every once in a while, the job guy gets a taste of glory. In March 1987, the hapless duo of Randy and Bill Mulkey — two pasty brothers with peroxide-blond hair and nary a muscle to be seen on either of them — scored a surprise win over the debuting masked team the Gladiators (South and Gary Royal under hoods) giving them their first nationally televised win, on SuperStation TBS. "Randy and Bill you beat 'em! You beat 'em! This is unbelievable. You beat the Gladiators!" announcer David Crockett exploded, setting off a short-lived fever of "Mulkey-Mania."

In May 1993, Sean Waltman (wrestling simply as "The Kid") scored a surprise pin on Razor Ramon on *Monday Night Raw*. He took on the name "The 1-2-3 Kid" following the win and went on to a major push, becoming a featured member of the NWO and DX, two of wrestling's most successful factions of the 1990s.

In July 1995, perennial enhancement talent Barry Horowitz surprised Bodydonna Skip (Chris Candido) with a three-quarter nelson cradle and scored an upset win. The win resulted in a small push for Horowitz and programs with Candido and Hakushi.

In October 2016, James Ellsworth — after declaring "any man with two hands has a fighting chance" prior to a lopsided loss to Braun Strowman that summer — scored an upset win over WWE world champion A.J. Styles on SmackDown, due to some decidedly impartial officiating by guest referee Dean Ambrose. Ellsworth remained a featured WWE performer through 2018.

There are, of course, many other examples of "enhancement talent" getting their hands raised as a tried-and-true way to surprise the fans or kick off a new storyline, but these are some of the most well-known examples. Allowing the "jobbers" to win every once in a while keeps fans interested in the match, even if they "know" who's going to win before the opening bell sounds.

"There's a place in wrestling today for these guys, without a doubt," former WWE writer and host of the *Something to Wrestle* podcast Bruce Prichard told RollingStone.com in a 2016 interview. "It's a better way to introduce new stars. If you're trying to get someone over with the crowd, you need to make them look great. Get them a dominant win. If you put a new guy in the ring with another guy the company is still high on, and they've got to go 50/50 in a match, no matter who wins they both lose."

"I refer to them as the guys who made the business," said Kevin Sullivan. "If you want to put a hall of fame in, it should be for the guys who got the guys over. The Jack Harts, the Mike Sharpes, the Barry Ortons of the world. The guys who put guys over the correct way should be in the hall of fame."

PART 6:
ROH and Rise of the Indies

If the 1990s represented the rise of the "Extreme," then the 2000s represented the influence of Independents.

Following the fall of both WCW and ECW in 2001, the small, independent promotions that ran shows in high school gyms, fire halls, and VFW posts saw an upsurge in available talent. Not only were former WCW and ECW wrestlers available for bookings, but a new generation who had grown up watching the Monday Night Wars between the WWF and WCW had trained, become wrestlers, and were eager to find an outlet to show their stuff.

The East Coast Wrestling Association, based in Delaware and headed by promoter Jim Kettner, established its Super 8 tournament in 1997, designed to showcase the best unsigned talent in wrestling. In 2000, All Pro Wrestling, based in California and headed by promoter Roland Alexander, held its first King of the Indies tournament. Inspired by these tournaments and the high-level of talent available, Rob Feinstein — owner of the pro wrestling video distribution company RF Video — established his own promotion named Ring of Honor.

In ROH, matches were conducted under a handshake "code of honor." Instead of bloody out-of-control brawls, the company mostly featured fast-paced chain wrestling and high-flying contests. Like ECW nearly a decade earlier, ROH established itself as an alternative for fans who were looking for something other than WWE, since WCW and ECW were no longer around.

ROH has managed to survive two decades and counting and is currently owned by the media powerhouse Sinclair Broadcast Group. Though ROH did sell out Madison Square garden on a joint show with

New Japan Pro-Wrestling in 2019, through most of its history, ROH has attracted a niche audience. Live events usually attracted between 300 and 1,000 fans, with DVD sales (and later Sinclair's funding) keeping the company afloat.

But in 2020, the influence of ROH and similar independent promotions is impossible to overlook. Daniel Bryan, Seth Rollins, CM Punk, Kevin Owens, Sami Zayn, and many others cut their teeth before moving on to WWE. All Elite Wrestling, established in 2019 and owned by Tony Khan, co-owner of the Jacksonville Jaguars, was virtually an outgrowth of ROH, as AEW's founding fathers Matt and Nick Jackson, Kenny Omega, and Cody Rhodes were all top players in ROH before forming AEW.

These are the wrestlers who forged their skill on the independents and helped drive what wrestling has become in the 2020s.

NIGEL MCGUINNESS

The wrestling gods are fickle. They can take a career with unlimited potential and snuff it out in the blink of an eye. Just ask Nigel McGuinness.

That isn't to say McGuinness didn't have a remarkable career in wrestling. For a period of time in the 2000s, he was one of the best in the world. He was ranked number six in the 2009 *Pro Wrestling Illustrated* 500, sandwiched between first-ballot Hall-of-Famers Randy Orton and Hiroshi Tanahashi. He held the Ring of Honor championship for an incredible 545 days and had epic feuds with Bryan Danielson and Chris Hero. And after he retired from the ring, he landed a high-profile announcer job with WWE as the color commentator for NXT. By any objective measure, McGuinness has had a wildly successful career in wrestling.

But for a wrestler with such technical ability, presence, and charisma, there will always be that niggling question . . . that *What if?*

What if his career hadn't ended prematurely? Could he have achieved the same level of success in WWE as his fellow ROH alumni Bryan Danielson (Daniel Bryan), Tyler Black (Seth Rollins), and Kevin Steen (Kevin Owens)? Could he have won the WWE world title? Headlined WrestleMania*? Just how far could he have gone?*

Steven Haworth was born in London, England, on January 23, 1976. He became a wrestling fan at the age of 12, idolizing the British Bulldogs and the Ultimate Warrior (he attended SummerSlam 1992 in Wembley Stadium wearing Ultimate Warrior face paint). After graduating college with a degree in chemistry, he wrote to wrestling schools listed in the back pages of a wrestling magazines and ultimately enrolled in Les Thatcher's Heartland Wrestling Association training school in Cincinnati, Ohio, to chase his dream of becoming a wrestler. He made his pro debut in September 1999 in a match that was featured in an ABC 20/20 feature on independent wrestling. But, with bills piling up from living abroad, he returned home to England and began working, squirrelling away money to return to the U.S. and continue his wrestling training.

"William Regal was the one that saw me and told me, in a very polite way, that I should probably go back to England and learn the British style, which is probably the best advice I'd ever had," McGuinness said. "When I went back there and met Robbie Brookside, I passed on the message that was what I was doing there, and he lent me this huge carry-on bag full of VHS cassettes of all the old World of Sport stuff. This was pre-YouTube so you couldn't just go online and see this stuff. So, while I was staying over there, I'd watch all of this old stuff — Johnny Saint, Steve Grey, Paul Mitchell, Mel Sanders, Fit Finlay, Marty Jones. That was really my education in the British style."

He returned to the HWA and was billed as the new European champion, a title he held twice. He also won the HWA heavyweight title twice. He debuted in ROH in August 2003 and captured that company's Pure Wrestling title with a win over Samoa Joe in August 2005. With its emphasis on workrate and influence from international styles, ROH was the perfect environment for McGuinness to thrive.

"ROH was sort of a family environment. When I left Ring of Honor, no one was making six figures, no one was doing it for a living — well, I mean, yes you were doing it for a living, but you weren't doing it for a *good* living — so there wasn't a whole lot of backstabbing or politics involved. If you were the top guy, yes, you made more than the midcard guys, but not so much that it was going to change your life drastically," McGuinness said. "I think that's why there was that family mentality. So many of us that were there had that mentality of just putting the art form, if you want, above the fame of it or the fortune of it, because there wasn't a whole lot of those necessarily, outside of the hardcore fan base. It was always a great environment when I was there in that regard. It was highly inspired by that All Japan, Pro Wrestling NOAH, late-1990s style. I remember watching those matches with Misawa and Kobashi and those guys. . . . A lot of inspiration also came from the ECW notion of putting out things that you couldn't see elsewhere or wouldn't see elsewhere."

McGuinness faced ROH champion Danielson several times, ultimately losing the Pure championship to Danielson in a title-versus-title match in August 2006. On October 6, 2007, he defeated Japanese super-heavyweight Takeshi Morishima to win the ROH title. McGuinness held that title for 18 months, but he paid a heavy price to be champion. He suffered a slew of injuries during his reign, including concussions, a compacted spine, a broken nose, and a torn biceps muscle. In September 2009, it was announced that McGuinness had signed a deal with WWE, the same day as his arch-rival and close friend, Bryan Danielson. It looked like the start of a new chapter in a rivalry that had lit the indies on fire, starting on the big stage of WWE. Instead, in October 2009, McGuinness debuted in TNA — not WWE — under the name Desmond Wolfe. WWE rescinded its offer after a pre-screening physical, with WWE doctors advising that McGuinness needed surgery to repair his biceps injury. It was a surgery he could not afford at the time, so his WWE dreams were put on hold.

McGuinness debuted in TNA under the name Desmond Wolfe and was immediately slotted into a program with Kurt Angle. But, as the months wore on, he slipped further and further away from the title picture. He formed a tag team with Magnus (Nick Aldis) before vanishing from TNA television completely. He resurfaced briefly in a commissioner role, but was released by TNA in June 2011. He went on a two-month retirement tour and wrestled his final match in December 2011. The abrupt end of his career was the subject of rumors and speculation — he had simply been too good of a talent to just walk away from the ring the way he did — until he finally revealed the reason for his abrupt retirement; he had been diagnosed with hepatitis B.

McGuinness addressed his frustration, disappointment, and depression in a self-produced documentary entitled *The Last of McGuinness* (available on YouTube). He went on to a color commentator and matchmaker role in ROH, then signed with WWE as an announcer in December 2016. WWE released a documentary on his career, entitled *Chasing the Magic: The Nigel McGuinness Story* on the WWE Network. In that documentary, Seth Rollins said he considered McGuinness a mentor and said it was a shame that the entire wrestling world didn't get an opportunity to see him in action, calling McGuinness, "one of the greatest performers that no one may ever know."

"Nigel McGuinness, now there's a guy that should have gone all the way," said Luke Williams. "He worked for years and years in England and was so good. It's terrible about the injuries. What a piece of talent he was!"

MERCEDES MARTINEZ

"Mercedes has the uncanny ability to make any wrestler look *good*," said WWE NXT star Shayna Baszler, who teamed with Mercedes in SHIMMER, the premier women's wrestling promotion in the U.S., prior to joining WWE. "I have seen her, on more than one occasion, take the most green wrestler — including me — sometimes being their first match in their career, and make them look like a viable and seasoned wrestler. I have said more than once, 'If Mercedes can't make you look good, you probably shouldn't wrestle.'"

Mercedes Martinez's career has been marked by her dedication to her craft and her refusal to compromise her ideals and values. "Mercedes Martinez, the wrestler, is not far from who I am in real life," said Martinez. "I speak my mind. I don't sugarcoat things. My style has never changed in 16 years. Strong style, technical wrestling. That's who I am and that's what I want people to see from me."

Born Jazmín Benítez on November 17, 1980, in Waterbury, Connecticut, she was a wrestling fan since childhood and was captivated by the larger-than-life personalities of Hulk Hogan, Randy Savage, and the Big Bossman. "I was the middle child out of five kids," she said. "I watched wrestling with my uncle and my brothers. Wrestling was big with them. Growing up, I followed it. I roughhoused with my brothers and wrestled in the backyard with them and the neighbors. Of course, I never for a moment thought that I was going to be a professional wrestler."

That changed when she discovered *GLOW: Gorgeous Ladies of Wrestling*, on television in the late 1980s. She found it empowering to see females given characters and promoted on television like their male counterparts.

While recovering from an injury that put her collegiate basketball career on hold, she discovered Jason Knight's pro wrestling school and began training, in part to rehab her injury and get back to basketball. "Wrestling just fell into my lap. I guess I was pretty good at it."

So good, in fact, that she wrestled her first match barely one month after beginning her training in 2000. Knight gave her the ring name Mercedes Martinez. "Here's your name, now go out there and work, that's all there was to it," she said.

She competed throughout New England, including Sheldon Goldberg's New England Championship Wrestling and Ian Rotten's IWA Mid-South. SHIMMER promoter Dave Prazak was impressed with what he saw and brought Martinez in to headline SHIMMER's first event, facing Sara Del Rey in 2005. Martinez and Del Rey wrestled a 20-minute draw. Ring of Honor brought her in as part of the Vulture Squad stable, starting a rivalry with Lacey.

"She and I broke in together and it was such a breath of fresh air to work with a woman who was as tough as nails and an absolute ring general from day one," said Allison Danger. "She commands, not demands, respect when she walks into a locker room. The poise with which she carries herself is a fantastic example for what young wrestlers — male or female — should strive for."

In 2006, Martinez was brought in for a look by WWE, wrestling Victoria in her tryout match. The agents watched her match and told her they wanted her to change the way she worked. "My style was too aggressive for them — too hardcore, too strong style. I had to tone it down and we could go from there. I didn't want to water down myself and be something they wanted me to be when I knew what I was capable of at that time."

So Martinez said thanks but no thanks and went back to the independents. "I don't regret turning them down because what they wanted wasn't right for me," she said. "If what's going on now (a greater emphasis on athleticism and workrate) had happened 10 years ago, I believe I would have been there."

She started in the New Jersey–based Women Superstars Uncensored in 2007 and took over the booking responsibilities. In 2009, she wrestled

Angel Orsini in a 71-minute bout, a match that originally had been conceived as a 30-minute Iron Woman match. "Iron Woman matches at that time were usually 30 minutes. We thought, we can do that, that's easy. Let's give the fans something they haven't seen, something that's never been done. We ended up going more than 70 minutes," she said. "At that time, there hadn't been anything like it. We were only supposed to go a little more than an hour. We went out there and beat the hell out of each other and let it all out. When you have the crowd behind you and you have enough gas in the tank, you just keep going until you can't go any more."

In 2011, she topped that record with a 73-minute match against Lexxus. And, in October 2018, she topped the record once again, beating Tessa Blanchard in a 75-minute Iron Woman match for RISE in Chicago. At a time when WWE women's matches were going three to four minutes, Martinez showed that a woman wrestler could take a match over an hour and keep the fans firmly invested from bell to bell.

Throughout the 2010s, Martinez was one of the most decorated women on the independent circuit, capturing titles throughout the U.S., Canada, Australia, and England. In 2011, she was named number two in the PWI Female 50, behind Cheerleader Melissa.

She took a sabbatical (reported as a retirement at the time) from wrestling in 2014, but returned in 2016 and immediately reasserted herself as one of the top females on the independents. She made a surprise return to SHIMMER in June 2016, beating Madison Eagles for the SHIMMER title and forming "The Trifecta" with Baszler and Nicole Savoy. Martinez held the SHIMMER title for five months, then regained it and had a one-year reign from November 2016 through November 2017. She also captured the Phoenix of RISE title in 2018 and the SHINE title in 2019.

"Her work, talent and attitude always pushed the promoters to give her an important role in the company," said former NCW Femmes Fatales promoter Stéphane Bruyere. "She's one of the best, if not the best, female wrestlers who was never signed by one of the main wrestling companies."

That finally changed in January 2020, when Martinez signed a deal with WWE. She had participated in the Mae Young Classic in 2017 and the second Classic the following year. She also made a couple appearances with All Elite Wrestling in 2019, which likely helped convince WWE it was time to sign her before she signed with the competition.

"Mercedes has battled for equality, battled for her place, and wears those scars like a badge of honor," Danger said. "Women's wrestling will feel her impact and touch long after she has hung her boots up for that final time."

A.J. STYLES

Roman Reigns had just tossed Rusev out of the ring and was catching his breath in the corner as the 15,000 fans in Orlando's Amway Center counted down the third entrant into the 2016 Royal Rumble. As the countdown hit zero and the buzzer sounded, there was a brief pause and the first sustained note of unfamiliar theme music. Then three words appeared on the Titan Tron over the entranceway, and the crowd came unglued.

"I Am Phenomenal."

A.J. Styles had arrived in WWE.

Orlando was an appropriate city for Styles to make his debut. He had spent the previous several years right up the road, competing in TNA Wrestling, based out of a soundstage at Universal Studios. He was, in fact, TNA's most decorated wrestler — a three-time NWA champion (when TNA recognized the NWA title as its top prize), two-time TNA champion, six-time X Division champion, and six-time tag team champion. He was literally voted "Mr. TNA" for the first three years of the company's existence. Universally lauded as a, well, *phenomenal* in-ring competitor, Styles had been the cornerstone of TNA for more than a decade. He had put on spectacular matches with Christopher Daniels, Samoa Joe, Kurt Angle, Abyss, and many other competitors of all shapes and sizes.

More than a decade earlier, Styles had declined an offer to join WWE's developmental system. "I couldn't support myself and my wife on that salary," he told Dan Murphy in 2003 interview in *The Wrestler*. "God first, family second. That's the way I was raised. Besides, if they like me now, I can't do anything but get better."

But industry insiders wondered whether the undersized, soft-spoken Styles could establish himself as a star in WWE. Less than eight months after his WWE debut, Styles was the WWE world champion.

Styles's rise to the top has had its fair share of twists and turns. Allen Neal Jones was born on June 2, 1977, at Marine Corps Base Camp Lejeune in Jacksonville, North Carolina. He had a hardscrabble childhood and left college to pursue his dream of becoming a professional wrestler. He trained under wrestler Rick Michaels and had his first match in 1998 in National Championship Wrestling which, despite its lofty name, was a tiny independent promotion in Georgia.

With his agility, athleticism, and work ethic, Styles rapidly improved and became a rising star in NWA Wildside, Bill Behrens's Georgia-based promotion that opened in 1999. Behrens had a working arrangement with WCW, and he was offered a WCW contract in 2001. But WCW folded before Styles could settle in. he ended up in NWA-TNA, an NWA-affiliated start-up headed by Jerry and Jeff Jarrett based in Nashville, Tennessee. He also wrestled a handful of dark matches for the WWF and started up with Ring of Honor, a new independent promoting athleticism and workrate over gimmicks and storylines.

In ROH and in TNA, where he was slotted in to the company's unique X Division, Styles was able to shine with his fast-paced, highspot style. On June 11, 2003, he took the NWA heavyweight title, winning in a three-way bout against Raven and Jeff Jarrett. The NWA title was not as prestigious as it once had been, but it was still a major coup for the 26-year-old who had grown up watching the NWA during its glory years.

In February 2014, Styles defeated CM Punk in a tournament final to become the first ROH Pure champion. The Pure title was contested under unique rules: each wrestler had only the rope breaks per match, closed-fist punches were banned, and count-outs were 20 seconds (instead of the traditional 10). By 2005, he had become one of the most emulated wrestlers on the independents with his signature finisher, the Styles Clash, being mimicked on indie shows everywhere.

There was no question that Styles was a superior wrestler, but TNA was reluctant to get fully behind him as the kingpin of the company. He dropped the belt back to Jarrett in October 2003. He won the NWA title twice more — one reign lasting 28 days and the next lasting 35. After that, the NWA and TNA heavyweight titles (recognized after TNA had ended its association with the NWA) bounced between former WWE and WCW wrestlers coming into the company. Rhino, Christian Cage, Kurt Angle, and Mick Foley all had runs with the title. Meanwhile, Styles went about his business, routinely wrestling the best match on the card and putting on a modern-day classic series with Christopher Daniels, a feud some compared to the Ric Flair/Ricky Steamboat feud of the 1980s.

A.J. Styles and Christopher Daniels were natural rivals.

PHOTO BY GEORGE NAPOLITANO

Styles finally got another world title run in September 2009, when he won a five-way bout to capture the title at No Surrender. This title reign lasted more than 200 days and showed promise, with Styles taking on Ric Flair as his manager and becoming the central figure in a new Four Horsemen–type stable called Fortune. But instead of embracing Styles as a long-time Flair-type champion, he dropped the belt to newcomer Rob

Van Dam, and more former WWE stars — Jeff Hardy and Mr. Anderson — came in and took over the world title picture.

Styles had one more world title reign in TNA, for one day in October 2013, but was stripped of the belt by TNA President Dixie Carter (he did, however, continue to defend the title in Mexico against El Mesías and in Japan against Seiya Sanada after he was stripped of the belt). He and TNA were unable to come to terms on a new contract and, in December 2013, he left TNA after more than a decade in the company. He returned to ROH and the independents before signing with New Japan Pro-Wrestling in 2014. New Japan pushed him immediately, putting him into a program with IWGP champion Kazuchika Okada. On May 3, 2016, he defeated Okada to win the IWGP championship. Styles also became the leader of the Bullet Club, New Japan's top heel faction.

Styles had two IWGP title runs and then signed with WWE in 2016, shortly before his surprise debut at the Royal Rumble. Styles was an unqualified success in WWE. His second WWE world title reign lasted more than a year in length. He was voted Wrestler of the Year for 2016, 2017, and 2018 by readers of *Pro Wrestling Illustrated*. He was also voted Wrestler of the Decade by *PWI* readers due to his consistency and in-ring excellence.

"I think I've matured so much in this business and understand what really draws people into a match, rather than just the crazy things that I did where you can get yourself hurt," Styles told *PWI*'s Al Castle in a 2020 interview. "The little things mean the most. And people don't realize these little things. They just know it was a good match. But it's the little things that can take a great match and make it an unbelievable one.

"I think, as I've gotten older I realized what's more important," Styles said. "You've got to sell. That means you can't do some crazy thing and come back like it never happened. I understand that there's a psychology that plays a huge part in what we do. That doesn't mean you can't do something cool. You've just got to make it make sense when you do it."

CHRISTOPHER DANIELS

It's impossible to overstate the influence Christopher Daniels had on the wrestling industry in the 2000s.

He wrestled in the main event of the first Ring of Honor card on February 23, 2002, in a triple-threat match against Bryan Danielson and Low Ki and — over the course of multiple runs there — he remained one of the cornerstones of that company for most of the next two decades.

His matches against A.J. Styles (and, in 2005, Styles and Samoa Joe) helped put Total Nonstop Action on the map. The three-way bout between Daniels, Styles, and Joe from Unbreakable 2005 remains (as of this writing) the only match in TNA history to receive the five-star treatment from *Wrestling Observer* publisher Dave Meltzer.

He was one of the most well-traveled, decorated, and respected wrestlers on the independent circuit, winning championships in dozens of promotions, large and small. But he may also be one of the most versatile wrestlers ever to lace up a pair of boots, able to work main events, openers, intense grudge matches, comedy, singles, and tags.

"Christopher Daniels will be, I think, a name that will pop up when you talk to anybody about Wrestlers' Wrestlers," said NXT color commentator and former ROH champion Nigel McGuinness, who competed alongside — and against — Daniels in ROH, TNA, and on the indies. "The top guys in Ring of Honor — Bryan Danielson, Samoa Joe, Christopher Daniels — those were the guys you could always rely upon to have good matches, which is why, arguably, they were put in those positions (on top) . . . How you conduct yourself outside the ring and in the locker room. There are other guys that had the presence and the bell-to-bell in spades but — I won't name them but I'm sure you can think of them off the top of your head — because of the way they behaved in the locker room, they weren't considered Wrestlers' Wrestlers. They didn't have that respect. That came from helping guys out, which Christopher Daniels would always do. He would watch almost every match and would always give feedback *if you went to him and asked*. He wasn't one of these guys who would come up and give you advice you didn't ask for. He'd keep to himself but give sound advice if asked. That's how he earned respect."

Born in Kalamazoo, Michigan, on March 24, 1970, Daniel Christopher Covell grew up in Fayetteville, North Carolina, where he discovered Mid-Atlantic Championship Wrestling. He graduated from Methodist College with a degree in theater and moved to Chicago to make it as an actor. In Chicago, he discovered the independent promotion Windy City Pro Wrestling and he decided to give wrestling a try. He trained at the Windy City school and made his pro debut in April 1993.

Daniels began barnstorming the independent scene, which was experiencing a boom at the time, particularly the Monday Night Wars between the WWF and WCW. He toured Puerto Rico in 1995, winning the World Wrestling Council tag title with Kevin Quinn.

In 1998, he signed a WWF developmental deal and reported to Dory Funk Jr.'s Funkin' Dojo training center in Florida. He was used as enhancement talent on television and in dark matches, but he was never signed to a full-time contract. He continued to wrestle on the indies, including the East Coast Wrestling Association's annual Super 8 tournament which received heavy coverage in *Pro Wrestling Illustrated*. He won that tournament twice, in 2000 and in 2004.

"'The Fallen Angel' Christopher Daniels was an interesting pick for the Super 8," said Brandi Mankiewicz, the managing editor of *PWI* at the time. "As the first West Coast guy in the tournament, he was a curiosity. His workrate reputation preceded him and he definitely did not let us down. His performance singlehandedly propelled the tournament into global recognition."

In 1999, he made his first tour of Japan for Michinoku Pro Wrestling, where he developed the "hot and spicy" Curry Man persona. While Curry Man was played for laughs, Daniels soaked up the Japanese style like a sponge.

At the start of the new millennium, Daniels seemed to be on the verge of a major breakthrough. He had made multiple appearances in the WWF, but the front office had nothing for him and released him from his developmental contract. He made appearances in Extreme Championship Wrestling and WCW, but both of those national companies were on their deathbed. The timing simply didn't work out.

But, while the national promotions didn't work out, Daniels had a home on the indies. In addition to the ECWA Super 8, he also won the inaugural All Pro Wrestling (California) in December 2000, beating Donovan Morgan in the finals. His work was also appreciated in Ring of Honor, a new upstart promotion that valued workrate and athleticism as an alternative to the convoluted, storyline-based matches that were in vogue in WWE at the time.

Daniels established himself as the top heel in ROH by spurning the "code of honor" that required both wrestlers to shake hands before and during each match. He became the leader of a stable called the Prophecy. He also debuted in another start-up promotion, NWA-TNA, Jeff Jarrett's attempt to build an alternative promotion out of the ashes of WCW. Daniels was placed in Vince Russo's Sports Entertainment Xtreme stable, but later broke out as a member of the X Division, which was built around smaller, high-flying competitors.

Daniels bounced between ROH and TNA/Impact Wrestling from 2002 through 2019. During that span, he captured almost every championship in both companies, with the notable exception of the TNA world title. Still, with a combined 10 tag titles (between both promotions), a short ROH heavyweight title run, four X Division reigns, and a run as ROH TV champion, "The Fallen Angel" was ensconced in the title picture for the better part of two decades.

In 2019, Daniels was one of the first wrestlers to be signed to All Elite Wrestling, where he has settled into a role as wrestler and mentor for a relatively young roster.

SAMOA JOE

Nigel McGuinness remembers the incident vividly.

"Delirious was having a match against Roddy Strong in Philadelphia (in Ring of Honor). Roddy pulled in a guardrail and pulled Delirious off of the top rope, and the back of his head hit the guardrail. He got knocked loopy, absolutely senseless," McGuinness said. "He got to the back and he had just about regained his faculties and he started freaking out, as you often do when you've been knocked out and have had a concussion. He was running around going 'What happened? Did I finish the match? Was it okay?' Because he couldn't remember anything. And I tried to talk to him and everybody tried to talk to him, his girlfriend tried to talk to him, and none of us could get through to him whatsoever. And we were starting to get a little bit worried because it was a worrisome situation. And Samoa Joe was walking past and he stopped and put his hand on Delirious's shoulder and said 'Everything's going to be all right.' And Delirious went 'Oh. Okay.' And he just sat down and stopped, perfectly calm. It was the craziest thing I've ever seen. That was the level of respect Joe had, that he could cut through this sort of concussion-induced anxiety to get right to the core of this guy who was really struggling with where he was. That is, to me, the sign of being a Wrestlers' Wrestler."

For most of his career, Samoa Joe has been seen as a locker room leader, from his days on the California independent scene, through his impressive title runs in ROH, Total Nonstop Action, and NXT, and on to the big stage of WWE. Nuufolau Joel Seanoa was born on March 17, 1979, the son of Pete and Portia Seanoa, both of whom were Polynesian dancers. He took up dance as a boy and performed in front of more than 93,000 attendees at the opening ceremonies of the 1984 Summer Olympics at Los Angeles Memorial Coliseum. A self-described "casual fan" of wrestling as a child, he got his first real exposure to pro wrestling when he joined the UIWA West Coast Dojo in search of an MMA gym to try to get in shape and slim down from his weight of 340 pounds. He attended a pro wrestling class at the dojo and got hooked. He wrestled his first match three months later in December 1999.

By 2000, Joe had earned a contract with Ultimate Pro Wrestling, which was then a developmental affiliate of WWE. Although he held the UPW heavyweight title for eight months in 2001 and had a few tryout matches for the company, WWE wasn't interested in Joe, so he turned his attention to Japan. Joe learned the stiff Japanese strong style during a 2001–02 run in Shinya Hashimoto's Pro Wrestling Zero-One promotion. In 2002, he debuted in ROH as a hard-hitting Samoan submission machine, mixing his Japanese influence with his training in judo and MMA. On March 22, 2003, he defeated Xavier to become ROH champion. He would hold that title for 645 days. In many ways, Joe became the poster boy for ROH. His style was stiff and aggressive. He didn't have the cookie-cutter bodybuilder look that was in vogue in WWE at the time. And he was *believable* in the ring.

"He had presence, so you don't see through the cracks," said McGuinness, who defeated Joe to win the ROH Pure championship, a now-defunct title that was contested under "pure wrestling" rules; a "Wrestlers' Wrestler" championship if ever there was one. "You see a Samoa Joe match or a Bryan Danielson match and you never have to go, 'Oh, I'm going to have to suspend my disbelief there and let that go.' Even if someone else is out there and kind of fucks up, because their presence is so strong, it just plays along flawlessly in what you're seeing. From bell to bell, you have to have that competency."

Joe signed with Total Nonstop Action in June 2005. On September 11, 2005, Joe faced Christopher Daniels and A.J. Styles in a three-way match for the X Division title. The match (which was won by Styles) was an instant classic, earning five stars from *Wrestling Observer Newsletter* publisher Dave Meltzer. Three weeks later, Joe faced Kenta Kobashi in ROH in another five-star spectacular. In fact, only six matches received the five-star treatment from Meltzer in the first decade of the 2000s;

three of them involved Samoa Joe (the third being an October 2004 ROH bout against CM Punk).

Joe went on an 18-month undefeated run (in singles competition) in TNA before falling to Kurt Angle at Genesis 2006, arguably the most highly anticipated singles clash in TNA history. However, injuries and uneven booking disrupted his momentum. He finally won the TNA world title by beating Angle in April 2008 and held the title for six months before dropping it to Sting. He remained with TNA until 2015 when — after a handful of matches in ROH — he joined NXT, WWE's developmental territory. He became the first wrestler to win the NXT title on two occasions in 2016. He joined the main WWE roster in 2017, where he has captured the U.S. title multiple times and remains a perennial title contender.

MIKE QUACKENBUSH

The independent wrestling circuit can be a dicey place.

When Mike Quackenbush was trying to get his foot in the door in the early 1990s, he learned that lesson firsthand.

"When I didn't know what I was doing, somebody would say to me, 'Hey, if you show up at this place with 50 bucks in your hand and give it to the guy at the door, someone will get in the ring with you for an hour and teach you something.' And when I started, that's what I needed; I needed anybody to teach me anything because I was just making it all up," Quackenbush said. "I would go places where I would take all the money I had that week as a high school or college kid, hand it to some dude at the door, then some guy would beat the absolute tar out of me for the next hour until my chest was raw and bleeding and I could barely pull myself off the mat. Then they would kick me out and say, 'Send in the next guy.' And they taught me nothing, other than maybe a threshold for pain."

Those early experiences left an indelible impression on the Reading, Pennsylvania, native. It inspired him to become a trainer himself one day, and ultimately led him to create a training school and promotion of his own . . . a promotion that would become one of the most influential independents of the 2000s.

A comic book fan from childhood, Quackenbush was drawn to wrestling for the first time when he saw Japanese star Jushin "Thunder" Liger in action. With his ornate horned mask and bodysuit and graceful, artful movements, Liger was a living comic book superhero. Quackenbush was hooked. He began wrestling in 1994, landing local independent bookings despite being entirely self-taught, mimicking the moves he saw on television.

"I have these three ill-formed, misshapen years in which I had the worst injuries of my career," Quackenbush said in a 2019 interview with the website one37pm.com. "I fractured the back of my skull. I had a seizure in the ring. I had a traumatic brain injury from that. It took months and months to recover. I was 19 at the time. So training doesn't really become part of my story until I've already had between 100 and 150 matches."

That's when Quackenbush met Ace Darling, who recognized the youngster's passion and took him under his wing. He received further instruction from Reckless Youth (Tom Carter) and Mexican wrestler and trainer Skayde (Jorge Rivera Soriano) and he soaked up the instructions like a sponge, developing a hybrid style that combined elements of Lucha Libre, British catch-as-catch-can, traditional American wrestling, and comic book action. He took the nickname "The Master of 1,000 Holds," and made a point to showcase as many new and unique moves as he could, earning him a strong fan following on the Northeast independent circuit.

Mike Quackenbush locks Ultimo Dragon in a modified surfboard.

What set Quackenbush apart from the thousands of aspiring pro wrestlers on the independent scene was his unique vision of what wrestling could be and his willingness to make that vision a reality.

In 2002, he and Reckless Youth opened the Wrestle Factory wrestling school. A few months later, they opened an associated wrestling promotion where they and their students could perform. CHIKARA was born.

Though it's a wrestling promotion, CHIKARA has more in common with comic books and sci-fi than traditional, kayfabe-conscious pro wrestling. The company has been home to a menagerie of bizarre characters (such as Los Ice Creams, the wrestling ice cream cones; the Proletariat Boar of Moldova; and the living masterpiece Still Life with Apricots and Pears), but it also featured some of wrestling's biggest stars, such as CM Punk, Bryan Danielson, Manami Toyota, the Young Bucks, and Johnny Gargano. CHIKARA fostered an atmosphere where anyone could be involved, regardless of size or gender. Women regularly were featured on equal footing against men, just as they would be in comic books. It sought to make wrestling fun, above all else, and attracted a fan following that has kept it in operation for two decades. It became, in many ways, an oasis from the shady indie scene that Quackenbush had survived in the 1990s. CHIKARA was one of the most influential independent promotions of the 2000s and managed to successfully utilize the internet to build and maintain a passionate international fan base.

Wrestling has taken Quackenbush around the world and has earned him several championships, including the Combat Zone Wrestling junior heavyweight title (twice), the Westside Xtreme Wrestling (Germany) heavyweight title, and the NWA junior heavyweight title. As a trainer, he has had a hand in training more than 100 wrestlers, including Cesaro, Alexa Bliss, and Orange Cassidy. He has also been a guest trainer and coach at the WWE Performance Center.

"I kind of divide it up into three categories," Quackenbush said of his philosophy on training wrestlers. "There is the mechanical piece — you have to be sure your bumps are correct and you are taking care of yourself and another human, as well. Then there's the performative pieces — it's about your character, your facial expressions, your vocalizations, and your body language. It's the way we create live combat theater. And then there is the structural piece — understanding the underlying psychology behind what you are doing, how you structure a story. It's not just in the context of a match. What if you realize you're going to be married to another performer (in a program) for the next five months? How do you tell a story that fills that time? You have to understand story structure and narrative to be able to do that.

"In the first several years of my career, I was sloppy and would not get the feedback I needed to help me develop," Quackenbush continued. "I would come back behind the curtain and the veterans would be lined up saying 'Kid, you don't know how to work' or 'You're so stupid. Who put you on this card? You're terrible.' Well, that's not helping me make my snapmare better. I went through a really long phase where I was just obsessed with cataloguing moves and variations, becoming a stickler for form. At my wrestling factory, there are seven coaches, and when it comes to the technical prowess, nobody grades harder than I do because that's my particular hang-up."

In 2020, Quackenbush announced he was shutting down CHIKARA after he was accused of making "misogynist, racist, and homophobic remarks" by a former CHIKARA Wrestle Factory trainee. Quackenbush was one of several wrestlers who was taken to task on social media during the #SpeakingOut movement. He has issued a public apology for any hurtful comments he made.

DAVE TAYLOR

In a 2012 shoot interview done for Highspots.com, Dave Taylor recalled a conversation he had with Sting following a match in WCW. "He said, 'You've got to stop putting me in those holds I can't get out of,'" Taylor remembered. "I said, 'I've never put you in a hold you can't get out of. Never in a million years.'"

Taylor was willing to let his opponent out of the holds. Whether or not they knew *how* to get out of the holds was a different question. Occasionally, a wrestler — such as Sting — discovered himself in a hold and found himself frozen in the headlights, unable to figure out a countermove, until Taylor coached him through it. It's a testament to Taylor's encyclopedic knowledge of catch-as catch-can grappling.

A third-generation pro wrestler, Taylor was one of the most underrated in-ring performers of the 1990s and 2000s. He was already 38 years old by the time he started with WCW in 1995. He would remain a dependable midcard performer on the national stage until 2008, when he was released by WWE.

David Taylor was born on May 1, 1957, in Yorkshire, England. His father, Eric Taylor, was the reigning British heavy middleweight champion when David was born. His grandfather, Joseph Taylor, competed in the 1932 Summer Olympics in the freestyle featherweight division before turning pro.

An accomplished amateur wrestler, he made his pro wrestling debut in 1974 (or 1977, depending on the source). He competed his first tour of New Japan Pro-Wrestling in 1977.

Taylor put in a good word for his countryman Steven Regal with the Catch Wrestling Association promotion in Hamburg, Germany, helping

Regal get booked in that country. A few years later, Regal would return the favor, helping Taylor get his foot in the door with World Championship Wrestling. In 1995, he signed with WCW as "Squire" David Taylor, part of the Bluebloods stable with Lord Steven Regal and Earl Robert Eaton (playing a snobbish Englishman by way of Huntsville, Alabama).

Taylor became a utility performer for WCW, stepping into contention for the tag team and TV titles periodically, working with younger talent, and very frequently putting over most of his opponents. In WCW, where many veteran competitors refused to do jobs, a veteran without an ego was a man in demand.

"Most of the guys (in WCW) wanted to win every match they were in," Taylor said in a 2014 interview with the *Inside the Ropes* podcast. "It's an American thing. They don't want to lose. I don't give a shit about losing. You know what I mean? If it was real, that's a different thing. But it's not. It's entertainment."

After WCW folded, Taylor was signed as trainer at Ohio Valley Wrestling, one of WWE's developmental territories at the time. He spent a short period of time in the Heartland Wrestling Association, another WWE farm system located in Cincinnati, before leaving and going back to Europe, where he split time between the United Kingdom and Germany.

In 2006, Taylor signed with WWE as a trainer at Deep South Wrestling, one of the company's developmental territories, but it quickly became clear that "The Squire" still had a bit more gas in his tank. He was brought up to the main roster, where he competed as part of the SmackDown brand, re-forming his tag team with Regal. The duo had memorable matches against the team of Paul London and Brian Kendrick, and competed in a fatal-four-way ladder match against London and Kendrick, Joey Mercury and Johnny Nitro, and the Hardy Boyz at Armageddon 2006.

When Regal was moved to the *Raw* brand, Taylor was paired with promising young prospect Paul Birchall, and later with Drew McIntyre, but it was clear that the veteran was there to mentor the young guys rather than get a push of his own. He was released by WWE in April 2008. He bounced around the independents, including a 2011 appearance in Ring of Honor, and ultimately announced his retirement in 2012.

"I had the pleasure of working with (Dave) in a Main Event in South Africa for WWE (September 2007 — the Highlanders against Dave Taylor and Paul Birchall)," said Derek Graham-Couch, who wrestled as Highlander Robbie McAllister. "It was the Scottish versus the English in the Durban Tennis Stadium. It was absolute magic from start to finish. I couldn't have asked to make magic like that happen with nothing called but the finish. It was one of my most enjoyable and memorable matches ever."

THE MASTERS OF TODAY

In April 2020, WWE held a pre-taped "empty arena" version of *WrestleMania* due to the outbreak of the COVID-19 coronavirus and the ban on large gatherings that made a traditional live event (let alone one as large as *WrestleMania*) an impossibility.

Without fans in attendance, WWE opted to push the boundaries and present a pair of unorthodox, decidedly non-traditional bouts: a "Boneyard Match" between the Undertaker and A.J. Styles and a "Firefly Funhouse Match" between "The Fiend" Bray Wyatt and John Cena.

The Boneyard Match was a nighttime brawl in a makeshift cemetery with dialogue, movie lighting, multiple cameras, a musical score, and special effects, ending with the Undertaker "burying Styles alive." The Firefly Funhouse match was even more bizarre, with Cena "teleporting" from ringside into Wyatt's funhouse sketch studio and then Wyatt and Cena, side by side, acting out surreal reimagined scenes from Cena's career. There was no attempt whatsoever to present "the match" as an athletic contest.

Both of these "cinematic matches" proved polarizing with fans. More traditional fans hated them and saw them as hokey, an insult to professional wrestling. But others saw them as the next step in the ongoing evolution of wrestling as entertainment. For these fans, pro wrestling has more in common with superhero movies than Greco-Roman wrestling. As the 2020s began, these cinematic matches (which truly originated with Matt Hardy's "Final Deletion" match in 2016) were becoming more ingrained in wrestling. Intergender matches between men and women where women overpower men two or three times their size are commonplace on the independents; Impact Wrestling had Tessa Blanchard win its world championship in January 2020.

There's no question that wrestling has changed dramatically, not only since Lou Thesz's heyday, but even over the past 20 years. Today's wrestlers are required to be "sports entertainers." Whether or not they can properly apply a hammerlock is less important than whether or not they can cut a promo or have a strong entrance routine. Wins and losses are less important than making memorable moments or — perhaps the ultimate accomplishment today — going viral online.

But there are a handful of wrestlers of today who still fit the mold as "Wrestlers' Wrestlers." They are wrestlers who have the technical know-how, presence, and wrestling mastery to have been stars 50 years ago, yet have been versatile enough to adapt to the new style and have success in the 2020s. These are all active wrestlers whose stories are still being written, but they deserve inclusion in any book about the masters of the craft of wrestling in any era.

KAZUCHIKA OKADA

They call him "The Rainmaker," and Kazuchika Okada has lived up to the moniker.

The six-foot-three Okada trained under Último Dragón and made his pro debut in August 2004. He moved on to New Japan, where he trained in the NJPW dojo, and in 2010 was sent to TNA Wrestling to continue his development in the United States. However, Okada was badly booked in TNA, where he was saddled with a gimmick lifted from the Green Hornet and barely used. He returned to New Japan in 2011, and while TNA had bungled its opportunity with him, New Japan pushed him as the company's top heel.

As "The Rainmaker," Okada melded together the different styles he had learned, incorporating the dropkicks and aerial attacks of Lucha Libre with the showmanship of the U.S. and the "fighting spirit" taught in the New Japan dojo.

In February 2012, Okada defeated Hiroshi Tanahashi to win the IWGP heavyweight title. For the next two years, the feud between Okada and Tanahashi carried New Japan, winning Feud of the Year honors from the *Wrestling Observer Newsletter* in 2012 and 2013. Okada had four *Observer* Matches of the Year in the 2010s (2013 and 2016 against Tanahashi; 2017 and 2018 against Kenny Omega). In 2017, he was the first Japanese wrestler ever to top the annual PWI 500 ranking of the top 500 wrestlers in the world.

"It's an indication that finally the world at large is realizing just how great Japanese wrestlers and Japanese wrestling is, and that's special," he told *PWI* through an interpreter. He also broke Dave Meltzer's vaunted five-star scale with a seven-star match against Omega in June 2018.

Okada posted five IWGP title reigns between 2012 and 2020, holding the title a combined 1,790 days. During that time, New Japan made significant inroads in the U.S., due in large part to Okada's big-money matches and drawing power. Already one of the top stars in New Japan history, he is poised to remain the company's franchise player for the foreseeable future.

CESARO

At six-foot-five and a chiseled 235 pounds, "The Swiss Superman" could have been a main-eventer in any era. Ironically enough, Cesaro has mostly been a utility player since joining WWE in 2012, but he has managed to capture six tag team titles, the U.S. title, and the inaugural Andre the Giant Memorial Battle Royal trophy between 2012 and 2020.

Under his birth name of Claudio Castagnoli, he garnered attention on the American independent scene in the mid-2000s. Born in Lucerne, Switzerland, he started his wrestling career in 2000 and competed throughout Europe, where he was exposed to multiple styles of wrestling. He received training under Dave Taylor and later under Mike Quackenbush at CHIKARA in the U.S.

"He is that guy who was in the gym daily, even at two a.m.," said retired wrestler Allison Danger. "Every day, he was watching tapes, learning more about nutrition, teaching himself how to sew his own gear, always thinking about that next step. He left his country, family, friends, and career behind in Europe to essentially start over in the U.S. and rebuild himself up from scratch. I remember being in awe of his work ethic, which was incredibly motivating to all those around him. To this day, he is one of the most inspiring people to be around, both inside and outside the ring."

With his size and power, Castagnoli could easily have become a one-dimensional strongman, especially on the independents, where he frequently stood head and shoulders above his opponents. Instead, he built a reputation as a workhorse, adept at a variety of different styles and able to work any opponent. In 2006, he signed a developmental deal with WWE but was released a short time later. He returned to the independents with stints in Ring of Honor and Pro Wrestling Guerrilla, as well as tours with Pro Wrestling NOAH in Japan, until finally re-signing with WWE in 2011.

Cesaro was voted Most Underrated Wrestler of the Year by readers of The Wrestling Observer *Newsletter* for four consecutive years (2013–16).

ZACK SABRE JR.

England has produced its fair share of wrestlers who were considered technical masters, from Billy Robinson to Nigel McGuinness. Kent native Zack Sabre Jr. is proudly carrying the banner of British catch wrestling into the new millennium.

ZSJ turned pro three months shy of his 18th birthday, in 2004. By the time he turned 19, he was already the NWA United Kingdom champion. A lean, lanky competitor, Sabre often looks out of place against larger, more muscular opponents, but his quickness and encyclopedic knowledge of submission holds more than make up for his lack of power.

Between 2004 and 2016, Sabre made his name in multiple British companies, including International Pro Wrestling UK, Triple X Wrestling, and Progress Wrestling. At every stop, he made waves and awed crowds with his pure technical ability and tenacity.

In 2014, Sabre was voted Best Technical Wrestler by readers of the *Wrestling Observer Newsletter*, breaking a nine-year streak by Daniel

Bryan. Sabre went on to win that award again in 2015 . . . and 2016 . . . and 2017, 2018, and 2019. He won the prestigious Pro Wrestling Guerrilla Battle of Los Angeles tournament in 2015.

In 2016, he participated in the inaugural WWE Cruiserweight Classic, advancing to the semifinals with wins over Tyson Dux, Drew Gulak, and Noam Dar before succumbing to Gran Metalik. But rather than sign with WWE, Sabre joined New Japan Pro-Wrestling. He won the 2018 New Japan Cup tournament, submitting the iconic ace Hiroshi Tanahashi in the finals.

Perhaps the best pound-for-pound pure wrestler on the circuit today, ZSJ has made submission grappling fashionable and has helped introduce catch wrestling to a new generation of fans.

NICK ALDIS

In May 2017, Billy Corgan — lead singer of the alternative rock band Smashing Pumpkins — bought the name, rights, trademarks, and championship belts of the National Wrestling Alliance from Bruce Tharpe, a Houston attorney who had owned the rights to the NWA brand since 2012. Once the premier name in wrestling, the NWA had become a loose alliance of small independent promotions under the NWA banner. It bore very little semblance to the NWA of the 1960s, 1970s, and 1980s. The brand had been in a virtual free-fall since breaking away from the Ted Turner–owned World Championship Wrestling in 1993.

With visions of resurrecting the NWA brand, Corgan sought a wrestler who could best represent the NWA and serve as a link back to the champions of the NWA's glory years. He chose Nick Aldis.

A native of Norfolk, England, Aldis made his pro debut in 2003. He made his way to the U.S. in 2008, when he signed with TNA Wrestling, where he debuted as Brutus Magnus (he dropped the Brutus name a short time later). He won tag titles with countryman Doug Williams and Samoa Joe and won a tournament for the TNA world title in December 2013. However, instead of becoming a long-term solution for TNA, he dropped the title to Eric Young after just four months.

TNA's loss proved to be the NWA's gain. Since beating Tim Storm for the NWA title in December 2017, Aldis has drawn comparisons to Dory Funk Jr. and Ric Flair. Technically proficient, Aldis is a ring general with expert timing and body language. He carries himself like a champion of a bygone era, exuding confidence and class reminiscent of a young Nick Bockwinkel. He has also proven to be a champion willing to travel to defend his title, defending the NWA championship in the United Kingdom, Puerto Rico, Australia, and throughout the U.S. and Canada. He has done a remarkable job representing the NWA in its latest incarnation.

JAY WHITE

To paraphrase Lincoln Steffens, we have seen the future, and it is Jay White. White, a New Zealander who is a superstar in Japan, has achieved a great deal in a short period of time. He began wrestling in 2013 and caught the attention of Prince Devitt (known as Finn Bálor in WWE). Devitt put him in touch with New Japan Pro-Wrestling and, in 2015, White began training in the NJPW dojo.

He moved on to the U.S. in 2016, competing in Ring of Honor, then returned to New Japan in November 2017, adopting the moniker "Switchblade." He was immediately positioned in a program against Hiroshi Tanahashi for the IWGP Intercontinental title. Though he failed to beat Tanahashi, he went on to beat Kenny Omega for the IWGP U.S. title in January 2017. He established himself as main-event talent during the 2018 G1 Climax tournament; though he did not win the tourney, he managed to score pinfall wins over New Japan's top two stars, Tanahashi and Kazuchika Okada. White became the leader of New Japan's top faction, the Bullet Club (a position formerly held by Devitt) and defeated Tanahashi to win the IWGP title in February 2019.

Though White's IWGP reign lasted only eight weeks (he lost the belt to Okada in April 2019), he went on to beat Tetsuya Naito to win the IWGP Intercontinental title in September 2019.

White's star power and talent continues to grow. He is among the new stars that help keep the wrestling business alive and exciting, and he's positioned to be one of wrestling's brightest stars in the coming years.

CHAD GABLE

A high school state wrestling champion in his native Minnesota, Charles (Chad Gable) Betts competed at the 2012 Summer Olympics, finishing in ninth place in the men's Greco-Roman 84-kilogram division. The following year, he signed a developmental contract with WWE.

"If you had taken 100 amateur wrestlers at that time and asked me who the *last* one I could imagine becoming a professional wrestler was, I would have said Chad Gable," said Kyle Klingman, former director of the National Wrestling Hall of Fame Dan Gable Museum. "He was always so locked in, he never showed any of the charisma or personality you need as a pro wrestler. But he was a Greco-Roman wrestler, and in Greco-Roman wrestling, you don't have to play to the crowd, while in pro wrestling the crowd is everything. Boy, was I dead wrong! He turned on the charisma, and I've become a huge Chad Gable fan. I'm hoping WWE gives him more of a push because I think he can be one of the next all-time greats."

In a previous era, a bona fide Olympic wrestler would have received a significant push out of the gate, but Gable (a ring name given in honor of legendary wrestler Dan Gable) had to put in his time at the WWE Performance Center before making his NXT network debut in January 2015. He was voted Rookie of the Year by *Wrestling Observer* readers in 2015.

Gable was paired with former NCAA wrestler Jason Jordan as American Alpha. They had chemistry and, in April 2016, they defeated the Revival to win the NXT tag title in a critically acclaimed bout. They were called up to the main roster and won the SmackDown tag title in December 2016.

Gable and Jordan parted ways in 2017, and Gable subsequently formed teams with Shelton Benjamin and Bobby Roode. In the summer of 2019, he changed his ring name to Shorty G, in acknowledgement of his five-foot-eight stature. *Observer* readers voted him Most Underrated Wrestler of 2019.

Still a relative newcomer to the pro ranks, Gable has the credibility to stand out and to elevate those around him.

DREW GULAK

Combat Zone Wrestling isn't a promotion known for catch-as-catch-can grappling and five-star technical matches, but that's where Drew Gulak cut his teeth. Gulak, a Pennsylvania native, trained at the CZW Wrestling Academy and made his pro debut in April 2005. In 2010, he won the company's Wired TV title and began a storyline where he campaigned against the blood-and-guts "ultraviolence" that was CZW's calling card. He defeated death-match specialist Masada to win the CZW heavyweight title in August 2013.

In 2016, Gulak competed in the WWE Cruiserweight Classic, where he defeated Harv Sihra in the opening round before being eliminated by Zack Sabre Jr. in round two. He officially signed with WWE later that year and was assigned to the 205 Live cruiserweight division. There, he adopted the role of a crusader against the rampant aerial maneuvers, starting a "No Fly Zone" campaign. Complete with PowerPoint presentations on how to improve 205 Live and on his No Fly Zone campaign, Gulak began to get over with 205 Live fans. In June 2019, Gulak won a three-way bout over champion Tony Nese and Akira Tozawa to win the WWE cruiserweight title.

Gulak truly got the chance to shine in 2020, when he faced Daniel Bryan at the Elimination Chamber pay-per-view. The story of the match was that Gulak was able to counter each hold Bryan could apply, putting over Gulak's technical ability and showcasing him as a credible wrestler, rather than comic relief. It was the start of a new chapter in Gulak's career and, in a sense, a passing of the proverbial torch from Bryan to Gulak.

THE REVIVAL

Since their debut in NXT in 2014, the team of Dash Wilder and Scott Dawson has earned praise for its throwback style, earning comparisons to teams like the Midnight Express, Jacko and Jerry Brisco, and the Andersons. In November 2015, the Revival won the NXT tag team championships from the Vaudevillains and went on to have a memorable series of matches against Chad Gable and Jason Jordan in 2016. Dawson and Wilder had two runs as NXT tag champions, and joined the main roster in April 2018. However, despite their success in NXT, the Revival quickly grew frustrated with their booking in WWE and reportedly requested their release in early 2019.

Perhaps as an effort to appease the team, the Revival won the *Raw* tag team titles in February 2019, only to lose the belts two months later to the unheralded team of Curt Hawkins and Zack Ryder at *WrestleMania* 35. In September 2019, they defeated the New Day to win the SmackDown tag titles, earning the distinction of being the first team ever to hold the NXT, *Raw*, and SmackDown tag belts. Their SmackDown reign proved to be just as brief, as they dropped the belts back to the New Day in November 2019.

In April 2020, the Revival got their wish and received their release from WWE, becoming two of the hottest free agents in the game.

"They are such a great tag team that they're on a level above most everyone else, but they have not been presented as that because tag teams are not presented as that in general in WWE," said Jim Cornette, an outspoken proponent of the Revival, on his *Cornette's Drive-Thru* podcast (episode 115). "The Revival has no clown show to 'em, so of course I'm sure the writers (wonder), 'What do we do with these guys? They just wrestle and talk like they're bad.'"

Wrestlers who wrestle and talk a convincing game. Who would have ever thought that would be a *liability* in professional wrestling?

PART 7:
The All-Time Masters of the Craft

Every wrestler included in this book has contributed a special piece to the art of professional wrestling. Whether they were amateur stand-outs who brought their knowledge of takedowns into the ring, master psychologists who made the audiences care about every little movement they made, expert bumpers who built up the fans' emotional investment, or smooth workers who made their opponents look like gold and delivered impeccable matches night in and night out, all of them have their lessons they can pass on to future generations of wrestlers and fans alike.

But some wrestlers have something else; an almost undefinable element that sets them apart. Their work can be viewed years later and stand the test of time. A viewer sitting down to watch wrestling for the very first time — one who doesn't know a suplex from a soufflé — can watch them work and intuitively understand that they are watching something special. And the experts, the wrestlers and students of the game, can watch their matches and appreciate them on an altogether different level, the way an artist or musician can appreciate the nuances and mastery of the greats in their given field.

Wrestling fans often like to debate their "Mount Rushmore" of wrestlers. This would be more like an all-star team of the best "Wrestlers' Wrestlers" ever to grace the squared circle; the unquestioned masters of the craft of professional wrestling.

KURT ANGLE

"He is, without question, the most gifted all-around performer we have ever had step into a ring. There will never be another like him."

—John Cena (from an interview on WWE.com)

There have been several Olympic athletes who have tried their hand in professional wrestling, but none have made such a seamless transition and achieved such remarkable success as Kurt Angle.

When Angle debuted in WWE, it was understood that he was a phenomenal technical wrestler. He knew all the moves. But when it came to *when to use* those moves, how to pace a pro style match, and how to develop a larger-than-life character, Angle proved to be a natural.

"I've never seen anybody get into the business of sports entertainment and learn it as fast as he did," said Steve Austin in a video package produced by WWE when Angle was inducted into the WWE Hall of Fame in 2017.

Born December 9, 1968, Angle grew up outside of Pittsburgh and began wrestling at the age of seven. He earned varsity letters in football and wrestling from Mount Lebanon High School. He moved on to Clarion University, where he became a two-time national collegiate champion. In 1995, he won gold at the FILA wrestling world championships and began training under Olympic gold medalist and amateur wrestling legend Dave Schultz for the 1996 Olympic Games. But shortly after Angle started at Schultz's Pennsylvanian Foxcatcher Club training center, Schultz was murdered by the organization's eccentric sponsor,

John DuPont. With Foxcatcher in turmoil, Angle left and joined the Dave Schultz Wrestling Club, which was not associated with DuPont.

In the weeks leading to the 1996 Olympic trials, Angle fractured two of his cervical vertebrae, herniated a pair of discs, and suffered several pulled muscles. "The doctors were like, 'You're done.' I was like, 'I can't be done. I have the Olympic trials and the Olympics,'" Angle recalled in an interview on TNA Wrestling. "They said, 'Do you want to wrestle there and end up in a wheelchair or do you want to live the rest of your life and be okay?' I said, 'Well, I don't want to end up in a wheelchair, but I'll take the chance.' Every time I'd go into the wrestling room, beforehand I'd go into (the doctor's) office, he'd stick me in the neck with 12 different shots of Novocain, I'd hurry up to the wrestling practice, I'd practice a little bit and go home."

In an incredible sign of his toughness and tenacity, Angle was still able to compete and won the trials to earn a spot on the Olympics squad. However, to cope with the pain, Angle developed a dependence on painkillers that would haunt him for much of his professional career and affect his life outside the ring.

On July 31, 1996, Angle defeated Abbas Jadidi of Iran in double-overtime to win the gold medal in the men's freestyle 100-kilogram division. As Angle would famously boast afterwards, he won the gold "with a broken freakin' neck."

Angle's underdog story and his incredible athletic pedigree caught the attention of pro wrestling talent scouts. Angle, however, had always found the pro game to be silly and had little interest in getting into the ring, especially after attending an Extreme Championship Wrestling event in Philadelphia where Raven staged a controversial "crucifixion" of the Sandman. However, after some back-and-forth discussions with WWF, Angle completed a tryout and, in 1998, signed a five-year contract with WWF.

Angled wrestled his first pro match in August 1998 against Tom Prichard, one of his trainers, in the World Wrestling Alliance, a Massachusetts independent that was affiliated with the WWF as a developmental territory. After a few months, he moved on to another developmental territory, Power Pro Wrestling in Memphis. In July 1999, he won his first pro wrestling title, beating J.R. Smooth for the PPW heavyweight title. He went on the WWF house show circuit that summer and finally made his television debut with a win over Shawn Stasiak at the 1999 Survivor Series pay-per-view.

In a previous generation, a clean-cut All-American Olympic gold medalist would have been the biggest natural babyface in the game. But Angle made his debut during the WWF's "Attitude Era," when anti-authority figures like Austin and D-Generation X were the WWF's most beloved acts. The fans were slow to embrace the relatively vanilla newcomer. In a prescient and bold move, the WWF changed course and turned Angle into a heel. With Angle calling himself the only "real" athlete in the WWF, the fans began booing louder, and Angle got over as one of the company's top villains.

Wearing replicas of his gold medal around his neck, Angle preached his "Three I's": Intensity, Integrity, and Intelligence, presenting a sanctimonious, self-righteous front as a heel. In February 2000, he won both the European and Intercontinental titles; he lost both belts without ever suffering a fall in a three-way match against Chris Jericho and Chris Benoit at *WrestleMania* 2000. He won the 2000 King of the Ring tournament and, in October 2000, he defeated the Rock to become WWF world champion, less than a year after his main roster debut.

"Almost overnight, Angle became a key player for the WWF's major pay-per-views," historian Larry Matysik wrote in his book *The 50 Greatest Professional Wrestlers of All Time* (Matysik ranked Angle number 33). "In the ring, he always delivered. At one point, I was talking with Jack Brisco, who told me of all the talent pushed to the top in that period, the person he would have wanted to work with most was Kurt Angle. 'Two amateur champions, combining the mat stuff at the level we'd be, along with the babyface-heel fireworks — we'd have brought down the house anywhere,' Brisco guaranteed."

"You knew from the beginning that Kurt was special. He was a special athlete," said former WWE referee Jimmy Korderas. "He was not one of those guys where you'd tell him something or try to explain something and he'd say, 'Yeah, yeah, yeah. I get it.' No. He'd listen and ask questions. 'Oh, how would I do that?' He genuinely wanted to learn and he just picked it up incredibly quick. Coming from that world of shoot wrestling into pro wrestling, it's a different animal. You're trained not to show fear, not to show pain. You don't want the other guys to know what you're feeling. Now you're going to a world where you have to register things, to show the audience. You have to be a little bit bigger so the people in the cheap seats are able to tell that you're selling. Coming from that world, he picked it up incredibly quickly."

Kurt Angle displays his power by hoisting Shawn Michaels with one arm at WrestleMania *21.*

PHOTO BY GEORGE NAPOLITANO

Between 2000 and 2006, Angle won the WWF/WWE world title five times, as well as the WCW title, the U.S. title, tag team title (with Benoit), and hardcore titles. In 2006, Angle was released by WWE due to concerns over his worsening substance abuse issues. He signed with TNA Wrestling and started a program with Samoa Joe. He won the TNA world title (TNA had previously recognized the NWA title until the NWA pulled its recognition of the TNA titleholders) in May 2017, winning a triple-threat match against Christian Cage and Sting.

Between 2007 and 2015, Angle held the TNA world title six times. He also had runs as X Division champion and two tag title reigns (with

Sting and A.J. Styles). In June 2007, as part of a co-promotion between TNA and New Japan, he won the IWGP title (Inoki Genome Federation version), beating Brock Lesnar for that championship.

In 2017, Angle returned to the WWE to be enshrined in the WWE Hall of Fame. He did a stint as on-screen general manager of the *Raw* brand. He had one final five-star match at *WrestleMania 34*, teaming with Ronda Rousey to defeat Triple H and Stephanie McMahon. He wrestled his retirement match at *WrestleMania 35*, losing to Baron Corbin.

"Kurt Angle, he really just is the best of the best," said Nigel McGuinness. "And that ability to get good matches — I've never seen a bad Kurt Angle match. He can't have one, you know?"

CHRIS BENOIT

Though his actions in the final days of his life will always overshadow his remarkable career in the ring, a book about "Wrestlers' Wrestlers" and masters of the art of wrestling would be incomplete without Chris Benoit. He was the embodiment of a Wrestlers' Wrestler. His style and technique can be used to teach a master's course in wrestling execution and psychology. He was arguably the best wrestler of his generation and one of the greatest of all time.

"(He was) the most intense and believable performer that I've ever been in the ring with. He could see things that would happen before they happened," said Benoit's longtime friend Chris Jericho in the 2020 Vice *Dark Side of the Ring* documentary on Benoit.

For roughly a 15-year period, Benoit was one of the most admired, respected, and emulated pro wrestlers in the game. Born May 21, 1967, in Montreal, he grew up in Edmonton. He saw the Dynamite Kid in action as a boy and immediately decided that *that* was what he want to be — he wanted to be a wrestler just like the Dynamite Kid. In 1985, he began training under Bruce Hart at the Hart family wrestling school (and Stu Hart's infamous "Dungeon") in Calgary. As a wrestler, he emulated the Dynamite Kid, adopting not only his signature moves (the snap suplex and diving headbutt) but also his mannerisms, the way he stood and positioned himself in the ring. Even as a rookie in Stampede Wrestling, he radiated a quiet, determined intensity.

At a generously billed five-foot-ten, Benoit lacked the size to become a national star in the 1980s, but he was determined to be the very best wrestler there was.

Benoit captured several midcard titles in Stampede, including the Stampede international tag team title and the British Commonwealth mid-heavyweight title, which he would hold four times.

"He was a huge fan of Dynamite Kid. He was very humble and, as a worker, he was a by-product of that time," said Bruce Hart. "Those guys — Benoit, Pillman, and some of them — they had a fire in their belly. I appreciated the fact that they were diligent and committed, always striving to be better. One of the hallmarks of their kind is they are never quite satisfied with their performance. Even if they gave a five-star match, they always thought there was something they could have done better, or wish they did. Benoit was like that."

In 1986, he began training at the New Japan Pro-Wrestling dojo, making his NJP debut in January 1987. The strict work ethic and aggressive and believable ring style practiced in New Japan made a tremendous impact on him and helped mold him as a performer.

Benoit received a moderate push as a junior heavyweight in New Japan as the masked Pegasus Kid. He also made tours of Mexico and Europe, gaining valuable international territorial experience in his first couple years in the business. In 1990, he defeated Jushin Liger to win the IWGP light heavyweight title. He eventually lost both the title and the mask back to Liger, but continued wrestling in NJPW as Wild Pegasus.

In April 1994, Benoit won the inaugural NJPW Super J-Cup tournament, an event featuring some of the finest light heavyweight wrestlers in the world, including Liger, Hayabusa, Dean Malenko, Eddie Guerrero (under a mask as Black Tiger), and the Great Sasuke. The tournament became an underground sensation with the VHS tape-trading community. In particular, the quarterfinal bout between Pegasus and Black Tiger was widely considered to be an instant classic. It was the beginning of a lifelong friendship between Benoit and Guerrero.

In the early 1990s, Benoit made a few appearances in World Championship Wrestling, including during the WCW's NWA tag team tournament in June 1992, when he and partner Beef Wellington lost to Liger and Brian Pillman, but a contract never came. He had a WWF tryout in 1995 with Ted DiBiase as his manager, but again was not offered a contract.

Ironically, his major break in the U.S. came in Extreme Championship Wrestling, a promotion known for violent brawls, blood, and the highest per capita number of panty-exposing catfights of any promotion in the country. At first blush, a no-frills wrestler like Benoit seemed wildly out of place in ECW. But his ice-cold in-ring demeanor helped get him over.

"Benoit was so intense. His principles just kind of reeked out of his aura," said Rob Van Dam, who worked alongside Benoit in ECW and also defeated Benoit for the WWE Intercontinental title in 2002. "He just seemed to know how intense he was and the value of that intensity he brought with him."

Chris Benoit was the embodiment of intensity and precision.

PHOTO BY GEORGE NAPOLITANO

In an example of ECW's promoter's ability to find a silver lining in a tornado, Benoit received a major push after an in-ring accident. Benoit threw Sabu, but Sabu bumped awkwardly and suffered a broken neck — a freak accident. Heyman looked to capitalize on the accident and christened Benoit "The Crippler." In February 1995, Benoit and Malenko won the ECW tag team title. Heyman planned to use Benoit as his top heel and main singles titleholder, but when Benoit's work visa expired, he returned to New Japan instead. WCW had a working arrangement with NJPW at the time, and WCW signed Benoit to become part of its burgeoning cruiserweight division.

By 1996, however, Benoit was moved into one of WCW's top storylines as the fourth member of the Four Horsemen, along with Ric Flair, Arn Anderson, and Brian Pillman. While this would have been a career-maker during the days of Jim Crockett Promotions, the WCW executive vice president was more focused on pushing new signee Hulk Hogan and saw the Horsemen as a vestige of a bygone era he had no interest in resurrecting. Benoit was moved into a program with booker Kevin Sullivan that saw Benoit steal Sullivan's real-life wife, Nancy.

Unfortunately, the lines between storyline and real life blurred when Benoit and Nancy began having a very real affair. Remarkably, given the real-life emotions at play, Benoit and Sullivan continued a heated (and very physical) in-ring feud. Benoit moved into a program with Booker T over the TV title and won the WCW tag titles with Malenko in another short-lived Horsemen reunion in 1999. He won the WCW U.S. title twice that year and, in January 2000, finally captured the WCW world title, defeating Sid Vicious for the title at the Souled Out pay-per-view . . . only to surrender the title and quit the company the same night.

Benoit, Malenko, Guerrero, and several other WCW wrestlers had grown increasingly frustrated with their role in WCW. They were the workhorses of the company but were largely shut out of the big-money contracts and main events that went to older stars like Sting, Hulk Hogan, Goldberg, and Kevin Nash. Nash had famously derided Benoit and Guerrero as "vanilla midgets," calling them bland and undersized compared to himself and other WCW main-eventers. Even though WCW had made him the world champion (for what would likely have been a brief reign, given that the WCW world title changed hands 13 times in 1999 and 25 times in 2000), Benoit surrendered the title and walked out of WCW.

Two weeks after winning the WCW title, Benoit (along with Guerrero, Malenko, and Perry Saturn) appeared in the WWF. The faction was dubbed the Radicalz, and all four received a major push out of the gate.

Benoit went on to win the Intercontinental title four times, the tag title four times, the U.S. title three times, and the world title, which he won by defeating Triple H and Shawn Michaels in the main event of *WrestleMania* XX.

WrestleMania XX, on March 14, 2004, seemed to be a symbolic turning point for WWE. Guerrero was the WWE champion (a world title that was excusive to the SmackDown brand). Benoit was the world champion (defended exclusively on *Raw*). Together, the two men, who had built their reputations for their hard work and athleticism in Japan and WCW, had captured the top two titles in pro wrestling. It signified that a new guard had taken over. The top titles in WWE were held by unabashed *wrestlers* — not "sports entertainers," one-dimensional brawlers, or wrestlers whose act had grown stale.

Tragically, 39 months later, both Guerrero and Benoit would be dead.

The circumstances of Benoit's death have been widely chronicled, in books as well as the aforementioned Vice *Dark Side of the Ring* documentary. In June 2007, Benoit killed his wife and seven-year-old son, Daniel, and then he killed himself. In post-mortem testing on Benoit's brain, it was found that he was suffered from advanced chronic traumatic encephalopathy (CTE) due to the many concussions he had suffered throughout his wrestling career. In his report, Dr. Julian Bailes, head of neurosurgery at West Virginia University, said Benoit's brain "resembled the brain of an 85-year-old Alzheimer's patient." That coupled with alcohol, drugs (including a substantial amount of steroids), and domestic issues ignited a latent powder keg that no one knew was smoldering.

Since the details of the murder-suicide became apparent, WWE has avoided mention of Benoit and use of his likeness across company platforms, with very few exceptions. As an in-ring competitor, he was one of the finest of his generation, and one of the most emulated and influential competitors during wrestling's boom period of the late 1990s and early 2000s. His achievements in the ring — while far eclipsed by his crimes — are still recognized, if not celebrated, in the wrestling world.

NICK BOCKWINKEL

He called himself "The Smartest Wrestler Alive," and every time he climbed between the ropes, Nick Bockwinkel taught a master's course in professional wrestling technique and presentation.

Bockwinkel was the AWA's standard-bearer from 1975 through 1987, carrying the company into the post-Gagne era and into the national expansion era of the 1980s. A second-generation wrestler, Bockwinkel was a true student of the sweet science of professional wrestling. The ultimate condescending heel, Bockwinkel exuded a 1970s-era machismo with his suits (the top two buttons of his shirt often undone to show off a manly swath of chest hair), his immaculate hairstyle, and the big gold belt around his waist. "Tricky Nick" was the epitome of the word champion . . . even if the fans wanted to see him get his tail kicked.

Born on December 6, 1934, he grew up in the wrestling hotbed of St. Louis, Missouri. He was raised in wrestling arenas, watching his father, Warren Bockwinkel, take on the likes of Lou Thesz, Buddy Rogers, and Yukon Eric. Nick earned a football scholarship to the University of Oklahoma, but his football career came to a premature end when he suffered a pair of severe knee injuries that both required surgery. With a professional football career out of reach, he gravitated towards wrestling and began training under his father, Wilbur Snyder, and Thesz (who Warren had helped train a few years earlier).

He made his pro debut in 1954 in the Los Angeles territory while working towards a degree in marketing at UCLA. He paid his wrestling dues by doing a variety of jobs for the office, including a stint where he worked as the driver for Yukon Eric, driving Eric's signature convertible around towns to advertise the wrestling shows that night. He wrestled a series of tag matches with his father and also had singles matches against established names like Thesz, Joe Blanchard, Gene LeBell, John Tolos, and Don Leo Jonathan.

Bockwinkel competed as a babyface mainly on the West Coast through the 1950s and early 1960s. He won his first major regional championship in 1963, when he upended Tony Borne for the NWA Pacific Northwest heavyweight title. After successful tours of the Hawaii territory and Jim Barnett's territory in Australia, he was brought into Georgia Championship Wrestling, where he worked his way up into a series of matches against world champions Gene Kiniski and Dory Funk Jr. Bockwinkel gradually turned heel in his feud with Funk, exhibiting frustration at his inability to defeat the champion. To portray himself as a proud, intelligent competitor coming unglued, he relied upon a prop — a well-worn dictionary he carried to enhance his loquacious public persona.

"Webster's Unabridged Dictionary, page 1,348, the far right column, the thirty-sixth word down," Bockwinkel said, brandishing the dictionary. "It is 'Funk.' F-U-N-K. Definition: To retreat in terror, to be afraid, to be not confident." Then he slammed closed the dictionary and stormed off. Simple but effective. Bockwinkel had recast himself as the patronizing and haughty heel that would be his bread and butter for the next decade and a half.

In 1970, Bockwinkel was recruited by Verne Gagne and started up in the AWA in Minneapolis. He was the perfect fit for Gagne — he was an athlete, a solid wrestler, and a marketable and colorful personality. Gagne and Wally Karbo decided to use Bockwinkel as a heel and paired him with Ray "The Crippler" Stevens and manager Bobby "The Brain" Heenan. Stevens, Bockwinkel, and Heenan gelled right away and became the AWA's top heel tandem, winning the AWA tag title three times and having legendary feuds with the Crusher and the Bruiser and the team of Gagne and Billy Robinson.

On November 8, 1975, Bockwinkel defeated Gagne to win the AWA world title in St. Paul, Minnesota, ending Gagne's seven-year world title run. It was a clean pinfall win; the torch had been passed. Bockwinkel held the title until 1980, when he dropped it back to Gagne in Chicago. He was awarded the title in 1981, when Gagne retired as champion. In August 1982, he dropped the belt to Austrian wrestler and promoter

Otto Wanz but won the belt back 41 days later. That third reign lasted until February 1984, when he dropped the title to the up-and-coming Japanese star Jumbo Tsuruta; Terry Funk was the guest referee.

Bockwinkel had plenty of highlights and memorable moments during those reigns. In March 1979, he wrestled WWWF world champion Bob Backlund to a double count-out in a rare champion-versus-champion bout in Toronto. "Nick had a great head for the game, a wonderful sense of ring psychology, and an uncanny ability to use his intelligence and cockiness to get under the people's skin," Backlund wrote in his 2015 auto-biography. "He was a very intelligent, well-spoken, and cocky heel, and his in-ring skills were right up there with the very best in the business."

Few had the swagger, the repertoire, or the vocabulary of the one and only Nick Bockwinkel.

In 1982, Bockwinkel seemingly lost the title to a promising greenhorn by the name of Hulk Hogan only to have the decision reversed after the fact and have the title returned to him. The same thing happened later that year in Memphis with Jerry "The King" Lawler. But Bockwinkel always managed to outsmart the system and came away with the title and even more heat.

Jim Cornette praised Bockwinkel's work on his *Jim Cornette's Drive-Thru* podcast in 2018, following Bockwinkel's passing. "Nick was so good and so fluid. He was such a physical specimen that even at that age — he was almost 50 when he was working with (Jerry) Lawler on top in those matches going 30 minutes or whatever. And he looked so good. He carried himself like a champion. The promo was there because it wasn't over the top. It was believable. You could buy this guy as the best in the business at what he does. He had the confidence. But he could work with anybody.... He could babyface, he could heel, he could sell, and he was fucking vicious when he needed it to look like he was roughing you up, it looked legitimate."

While Bockwinkel was believable as one of the best wrestlers in the world, he himself would admit he wasn't a shooter. "I knew how to wrestle a little bit, but I was not a Danny Hodge in any capacity," he said to Steve Johnson and Greg Oliver in an interview for their book *The Pro Wrestling Hall of Fame: The Heels*, which was conducted long after Bockwinkel had retired; he would never have publicly claimed to be anything other than the best around during his wrestling days. "I worked hard, I worked enthusiastically. I didn't want anybody to see any holes in my work. By that, I mean the guy at ringside, the tenth row of ringside, the fifteenth row of ringside. So I laid them in. Now I didn't lay them in with the knuckles as much as the whole forearm. Well, if you can't take the pounding . . . then God almighty, it's not a sewing circle."

Bockwinkel expanded the footprint of the AWA well behind its Midwest/Minnesota base, defending the title in Houston, San Antonio, Memphis, and Japan.

There was a time when Bockwinkel was considered a viable candidate for the NWA world title, which had a greater national and international exposure and was more lucrative than the AWA could afford. Bockwinkel turned it down. He was content with the AWA schedule and his position. In the cutthroat world of wrestling, saying "no thank you" to an offer to be the highest-paid player in the game is virtually unheard of, but that's the kind of person Bockwinkel was. He was content and confident where he was.

Bockwinkel became AWA world champion a fourth time in 1986, when Stan Hansen was stripped of the title after a despite with Gagne over working dates for All Japan. By that point, Bockwinkel had become a fan favorite. He was an iconic performer who — like Ric Flair — was so good at being bad that eventually the fans just *had* to cheer him to express their appreciation. He held the title for almost 12 months before dropping it to Curt Hennig in a controversial match that saw Larry Zbyszko hand Hennig a roll of dimes to deliver a knockout punch to Bockwinkel. Just a few months before that title change, Bockwinkel (who was just shy of 52 years old) wrestled Henning to a one-hour draw in a match that was shown nationally on ESPN and was referred to by *Wrestling Observer Newsletter* publisher Dave Meltzer as "one of the best matches of the 1980s."

Bockwinkel retired from wrestling shortly after that match, though he did wrestle a handful of exhibition matches in subsequent years. He competed in a "legends battle royal" at a WWF show in November 1987 that was won by Thesz. He faced Billy Robinson in a tense 10-minute exhibition bout for the fledgling Union of Wrestling Force International promotion in Japan in 1992. And in 1993, he wrestled his old NWA rival Dory Funk Jr. to a 15-minute draw at WCW's Slamboree pay-per-view, marking his PPV debut. It was also his final match.

After his wrestling career was done, he had stints with the WWF as a road agent and color commentator. He became on-screen commissioner of WCW in 1994, and later became an on-screen commissioner for the shoot-style Japan Pro Wrestling Alliance. But he was most closely associated with the Cauliflower Alley Club, where he served as president for several years before stepping down in 2014.

He died on November 14, 2015, after a battle with Alzheimer's disease. He was 80 years old.

JACK BRISCO

On September 21, 1941, a Native American legend was born.

A descendant of the Choctaw and Chickasaw tribes of Oklahoma, Jack Brisco would grow to be one of the most gifted and respected wrestlers of all time. Growing up in the small town of Blackwell, Oklahoma, with its population of less than 10,000 people, a young Brisco dreamed of growing up to be like his idol, the great Lou Thesz.

"Jack and I were huge wrestling fans," Jack's brother Jerry said in a 2017 interview with *Pro Wrestling Illustrated*. "My sister worked at the drugstore and she would call us when the new wrestling magazines came in every month, and we'd run down there to be first in line to read them. We couldn't buy them because we couldn't afford the 25 or 30 cents they cost, but we'd read them cover to cover."

He excelled at amateur wrestling and football and, as he matured, he was viewed as one of the state's best high school athletes. After graduating high school, he was offered a football scholarship to the prestigious University of Oklahoma. However, the wrestling coach at Oklahoma State University also had his eye on Brisco. When the wrestling coach discovered that Brisco was a pro wrestling fan, he called in a favor with the local promoter, Leroy McGuirk.

"McGuirk had Grizzly Smith and Big Leroy Brown stop down at our house on their way out to another town, and they told him that if he went out and won a national title at Oklahoma State, McGuirk would have a spot there waiting for him," Jerry said.

Jack enrolled at Oklahoma State and went on to win the NCAA national title in 1965, becoming the first Native American ever to do so. Amazingly, not one opponent that entire season was able to take him down. Later that year, Brisco began his pro wrestling career. In October 1965, Brisco won his first *pro* wrestling title, beating Don Kent for the NWA Missouri junior heavyweight title.

After his trial run in Missouri, McGuirk brought his new protégé to NWA Tri-State and gave him his first big push, having Brisco win both the Oklahoma heavyweight championship and the Arkansas heavyweight championship. McGuirk also turned Brisco into a marketable tag team wrestler, first teaming him with Haystacks Calhoun to win the Tri-State tag team titles, followed by a second run as tag team champions with Gorgeous George Jr.

According to Terry Funk, Jack Brisco was "one of the best amateurs to ever come into this business."

PHOTO COURTESY *PRO WRESTLING ILLUSTRATED*

Brisco was gaining a reputation, and it wasn't long until the big time was calling. Eddie Graham's Championship Wrestling from Florida was a haven for hard-nosed tough guys. Fans were rabid and wild and loved their wrestling. Brisco came in as a different animal: a pure wrestler with a distinguished amateur background.

"Eddie Graham loved wrestling, real wrestling," said Ron Fuller. "He loved to have his guys wrestle a lot. And when he got his hands on Jack Brisco, out of Oklahoma, as a young guy, he said 'This is the direction I want to go,' and pushed him to being world champion. And he emphasized Jack Brisco is not a brawler, Jack was a pure wrestler."

Brisco won the Southern Florida heavyweight title and also the NWA Florida tag team title (with Ciclón Negro), but by 1969 Brisco decided to leave Florida to travel the world. Stops in Japan and Australia followed, and by the time he returned to Florida, two years later, and this time with his younger brother Gerald, whom he had trained, Jack Brisco was experienced and ready to make his true impact.

"He was so fast and he was so smooth," Fuller said. "There were a lot of shooters in the old 'snake pit' (of Championship Wrestling from Florida), and they would try to shoot on Jack, and he was such a good wrestler he was able to get away and out-shoot and beat the shooters. He would fireman's carry. That was his specialty, and he was the best at that move I ever saw. And what made him so good was he could do it from either side. He would tell you if you were shooting, 'I'm going to fireman's carry you, right-handed,' and you knew it was coming but he was so damn good he would still get it. And you know, when you're that good it really impresses guys that are working with you because you're at another level. He was on a level all his own."

Being at that elite level as a grappler and takedown specialist earned him the respect of the locker room, Fuller said.

"Guys didn't want to mess with him," Fuller said. "And also, Jack was a very personable guy, a really nice guy. He was soft-spoken, never raised his voice. And to the fans in Florida he was a god, I mean because they put him over everybody. He beat 'em all over the course of his three or four years (in Florida) while preparing him for that world title. And they were smart. They brought a lot of guys through there who were not part of the normal crew, and they gave them to Jack. Jack got to eat up some of the greats of the business during his run to the world title, so by the time he became champion he was known pretty much everywhere."

Within a few years, Graham's plan was to come to fruition, but with a catch. Brisco had a longstanding feud with Dory Funk Jr. and was scheduled to meet Funk for the title before Dory was hurt in a truck accident.

Dory's younger brother, Terry, was to replace him and face Brisco in several matches, igniting a feud with both brothers. Conspiracy theorists often claim that Funk faked his injury to avoid dropping the belt to Brisco, but regardless of whether that was fact or fiction, it added an intriguing element to what would become a long and profitable "family feud" between the Briscos and the Funks.

While Jack and Terry were traveling around putting on amazing shows, Dory came back and lost the NWA title to Harley Race, who, if the legend is true, Dory felt was a more "face saving" choice to lose to. Be that as it may, soon enough Harley Race did what he was supposed to do: he did the job for Brisco on July 20, 1973, in Houston.

For the next two and a half years, NWA world champion Jack Brisco traveled the territories and the world, defending the belt against some of the biggest names in the business. There was a brief title change in December 1974, when Brisco lost the title in Japan to Giant Baba, the Japanese superstar, only to regain the title one week later by defeating Baba in the rematch.

"Jack realized that to hold that title he had to be the best, not only in Florida, but also worldwide, including Japan and Canada. He took that very seriously," Jerry said.

In December 1975, Brisco defended his title against his old rival Terry Funk in Miami Beach. In a classic match, the younger Funk brother brought the title back to the Funk family, and this helped keep the feud between the two families alive and well for several years to come.

Many people to this day believe there was genuine hatred between the Funks and the Briscos. This is part of what makes them so special. They truly made us believe. The truth is there was nothing but respect between them.

"Jack Brisco was a great, great amateur wrestler. One of the best amateurs to ever come into the business," Terry Funk said. "He was so smooth, so fast, and so slick it was unbelievable. He was a phenom, he really was. And I really mean that about the guy. I loved him. He was so damn good."

After his historic run as NWA champ, Jack Brisco traveled through multiple territories, always making an impact and winning titles wherever he went both as a singles main-eventer and as part of a tag team with his brother Gerald. And Jack was loved and respected everywhere he went. From Georgia, to Puerto Rico, Florida again, and even to Memphis, where he got over on local hero Jerry Lawler.

In the early 1980s, the Brisco brothers had a run in Mid-Atlantic Championship Wrestling, where they feuded with Ricky Steamboat and Jay Youngblood over the tag team title. The feud was one of the featured matches at the first *Starrcade* event, in November 1983, which saw Steamboat and Youngblood defeat the heel Briscos for the NWA tag title.

By 1984, the Brisco brothers had begun to turn their attention to the business side of wrestling and had acquired a minority share in Georgia Championship Wrestling, buying shares from Lester Welch. They, along with several other shareholders, sold their stake in the promotion to Vince McMahon, giving McMahon a foothold on the cable powerhouse SuperStation TBS. Fans in the territory rejected McMahon's entertainment-based style of wrestling, prompting McMahon to eventually sell the time slot to Jim Crockett Promotions, but by orchestrating the initial deal, Jack and Jerry received positions in the WWF, first as wrestlers and then backstage. After a short tag team program against WWF champions Adrian Adonis and Dick Murdoch, Jack decided to retire from the ring in February 1985.

He was inducted into the WWE Hall of Fame in 2008 and is a charter member of the *Wrestling Observer* Hall of Fame. He died in 2010 following open heart surgery.

Jack Brisco came along at a time where wrestlers of Native American heritage were often labelled "Chief" or some other stereotypical "Indian" name, and would wear a headdress and carry a tomahawk while dancing around the ring. Not Jack Brisco. Brisco held his head high, and was simply Jack Brisco, or rather, he was remarkably Jack Brisco, as there was nothing simple about this great performer.

"When you look at Ric Flair, you think of entertainment. When you look at Jack Brisco, you think of wrestling," Gerry said. "His legacy would have to be his consistency — consistently one of the best all-around technical wrestlers ever to set foot in the ring — and his humility. He was as humble as a person could be. He was proud of his ability and he was proud to have the opportunity to elevate the guys around him."

DANIEL BRYAN

For years before he signed with WWE, Daniel Bryan — or, should we say, Bryan Danielson — had already been the consensus choice as the best wrestler in the world.

From 2005 through 2013, Danielson was voted Best Technical Wrestler by readers of the *Wrestling Observer Newsletter*. From 2006 through 2010, he was voted Most Outstanding Wrestler. And, in 2010, he was named Most Outstanding Wrestler of the Decade.

Born May 22, 1981, in Aberdeen, Washington, Danielson became a wrestling fan as a boy, discovering the mat game through wrestling magazines shared by a friend from school. He began watching WWF television on weekends, whenever it didn't conflict with the Seattle Seahawks games that his dad watched on the family's one TV.

By the time he was a senior in high school, he had decided that he was going to set out to become a professional wrestler. Having read several of the mail-order pamphlets on "How to Make it in Wrestling" from the back pages of the wrestling magazines, he had discovered the Malenko School of Wrestling Florida, but since that school had closed, he decided to enlist in Shawn Michaels's Texas Wrestling Academy in San Antonio.

"I spent as much time as I possibly could mentally and physically preparing for wrestling the best I knew how," he wrote in his auto-biography. "I wanted to get in the best shape possible, so I developed my own training regimen, which meant working out on my own time and not during phys ed. I read books on strength training. I worked on bridging to strengthen my neck and worked on backflips because I thought I'd have to be a high-flyer. I bought Japanese and Mexican wrestling tapes through a catalogue I found on the internet. I watched as much wrestling and I could and I wrote down every move I saw in a binder filled with things I wanted to learn."

Danielson negotiated payment terms on the $3,900 tuition and drove the 2,300 miles from Aberdeen to San Antonio. He was part of the academy's first class, which also included Brian Kendrick and Lance Cade. Rudy Gonzalez handled most of the training, but Michaels popped in to keep an eye on the students' development. Michaels gave Danielson the nickname "The American Dragon," saying that he thought he "wrestled like a Japanese guy." Danielson made his pro wrestling debut in December 1999 and, a short time later, went on his first tour of Japan, wrestling some dates for Atsushi Onita's Frontier Martial-Arts Wrestling promotion.

In 2000, he was fast-tracked to a WWF developmental contract and assigned to feeder-system Memphis Championship Wrestling. He won the MCW light heavyweight and tag team titles (with Kendrick) but was released from his WWF contract in July 2001. However, while stationed in Memphis, he met a man who would become a wrestling mentor, William Regal.

"(Regal) introduced us to the European style of wrestling, which was heavily based on submission holds, counters, and advanced mat-based wrestling — something I had never seen before, particularly as it became increasingly more difficult to find European wrestling videotapes that would work in a U.S. VCR," he wrote.

In February 2001, Danielson made it to the finals of the East Coast Wrestling Association Super 8, losing to Low Ki. The Super 8 was widely covered the by the *Pro Wrestling Illustrated* family of magazines and earned Danielson national attention in the same magazines that had sparked his interest in wrestling a decade earlier. In October 2001, he won the second annual All Pro Wrestling King of the Indies tournament, a 16-man event featuring some of the top unsigned young talent in wrestling. With both WCW and ECW having closed down earlier in the year, fans who were unsatisfied with the WWF's brand of sports entertainment were turning to the indies for an alternative, and wrestlers like Danielson were hungry to provide it. Danielson defeated Low Ki in the finals of a tournament that also featured up-and-comers A.J. Styles, Christopher Daniels, and Samoa Joe.

In 2002, Danielson joined the newly established Ring of Honor, where his technical prowess and international influences were appreciated by fans and peers alike. There, he had programs with Austin Aries and Homicide, and balanced tours of Europe and New Japan Pro-Wrestling, where he won the IWGP junior tag team title with Curry Man (Daniels) in 2004.

In 2005, with CM Punk and new ROH champ James Gibson leaving ROH for WWE, ROH booker Gabe Sapolsky decided to make Danielson the centerpiece of ROH. In September 2005, Danielson defeated Gibson for the ROH heavyweight title in Lake Grove, New York. As he began what would be a 462-day title reign, Danielson began exploring the idea of using different moves to end his matches instead of a set "finishing move."

"A standard wrestling trope was that you beat guys with your 'finisher,'" he wrote. "Some guys have two, but very rarely do people have more than a couple of moves that they will actually beat guys with. For the more astute fans, matches become more predictable: They know that even if a wrestler hits another with a big impact move, if it's not his 'finisher,' it won't end the match. I wanted people to think that a match could end at any time."

He began using a variety of moves to retain the title, including referee stoppages, a finish which had become more accepted and understood with casual fans with the rise of UFC. Danielson's talent for counter-wrestling and reversals, and deep moveset honed from his early days of jotting down notes in a binder, was on full display, and he began to develop a reputation as the "best in the world."

"Footing and time work and selling and being there for your opponents. It's stuff like when you're going into a spot, you'll notice he'll always be in the right place so there's no clunkiness," Colt Cabana said, describing what makes Bryan special. "That's why the ebbs and flows are so perfect — because of the wrestler. In the match, the emotion has got to the point where the fans love it, but if you let it dip for a second, it can really ruin the ebb and flow of it. Most people don't realize that. The ones that do are the ones that have been sitting in it and doing it and training in it and performing it for years. Those are the ones that appreciate guys like Bryan that do it."

After dropping the ROH title to Homicide in December 2006, he had memorable feuds with Nigel McGuinness and Takeshi Morishima, and had a brief run as Pro Wrestling NOAH junior heavyweight champion through a working arrangement between ROH and NOAH. In August 2009, Danielson — having won worldwide acclaim for his run in ROH and internationally — signed a new deal with WWE. However, after a brief stint in the Florida Championship Wrestling feeder system, he was brought up to the main roster not as an internationally proven superstar but as a "rookie" on WWE's newest series, NXT.

Now known as Daniel Bryan, he was paired with a "pro," the Miz, ostensibly to show him the ropes of the big leagues of WWE. Along with seven other developmental talents and their "pros," Bryan had to compete for a roster spot. Fans familiar with Bryan's body of work were outraged — it was like asking Derek Jeter to prove himself on a high school team and to sell his share of fundraising candy bars before giving him a shot. Each week, announcer Michael Cole would downplay Bryan's accomplishments on the independents and portray him as bland, nerdy, and uncharismatic. Instead, it made Bryan the most sympathetic figure on the show.

In June 2010, Bryan was a part of WWE's top angle as he and the rest of the NXT "rookies" savagely attacked John Cena and destroyed the ringside area to end an episode of *Raw*. In part of the orchestrated anarchy of the segment, Bryan "strangled" ring announcer Justin Roberts with his own necktie. That crossed the line with WWE, who fired him for "excessive violence," fearing it would offend advertisers.

Bryan returned to the independents, where he was touted tongue-in-cheek as being "too violent for WWE." But he was brought back to WWE just two months later as the mystery partner of John Cena's Team WWE against the Nexus, his former NXT teammates. One month later, he defeated his former NXT "pro," the Miz, to win the U.S. title.

In December 2011, Bryan won the world title by cashing in his *Money in the Bank* title shot and pinning the Big Show. He made a gradual heel turn, acting overconfident and mistreating his valet, AJ Lee, and lost the title at *WrestleMania* 28 when he was pinned by Sheamus after an

18-second match. While Bryan held the world title, that championship was presented as a lesser title than the top prize in the company, the WWE title. Bryan moved into a feud with CM Punk over the WWE title, then into an "odd couple" pairing with Kane dubbed "Team Hell No." Bryan and Kane exhibited tremendous chemistry, and their hug-it-out antics and backstage skits got the team over big with fans.

In the summer of 2013, Bryan was quickly becoming WWE's most popular competitor. Accompanied by the bombastic strains of "Ride of the Valkyries," Bryan would gallop down the entrance ramp, pumping his arms in the air and chanting "Yes!" The fans followed suit, and arenas across the country were packed with fans chanting "Yes!" in unison. In acknowledgement of Bryan's rising popularity (despite his not having received a major push from WWE to that point), Cena selected Bryan as his opponent for SummerSlam 2013. Bryan defeated Cena to win the WWE title, only to have special referee Triple H attack him immediately after the bout, allowing Randy Orton to steal the title.

In a promo the following night, Stephanie McMahon denigrated Bryan as a "B-plus player." It was a particularly effective promo, because it contained more than a grain of truth. "Really, Daniel, you're like what, five-foot-eight? Maybe 200 pounds? And, well, we can't all be supermodels," McMahon said. She claimed Triple H orchestrated the title change because it was "best for business." Bryan didn't have the look or aura of the typical WWE standard-bearer. Bryan was cast as "the ultimate underdog," and the fans responded in spades. Bryan was the everyman battling against the Authority.

At *WrestleMania* XXX, Bryan defeated Triple H in a grudge match to earn his way into the WWE championship main event between Randy Orton and Batista later that night. In the main event, Bryan submitted Batista to win the WWE title, the culmination of what WWE billed as "The Yes! Movement."

Bryan's reign would last only two months, as he was forced to vacate the title due to injury. He was out of action until January 2015, and when he returned, he was slotted firmly back into the midcard, out of the WWE Championship picture.

"I think the hearts and minds of the wrestling fans are with Daniel Bryan," Bret Hart said in a 2015 interview with *Live Audio Wrestling*.

"His workrate in the ring and what he gives through the match just means so much more to the wrestling fans than anything else."

Throughout 2015, Bryan was plagued by a series of injuries and, in February 2016, he announced his retirement due to the cumulative effects of at least 10 known concussions throughout his wrestling career.

Bryan spent two years as the on-screen SmackDown general manager, then — after consulting with a string of doctors — he was cleared to return to the ring in March 2018. Remarkably, after being one of WWE's most popular stars and an incredible comeback story, Bryan was able to make a successful heel turn and won the WWE Championship once more in November 2018, beating A.J. Styles. As an evil environmentalist character, he debuted a new version of the WWE title made of wood, hemp, and other environmentally sustainable materials. He also adjusted his ring style to avoid the big, high-risk bumps and shots to the head.

Because of the depth of his wrestling moveset and his incredible versatility, Bryan had enjoyed a hall-of-fame-caliber career. He remains one of the most influential and imitated wrestlers in the game today.

THE DYNAMITE KID

"All I ever wanted was to be the best wrestler I could be. I wasn't interested in gimmicks, or being a great talker; I wanted to be remembered for my ability in the ring."

—Tom Billington, from his autobiography, *Pure Dynamite: The Price You Pay for Wrestling Stardom.*

By his own admission, Tom Billington could be a cruel and evil human being. He once held a shotgun to his ex-wife's head during an argument (whether or not it was loaded depends on whose story you choose to believe). He was well known for mean-spirited "ribs" that under today's standards would be considered bullying, harassment, and assault.

But inside the ring as the Dynamite Kid, he changed the face of wrestling and became one of the most influential pro wrestlers of all time.

"The modern WWE style, the modern style of professional wrestling, is very largely based on what Dynamite Kid did," Daniel Bryan said in a 2019 interview with Sky Sports. "He changed the landscape for what it means to be a small man in professional wrestling. He wasn't necessarily a super high-flyer in that era. Sayama, who was the Tiger Mask, he was doing more high-flying stuff. Dynamite Kid was just so intense and aggressive, and that's something I try to transfer into my wrestling all the time."

"Every wrestler under 200lbs likely owes a debt of gratitude to The Dynamite Kid," Lance Storm tweeted following Billington's death in 2019. "He inspired so many and help(ed) change the sport. In the ring he was incredible."

Billington was born on December 5, 1958, in Golborne, Lancashire, a stone's throw away from the infamous wrestling town of Wigan. He was born into a family of boxers: his grandfather had been a bare-knuckle fighter. As a boy, he excelled in wrestling and gymnastics and trained in boxing. He began attending wrestling shows in Wigan and was drawn to the sport. It was, after all, a much more appealing profession than working in the coal mines. He began training under Ted Betley and wrestled his first match in December 1975 for promoter Max Crabtree at the age of 17.

He captured the British lightweight title in April 1977 and won the welterweight title in January 1978. Already a highly touted youngster in England, he caught the eye of Bruce Hart, who arranged to bring him into Stu Hart's Stampede promotion in 1978.

"Stampede Wrestling was dying and Stu Hart was about to shut it down," Heath McCoy, author of *Pain and Passion: The History of Stampede Wrestling*, said in a 2018 interview with the *Calgary Sun*. "Bruce Hart saw (a) skinny, young Dynamite Kid wrestle in England and was so blown away by his performance that he begged his father to bring the kid to Calgary. Stu took one look at Dynamite's tiny frame and wanted nothing to do with him, at first, until he saw Billington wrestle. He was explosive, agile, dynamic, high-flying, and like nothing the Harts or, for that matter, western Canadian wrestling fans, had seen before."

"I met him in the late 1970s. He was skinny and understated at cutting promos, like most of those British guys were, but he was so good in ring making guys look good," Bruce Hart said. "About three-quarters of what he did in the ring was about getting the other guy over. Most of the bumps he took were designed to make who he was working with look good. I remember more than a few times working with Dynamite and you would give him these spectacular arm drags or throw him into the turnbuckle, and he would go in upside-down. After that, when you work with a mere mortal who wasn't capable of making it look that good, the fans would come up to you like you had a night off or weren't really trying. In those so-called pre-kayfabe days, Dynamite could make you look better than you deserved to look."

At five-foot-eight and about 160 pounds, Billington found himself undersized compared to the top stars in Stampede, and he began using the steroid Dianabol to bulk up. It was the beginning of a long relationship with steroids and other drugs that would affect him for the rest of his life.

In June 1978, he was crowned Stampede's British Commonwealth mid-heavyweight champion, a title basically designed to showcase him against light heavyweight opponents. He would hold this title four times between 1978 and 1980. In July 1979, he made his first tour of Japan for International Pro Wrestling, then started with New Japan in 1980 after Hart and Inoki developed a working relationship. The Dynamite Kid felt at home in Japan, where workrate and effort were valued by fans and promoters alike.

"Unless you were six-foot-six and built like a brick shithouse, you have to work very hard to keep your place on the card . . . standards of wrestling were definitely higher in Japan, for the simple reason that good wrestlers were in the majority," he later wrote.

It was in New Japan that the Dynamite Kid clashed with the original Tiger Mask, Satoru Sayama. The pair put on incredibly fast-paced contests filled with aerial attacks, lightning-quick reversals, and innovative moves, and the entire wrestling world took notice. An August 1982 bout between the two was voted Match of the Year by subscribers of the *Wrestling Observer Newsletter*. It was the first in a string of accolades for the Kid from readers of the *Observer*. He was voted Most Underrated (1993), Most Impressive Wrestler (1983, 1984, and 1985), Best Technical Wrestler (1984, tied with Masa Saito), and Hardest Worker (1983). The series against Tiger Mask caused a huge boom in the popularity of the junior heavyweight division. It made the matches between plodding heavyweights — matches loaded with rest holds and stalling — look like they were happening underwater. The entire wrestling business had to adjust its game.

"The whole junior heavyweight division really stems from (Dynamite Kid and Tiger Mask) getting over," Dave Meltzer said in a 2018 appearance on the *Talk Is Jericho* podcast. "With you (Jericho), you had to combat being smaller early in your career, but . . . he had it 10 times worse because there was no Dynamite Kid when he started. You at least (had) guys who had made it that were already there, but . . . he shows up in the dressing room of Madison Square Garden and he's 175 pounds legit and everyone there is 240. And he walks in and they're all laughing at him, right? Here's a guy who is on the show because New Japan sent him. It's not like he's a WWF guy. And then he goes out there and out-works everyone by 10 times. He had that built-in resentment.

"He had that chip on his shoulder that made him such an incredible performer because he had to prove himself," Meltzer said.

"Smart" fans all over were watching the Dynamite Kid, and they were impressed. His crisp offense had a sort of poetry about it. The snap suplexes were delivered with an explosive pop of the hips. The way he hit the ropes and came crashing, flying back had an aggressive edge, as if he had been fired out of a cannon. His reversals (cartwheeling through a wristlock to create space and then seizing the inside wrist and reversing the hold) happened with such speed and grace that they were literally breathtaking. In their series, Dynamite and Tiger Mask managed to blend American-style pro wrestling with British catch-as-catch-can, Lucha-style acrobatics, and Japanese-style intensity and athleticism in a way no one had done before.

"There's something I was taught when I was training, and that's 'no wasted movement.' An example they would always give would be Dynamite Kid," said Colt Cabana. "There's no wasted movement. Sometimes there's a lot of wasted movement of just getting to a place or meeting someone somewhere in the ring. If you're good, you sell into a position where once that person is ready to go into something, you don't have to clunk around. Your opponent is right there. That wrestler is there to set you up for it so you can ride the momentum of the match and you're not wasting time or hurting the momentum of the match. Dynamite Kid was the model of how to do it right."

On February 7, 1984, Kid won a tournament to win the WWF junior heavyweight title, a title that had made its way to Japan in 1978 and was defended in New Japan. He held the title for nine months until he signed with the WWF, vacating the title and leaving NJPW. In his first televised match after signing, Kid teamed with his brother-in-law, Bret Hart. However, instead of keeping the former Stampede rivals together as a team, the WWF put Kid with his cousin, Davey Boy Smith, while Hart was teamed with another brother-in-law, Jim Neidhart.

The Bulldogs were quickly pushed by the WWF, winning the tag team title at *WrestleMania 2*, defeating Greg Valentine and Brutus Beefcake as heavy metal icon Ozzy Osbourne cheered them on from their corner. The Bulldogs became one of the most popular acts in the WWF, and their flashy style, speed, and teamwork set them apart from slower teams like Valentine and Beefcake and Nikolai Volkoff and the Iron Sheik.

The Dynamite Kid (right, next to his brother-in-law, Davey Boy Smith) revolutionized light-heavyweight and tag team wrestling in the early 1980s.

PHOTO BY GEORGE NAPOLITANO

Dynamite's life would change in an instant on the evening of December 13, 1986. The Bulldogs were defending the tag title against Bob Orton Jr. and Don Muraco in Hamilton, Ontario. It was a routine house show match until Kid suffered a freak injury. As he came off the ropes, Orton dropped down to the mat. Dynamite jumped over him but landed awkwardly and immediately felt a sharp, intense pain in his back. He continued into the ropes, where Muraco (standing on the apron) landed a soft, worked knee to his back. Dynamite crumpled to the mat in agony. Unable to stand, he dragged himself to the corner and managed to tag in Smith who finished the match while Dynamite remained prone on the mat.

Dynamite underwent surgery but defied doctors' orders and returned to the ring just one month later so he and Smith could drop the tag belts to the Hart Foundation. Barely able to stand under his own power, Dynamite was carried to the ring by Smith and was "knocked out" by a megaphone shot by Jimmy Hart at the start of the match, allowing him to lie on the floor at ringside for the entire "match."

Kid remained with the WWF until late 1988, but he was nowhere near the same wrestler as he had once been. He compensated for his lack of mobility with an overabundance of steroids (bulking up to a freakish level, given his frame) and painkillers. He became exactly what he did not want to be: a gimmick wrestler, complete with a mascot, Matilda the bulldog, that would accompany the team to the ring.

In November 1988, following a backstage skirmish with Jacques Rougeau (Rougeau sucker-punched Dynamite with a roll of quarters as payback for his bullying behavior, causing Dynamite to lose several teeth), the Bulldogs left the WWF and returned to what remained of Stampede Wrestling.

When Smith returned to the WWF for a singles run in 1990, Dynamite began teaming with Johnny Smith as the British Bruisers in All Japan Pro Wrestling. However, the injuries and drug abuse had taken a heavy toll and, in 1991, he announced his retirement. He returned to the ring for a time in the early 1990s and wrestled his final match in October 1996, teaming with Dos Caras and Kuniaki Kobayashi against Tiger Mask, Mil Máscaras, and the Great Sasuke in Tokyo.

By the end of the 1990s, Billington was confined to a wheelchair due to the cumulative spinal injuries sustained during his career. He published his controversial but fascinating and unapologetic autobiography, *Pure Dynamite,* in 2001. He died on his 60th birthday, December 5, 2018.

"The legacy of the Dynamite Kid is a complex one to digest," Dave Melzer wrote. "Perhaps the most succinct way of putting it came from Julie Hart, his former sister-in-law, who one day told me, 'Really, he was the best wrestler there ever was . . . And as great as he was as a wrestler, he was every bit as miserable of a human being.'"

RIC FLAIR

Buddy Rogers may have been the original "Nature Boy," but Ric Flair was the one who introduced us to Space Mountain and the stylin', profilin', limousine-ridin', jet-flyin', kiss-stealin', wheelin'-and-dealin' lifestyle we associate with "The Nature Boy."

According to WWE's count, Flair was a 16-time world champion, but if you choose to count some of the unacknowledged title switches and reversals, the number rises up into the 20s. He was named Wrestler of the Decade for the 1980s, over Hulk Hogan, by *Pro Wrestling Illustrated*. Hogan epitomized the cartoonish, gimmicky musclemen of the 1980s. Flair epitomized old-fashioned *wrestling* — 60-minute matches, masterful storytelling, and the fine art of drawing heat.

Fittingly for a worker of his caliber, his "retirement match" (technically, he wrestled a handful of matches afterward for TNA, but those are best left forgotten) against Shawn Michaels at *WrestleMania* XXIV was voted Match of the Year by *PWI* readers; he was 59 years old.

For two decades, Flair represented the standard of excellence in professional wrestling. He carried the NWA banner through the 1980s, through the transition from Jim Crockett Promotions to Ted Turner's World Championship Wrestling. He had a pair of world title runs in the WWF in the early 1990s, then returned to WCW, where he remained a featured star until the promotion closed in 2001. He returned to the WWF as a living legend, maintaining a high-profile position as a wrestler, on-air authority figure, and manager. Few wrestlers can match Flair's star quality, list of championships, or effect on popular culture.

Born February 25, 1949, he was adopted by Dr. Reid and Kathleen Fliehr through the Tennessee Children's Home Society. This was an organization run by the notorious child trafficker Georgia Tann and was actually a black-market baby-selling scam that ran for nearly 30 years. Richard Fliehr grew up in Minnesota, where he grew into a high school athlete, participating in wrestling (winning the private-school state title), football, and track and field. He attended the University of Minnesota on a football scholarship but dropped out and began working as a bouncer.

In 1972, Fliehr enrolled in Verne Gagne's training camp outside of Minneapolis, where he trained alongside fellow students Greg Gagne, the Iron Sheik, Ken Patera, and Jim Brunzell. He wrestled his first pro match in December 1972 for Gagne's AWA.

"I actually had his second match, and even then he was pretty good — at least the match we were in got over," said Baron Von Raschke. "Then he got that break down in the Carolinas with the Crocketts and they really liked him, and he worked really hard and he really blossomed."

Flair completed his first tour of Japan the following year, wrestling for the International Wrestling Enterprise promotion, which had a talent exchange agreement with Gagne.

In 1974, Flair left Gagne's AWA and started working in the Mid-Atlantic territory for NWA promoter Jim Crockett. In February 1975, he defeated Paul Jones to win the Mid-Atlantic TV title, his first singles championship. Flair had made the big time, but it almost ended as soon as it began. On October 4, 1975, Flair — along with David Crockett, "Mr. Wrestling" Tim Woods, Johnny Valentine, and Bob Bruggers were on a plane that crashed in Wilmington, North Carolina. The pilot was killed and Valentine was left paralyzed, while Flair had his back broken in three places. It wasn't clear if Flair would ever walk again, and the doctors said there was no way he would be able to wrestle again. But Flair was determined. After 32 weeks of recovery and rehabilitation, he was able to resume his budding wrestling career.

The injury forced him to modify his ring style. Flair had been a brawler — a hard-nosed tough guy, a bad-ass. This wouldn't fly with his new physical limitations, so he used his brain as well as his brawn and he morphed into the new "Nature Boy." He started using Buddy Rogers's technique, his psychology, his mannerisms, and even his famous submission move, the figure-four leglock. He won the NWA U.S. title in July 1977, a title he would hold five times between 1977 and 1980.

Flair's use of the Nature Boy nickname led to a bout against Buddy Rogers. "The Battle of the Nature Boys" took place on July 8, 1979, in Greensboro, North Carolina. Flair won the bout, successfully defending the U.S. title over the original "Nature Boy."

"Rogers put Flair over because it was good for business," Terry Funk said. "Buddy knew what was good and what was right. Plus, Ric was very respectful of Buddy. I'm sure that helped, because Buddy would have spit in his eye if he wasn't."

The win over the former world champion gave Flair credibility in the fans' eyes and helped elevate the prestige of the U.S. title. In addition to his U.S. title runs, Flair had world tag title reigns with Greg Valentine and with Blackjack Mulligan. But Flair's skill on the microphone was getting attention.

"What got Flair over more than anything were his interviews. His interviews were unbelievable," said Buddy Colt.

"Ric could talk. Boy, he was a wild one," Funk said. "Lots of energy, never knew how he didn't lose his voice. You've got to remember, he did that stuff in every city. We had some good matches, too. Flair was a better worker than people give him credit for, but he was wild. Lots of guys were then, but he really liked to have a good time."

On September 17, 1981, Flair defeated Dusty Rhodes to win the NWA world title in Kansas City. Lou Thesz was the special referee. Officially, Flair's first reign lasted until June 1983, when he dropped the belt to Harley Race, though in actuality, Fair had lost and regained the belt to Rhodes (as the Midnight Rider in Florida), Jack Veneno (on a tour of the Dominican Republic), Carlos Colón (in Puerto Rico), and Victor Jovica (in Trinidad), but none of those "title changes" were acknowledged on television. All of those matches built up the local babyfaces and gave them credibility by having them "beat the champ," ensuring good business going forward, even if the NWA world champion wasn't on the card. Throughout his reigns, Flair played a vital role in helping to build up the NWA territories while still managing to keep the spotlight on himself and not losing any of his drawing power.

Flair, now a full-fledged babyface after a heated feud with former tag partner Valentine, defeated Race to regain the title on November 24, 1984, in the main event of the NWA's inaugural *Starrcade* supercard, fittingly dubbed "A Flair for the Gold." Gene Kiniski served as the special referee for the championship bout.

Flair and Race traded the world title again in the spring of 1984, then, in May 1984, Flair defended the title against Kerry Von Erich at Texas Stadium. The World Class territory was still reeling from the death of David Von Erich, who died of enteritis while on a tour of All Japan on February 10. David's name had been brought up as a potential world champion. After his passing, Fritz Von Erich used his influence with the NWA to bring in Flair to face his son Kerry in the main event of the David Von Erich Memorial Parade of Champions event. Flair put on Erich over in front of an announced crowd of 50,123, providing a feel-good moment and an explosive pop when Kerry pinned his shoulders to the mat with a backslide. Flair regained the title two weeks later in Yokosuka, Japan.

In 1985, Flair partnered up with Ole and Arn Anderson, Tully Blanchard, and Tully's manager, J.J. Dillon, to form the Four Horsemen, the heel stable by which all other heel stables since are measured. Ostensibly formed to protect Flair's world title, the Horsemen — decked out in tailored suits and finery — were wrestling's version of Gordon Gekko from the movie *Wall Street*. With the Horsemen by his side, Flair took his promos to a new level. "Diamonds are forever, and so is Ric Flair," he would say. And, in a phrase he would use as the title of his autobiography, "To be the Man, you have to beat the Man."

Flair feuded with working-class heroes like Rhodes, Ron Garvin, the Road Warriors, Ricky Steamboat, and Sting through the late 1980s and into the 1990s. In 1991, Flair left WCW after refusing to take a pay cut and change his gimmick, which the new WCW President, Jim Herd, had ordered. In August 1991 — in a truly shocking moment at the time — Flair showed up on WWF television with the WCW world title belt (he had been stripped of the title but still had physical possession of the "ten pounds of gold" physical belt itself). Meanwhile, WCW attendance dwindled and fans loudly chanted "We Want Flair" at WCW events. Calling himself "The Real World Champion," Flair was positioned for a "dream match" series against Hogan.

Somehow, however, Vince McMahon dropped the ball on the biggest bout of its era. After drawing disappointing attendance on a handful of

*The Ric Flair/Ricky
Steamboat series is still
widely considered to
be the gold standard in
classic match-ups.*

PHOTO BY GEORGE NAPOLITANO

house shows (without any angle to build), McMahon got cold feet over
having Hogan versus Flair headline *WrestleMania*. Perhaps he didn't want
to portray a "WCW wrestler" as being a credible opponent to Hogan.
Instead, Hogan was stripped of the title after a controversial match with
newcomer the Undertaker, and Flair won the vacant title by winning the
1992 Royal Rumble. Flair lost the belt to Randy Savage at *WrestleMania*,
won it back five months later, and then dropped it to Bret Hart on a
house show in October 1992. He jumped back to WCW in January 1993
without the big "dream match" against Hogan ever taking place.

Flair returned to WCW as a huge fan favorite. He feuded with
Barry Windham, Rick Rude, and Big Van Vader and resumed his place
as world champion. But, in 1994, new WCW executive producer Eric
Bischoff signed Hogan to WCW and looked to push Hogan over Flair,
believing Flair had grown stale on top. It was the start of a contentious
and volatile relationship between Flair and Bischoff that would last

until the dying days of WCW. Hogan defeated Flair for the world title in July 1994.

In 1995, the Horsemen reunited (this time as Flair, Arn Anderson, Brian Pillman, and Chris Benoit). He had five brief WCW world title reigns between 1995 and 2000, the longest being a 71-day reign in 1996, the shortest being a one-night reign in 2000, when the title was switched almost every week.

He returned to the WWF in 2001, after WCW folded, as an on-air authority figure and later served as the manager of Triple H's Evolution stable. He had a short Intercontinental title reign and three tag title runs (two with Batista and one with Roddy Piper). In 2008, McMahon booked Flair in a storyline where he would have to retire with his next loss. After pulling off some upset wins, Flair was booked to face Shawn Michaels in a "career-threatening match" at *WrestleMania* XXIV. In an emotional classic, a reluctant Michaels took down his hero with a super-kick, forcing Flair into retirement.

In 2010, Flair jumped to TNA Wrestling as a manager and occasional wrestler. However, it was sadly apparent that Flair was well past his prime as a performer. He later called his time in TNA "the biggest regret of his career," feeling he should have hung up the boots for good following the loss to Michaels. Officially, his final match took place on September 12, 2011, with a loss to Sting in Orlando.

Among his lengthy list of accomplishments, Flair had five matches voted Match of the Year by *PWI* readers and four matches voted Match of the Year by readers of the *Wrestling Observer*. He is a member of every wrestling hall of fame there is and is widely considered to be the greatest wrestler of the second half of the 20th century. Still, Flair has his critics who say all of his matches follow the same script.

"Ric has never been able to do anything but his one routine match, which consists of cartoon high spots borrowed from Jackie Fargo and midget wrestlers, along with an assortment of tired old ripped off Buddy Rogers' high spots. My dad always called Flair a 'routine man' — because he did the exact same routine every night and was forever stuck with it," Bret Hart wrote in a 2004 online column.

Others have criticized aspects of Flair's game, including the repetitive signature spots, although during his early days on top, his matches weren't shown on national television and it was less noticeable if he was repeating spots from match to match. Still, Flair had a masterful ability to make any opponent look like a world-beater. From Sting and Lex Luger to Ricky Morton, Nikita Koloff, Kerry Von Erich, and many, many more, Flair was able to make stars, go the distance, and keep fans coming back like very few others.

BRET HART

His catchphrase was "I am the best there is, the best there was, and the best there ever will be." And, while the veracity of that particular claim might be subject to debate, there's no question that Bret "The Hitman" Hart is near the top of the list of the all-time greats.

Born July 2, 1957, Bret was the eighth child of Stu and Helen Hart. Stu had grown up in poverty and had carved out a livelihood in wrestling, first as an amateur (having qualified for the 1940 Olympics, which were ultimately cancelled due to World War II) and then as a professional, starting in New York for Toots Mondt before buying into his own promotion in his native Calgary, which would become Stampede Wrestling.

Wrestling was near and dear to the Hart family, and Bret followed in the footsteps of his father and older brothers Smith, Bruce, Keith, Wayne, Dean, and Ross, starting amateur wrestling at the age of nine. He joined the high school wrestling team "for the sole reason that my dad expected me to . . . no one asked me to," he said in the 2005 WWE-produced documentary *The Bret Hart Story*.

Like many second-generation wrestlers, Bret was immersed in pro wrestling growing up: the Harts had wrestlers coming to their home, training with Stu down in the basement "Dungeon," where Stu would stretch aspiring wrestlers and the Hart children could hear their screams of agony coming up through the heating vents. Wrestling was not their dad's job; it was their daily life.

Bret excelled as an amateur, becoming a collegiate champion at Mount Royal College by 1977. He was also helping the family business by working as a referee for Stampede, and eventually, his interest in becoming a pro wrestler overpowered his desire to continue college or a potential berth in the Olympics. He wrestled his first pro match in 1978 as a stand-in when another wrestler was unable to compete.

Bret worked tag team matches with his brother Keith but was often used as an undercard babyface putting over other talent. Hart took pride in his ability to sell, but he could also match elite wrestlers move for move. By the early 1980s, Bret had developed into one of Stampede's most versatile and valuable wrestlers, with multiple runs as British Commonwealth mid-heavyweight champion, international tag team champion, and North American heavyweight champion.

In December 1983, Bret was teamed with Davey Boy Smith and Sonny Two Rivers in a six-man tag match against Bad News Allen (one of Bret's top in-ring rivals in Stampede), the Stomper, and Jeff Gouldie at the Victoria Pavilion in Calgary when a riot broke out during the match. The City of Calgary shut down Stampede for a six-month period, and for Stu Hart, the time seemed right to finally work with Vince McMahon, who was buying out established territories in his quest to take the WWF international. Stu sold Stampede to McMahon in the summer of 1984, and McMahon took Bret, Smith, Jim Neidhart, and the Dynamite Kid, all of whom had been working for Stampede.

Hart was paired with Neidhart in a tag team and put with manager "The Mouth of the South" Jimmy Hart in the Hart Foundation, while Smith and Kid were paired as the British Bulldogs, managed by Captain Lou Albano. Hart adopted the nickname "The Hitman" (inspired by boxer Thomas "Hitman" Hearns), while Neidhart was dubbed "The Anvil." In January 1987, the Hart Foundation defeated the British Bulldogs to win the WWF tag team title (the Dynamite Kid had previously been injured, making the title change a necessity). With the aid of "crooked referee" and eventual Hart Foundation member Danny Davis, the Hart Foundation (and their Hart Attack elevated clothesline lariat double-team finisher) ran roughshod over the Federation's top babyface tandems, including the Bulldogs, Jacques and Raymond Rougeau, the Killer Bees (B. Brian Blair and Jim Brunzell), and the Can-Am Connection (Rick Martel and Tom Zenk). They held the tag belts until October 1987, dropping them to Strikeforce (Martel and Tito Santana).

Hart was beginning to show promise as a singles competitor, even though, at six feet and about 220 pounds, he was considered too small to be a viable singles competitor in the WWF at that time. Hart and Randy Savage put on an impressive singles match on a November 1987 edition of *Saturday Night's Main Event.* Then, in January 1988, Hart was the "iron man" in the 1988 Royal Rumble, lasting nearly 26 minutes. But Hart's true WWF singles career took off at *WrestleMania* IV, where he and Bad News Brown were the last two men standing in a battle royal. After seemingly agreeing to share the victory and split the winnings, Brown sucker-punched Hart with a "Ghetto Blaster" enzuigiri and tossed him out of the ring. An enraged Hart smashed the massive trophy for the match, igniting a hot feud between Hart and Brown, rekindling their program from Stampede. Hart had become a babyface.

Hart and Neidhart continued teaming, regaining the tag belts in August 1990 with a win over Demolition (consisting of Smash and Crush). But Hart received a few scattered singles opportunities and shined in matches against Curt Hennig, Shawn Michaels, Randy Savage, and Rick Martel (including a 20-minute draw at Madison Square Garden). The Hart Foundation lost the belts to the Jimmy Hart–managed Nasty Boys at *WrestleMania* VII, and the team disbanded shortly afterward.

In August 1991, Hart won his first WWF singles title, beating Hennig for the Intercontinental title at SummerSlam. Ironically, Hennig was suffering from a back injury and needed to drop the belt, just as the Dynamite Kid had four years earlier. Hart went on to win the King of the Ring tournament, giving him further credibility as IC champion. He dropped the belt in an upset to the Mountie (Jacques Rougeau doing a silly RCMP gimmick), but that led to Hart beating Roddy Piper (who had won the belt from Rougeau) for the championship in a rare babyface-versus-babyface match at *WrestleMania* VIII.

On August 29, 1992, Hart lost the title to his brother-in-law, Davey Boy Smith, in the main event of the *SummerSlam* pay-per-view held at Wembley Stadium in London before an announced attendance of 80,355. Hart and Smith delivered an absolute classic of a match, with Smith countering a sunset flip into a cradle for the out-of-nowhere pinfall. The match was voted Match of the Year by readers of *Pro Wrestling Illustrated,* and Hart has called it his favorite match of his career.

"Bret didn't just do moves to do moves. Everything he did meant something," said former WWE referee Jimmy Korderas. "It was part of his, for lack of a better term, storytelling in the match. He didn't just drop an elbow because he could. He didn't do that snap legdrop just because he knew it looked good. He did it because it fit in the context of the match and the context of the story he was telling during that match. It wasn't, 'Hey, I can do a diving headbutt off the top rope.' He could do all that stuff, but he didn't do it because it didn't fit his character and it didn't fit the way he wanted to present himself."

"The Excellence of Execution." Bret Hart traps Mankind in a sharpshooter.

PHOTO BY GEORGE NAPOLITANO

In October 1992, with Ric Flair's WWF contract nearing its end, Vince McMahon made the decision to put the WWF world title on Hart, but the title switch didn't come on a pay-per-view, or even with any advance build-up. On October 12, 1992, Hart defeated Flair on a house show in Saskatoon, Saskatchewan. The match was included on the WWF's home video series to try to drive sales in videocassettes as a revenue stream. Hart proved to be a popular world champion, though with the WWF's overall business in a downturn, he drew significantly less than previous babyface world champions Hulk Hogan and Randy Savage. Hart was set up to be a transitional champion, dropping the belt to Yokozuna at *WrestleMania* IX, setting the stage for Hogan to beat Yokozuna in an impromptu championship match immediately afterward.

But Hogan, wrestling a part-time schedule and looking virtually deflated after getting off steroids in light of the federal government's impending investigation of the WWF, was a flop as champion. McMahon picked Lex Luger as the heir apparent, giving Luger a major push and building for a big-money "Hogan versus Andre"–style title match. Hart won his second King of the Ring tournament and was slotted into a program with Jerry "The King" Lawler. Yet despite McMahon's heavy-handed push and a red-white-and-blue-themed bus tour across the country, the fans never quite took to Luger. McMahon decided to hedge his bets.

At the 1994 Royal Rumble, Hart and Luger were the last two competitors and went over the top rope simultaneously. They were declared "co-winners" and both received a title shot at *WrestleMania* X. In the weeks leading to the match, it was apparent that Hart was receiving louder reactions from fans at live events, and Hart was a much more versatile and talented pure wrestler.

At *WrestleMania* X, Bret opened the show facing his "estranged" brother, Owen. Owen got the pin over his brother in a tremendous technical bout. Luger got the first crack at the world title but lost to Yokozuna by DQ. In the main event, Hart defeated Yokozuna to become a two-time world champion. A feud with Owen was already set to go.

Hart would have three more reigns as WWF world champion. He proved to be both an effective babyface and an effective heel, making an unforgettable heel turn in his *WrestleMania* 13 "submission match" against Steve Austin, a match that would get the five-star ranking by Dave Meltzer. By 1997, Hart had formed a new Hart Foundation with Owen, Neidhart, Smith, and Brian Pillman. Hart was an anti-American heel yet was still very much a hero in his native Canada, locked in a feud with Shawn Michaels. Real-life bad blood between Hart and Michaels festered, but they still delivered magic every time they stepped between the ropes together.

Hart had been so valuable to the WWF that McMahon had locked him into a 20-year deal in 1996, but McMahon — losing the ratings war against WCW — was having buyer's remorse. McMahon encouraged Hart to accept a deal with WCW to cut costs. Hart worked out a three-year, $2.5 million deal with WCW but balked when McMahon asked him to drop the belt to Michaels in Montreal. In what has become known as "The Montreal Screwjob," McMahon had referee Earl Hebner prematurely ring the bell when Michaels had Hart locked in the Sharpshooter submission hold at the 1997 Survivor Series, ending the match early and making Michaels the new champion. Following the match, Hart spit in McMahon's face and allegedly punched him in the eye backstage (as recorded in the documentary *Hitman Hart: Wrestling with Shadows*).

Hart moved on to WCW, debuting in December 1997. However, WCW bungled Hart's push. Wildly popular and seen as a sympathetic character after the "screwjob," Hart was turned heel in April 1998 and made into a toady to Hulk Hogan. Hart won the company's secondary singles title, the U.S. championship, four times between July 1998 and October 1999. When he finally won the WCW world title in November 1999, WCW was in a tailspin and Hart's momentum from jumping from the WWF had come to standstill. Hart had two brief runs as WCW world champion, each lasting less than 30 days. In December 1999, Hart suffered a severe concussion from an errant kick to the head by Bill Goldberg. It proved to be the beginning of the end of his wrestling career.

Hart wrestled a handful more matches for WCW, including a hardcore match against Terry Funk, before he was forced to sit out due to the injury. He announced his retirement in October 2000 after being released by WCW while injured.

In July 2002, Hart suffered a stroke while riding a bike in Calgary, making a true comeback an impossibility. Nevertheless, in 2009, he returned to WWE for a farewell tour that saw him defeat McMahon in a "no holds barred" match at *WrestleMania* XXXVI and embark on a surprise U.S. title run, beating the Miz and then vacating the title. Hart took virtually no bumps in these matches and was positioned as a nostalgic figure making a hero's return and righting the wrongs of the "screwjob."

Perhaps the biggest criticism of Hart was that he took wrestling too seriously. He strove to be believable at all times and was arguably the most consistently excellent in-ring competitor of the 1990s.

"I think I was the guy that made wrestling real again," Hart said in a 2003 interview with *Pro Wrestling Illustrated*. "I had my share of ridiculous storylines . . . but when I look back on my career, people believed the realism of my matches against Curt Hennig, Roddy Piper, The British Bulldog . . . I was able to give wrestling fans the most realistic kind of matches. Even against guys like Jerry Lawler, who weren't really known as being 'real.' But when I used to bump (for) him all over the ring, people were ready to lynch him. It kind of brought the realism back. I think that when Steve Austin and I wrestled, wrestling was at its all-time peak."

SHAWN MICHAELS

Only a fool would say Shawn Michaels wasn't an incredible performer. With three matches winning Match of the Year honors from readers of the *Wrestling Observer Newsletter* and 11 matches voted as Match of the Year (including a remarkable stretch of seven consecutive years from 2004–10) by readers of *Pro Wrestling Illustrated*, Michaels has earned the sobriquet of "The Showstopper."

But, whether he's a true "Wrestlers' Wrestler" really depends on what version of "The Heartbreak Kid" you're referring to: Shawn Michaels up to his 1998 retirement, or Shawn Michaels after his 2004 comeback.

"Shawn always pushes the envelope," said Vince McMahon in a 2002 interview on WWE Confidential. "From a creative standpoint, he would drive you insane, but simply he wanted to be the very best. He had this burning desire in his heart to be the absolute best that he could possibly be at anything he was going to do."

Jim Cornette put it a different way.

"Great in the ring but horrible for business," Cornette said in a Kayfabe Commentaries interview with Sean Oliver.

For all the remarkable matches Michaels had during the first part of his career, there was an equal number of temper tantrums, refusals to do jobs, backstage political maneuvers, and other examples of unprofessional behavior. "You name it, I tried it," Michaels wrote in his 2015 memoir *Wrestling for My Life*, in reference to his drug and alcohol abuse. "And most of what I tried I kept doing. The worse my lifestyle became, the more difficult I became to work with. It's fair to say that I was a jerk to many people in the business."

"Quite honestly, Shawn could be a handful back in the day. And, well, he was a prick. He was not nice to people," said former WWE referee Jimmy Korderas. "He never treated me badly, but I saw him treat others not so well. I think a lot of people's perceptions of him are skewed because of that. From an in-ring standpoint and a talent standpoint, he belongs in that group of Wrestlers' Wrestlers because he took the technical aspect and took it to a new level. Being able to do some of that stuff, like that ladder match (against Razor Ramon at *WrestleMania* X) and some of that high-flying stuff, and incorporating it and telling a good story while he's doing it. But because of his attitude back in the day, I think he rubbed some people the wrong way."

Born Michael Hickenbottom on July 22, 1965, he grew up in San Antonio, Texas. By the time he was in middle school, he had already determined he wanted to be a professional wrestler. After graduating from high school, he trained under José Lothario and made his pro debut in October 1984. After starting out in Mid-South Wrestling, Michaels bounced around World Class, Central States Wrestling, and Texas All-Star Wrestling before landing in Verne Gagne's AWA. Michaels was paired with Marty Jannetty (with whom he had teamed in the Central States territory) and the duo was given the gimmick the Midnight Rockers, Gagne's attempt to capitalize on the popularity of the Rock 'n' Roll Express.

The gimmick was that Michaels and Jannetty partied well past the midnight hour, and both men lived the gimmick. "Even though I was only 19, I began going out drinking with other wrestlers after matches," Michaels later wrote. "That was the beginning of a long slide into losing control of my life."

The Rockers defeated Buddy Rose and Doug Somers to win the AWA tag team title in January 1987. By spring, the WWF had already come calling and the young Rockers jumped ship, but just two weeks after starting with the WWF they were fired for becoming unruly at a bar, victims of their youthful partying ways. They returned to the AWA, where they regained the tag titles, beating the "original" Midnight Express (Dennis Condrey and Randy Rose) in the AWA's version of the Rock 'n' Roll Express/Midnight Express feud.

In July 1988, Michaels and Jannetty got a second chance with the WWF. Now known simply as the Rockers, they were positioned as a mid-level babyface team. But Michaels's singles career was kickstarted (pun, sadly, completely intended) in December 1991, when Michaels turned against Jannetty, hitting him with a superkick that sent Jannetty through a glass window during a "Barber Shop" interview segment with Brutus Beefcake.

As "The Heartbreak Kid," Michaels got a singles push, beating Davey Boy Smith for the Intercontinental title in October 1992. He lost the belt to former partner Jannetty and regained it three weeks later with an assist from his new bodyguard, Diesel (Kevin Nash). In 1994, he wrestled Ramon (Scott Hall) in a ladder match at *WrestleMania* that reinvented the ladder match as a gimmick attraction. The match was his first *Wrestling Observer* Match of the Year and it propelled him into the main event picture in the WWF.

However, there were other factors at play as well. With the WWF reeling from a federal steroid investigation and the defection of long-time WWF star Hulk Hogan from the WWF to the rival WCW, there was a vacuum on top. In the spotlight of the federal government, Vince McMahon moved away from featuring superhumanly muscled competitors as his main-eventers. Instead, he turned to a pair of younger, smaller, more athletically gifted competitors: Michaels and Bret Hart. At *WrestleMania* XII, Michaels (with Lothario in his corner) defeated Hart in a sudden-death overtime of a 60-minute iron man match to win the WWF world title.

Michaels had twice vacated the IC title, once after allegedly failing a steroid test and once after getting injured in a bar fight in Syracuse. He was developing a reputation for refusing to job and using his backstage influence with Vince McMahon to keep rivals (such as Shane Douglas) from getting a push. In May 1996, a month after Michaels's title win, Michaels joined Nash, Hall, and Triple H (members of his so-called Kliq) in the ring at Madison Square Garden for a kayfabe-breaking "Curtain Call," where they said farewell to Hall and Nash as they were headed to WCW. The incident generated nuclear heat backstage and reinforced some of the growing ill will on Michaels. In February 1997, Michaels once again surrendered his title rather than do the job for Hart, claiming a knee injury and saying he had "lost his smile," teasing retirement.

The incident exacerbated the bad blood between Michaels and Hart and, on November 9, 1997, the situation came to a head with the "Montreal Screwjob," where McMahon orchestrated a title switch, taking the belt off Hart and putting it on Michaels before Hart jumped to WCW. As the heel leader of D-Generation X, Michaels was once again the WWF's standard-bearer as the Monday Night War between the WWF and WCW continued to rage.

At the 1998 Royal Rumble, Michaels suffered a severe back injury while taking an awkward bump on a wooden casket at ringside in a match against the Undertaker. Michaels finished the match, but his condition worsened. At *WrestleMania* XIV, he cleanly put over Steve Austin for the world title and then went into a quiet retirement due to the back injury.

But there would be a major second act to the Shawn Michaels story. He had a one-off match against Paul Diamond in 2000 in conjunction with his training school in San Antonio. He returned to WWE in 2002 and beat Triple H in an "unsanctioned street fight." The brawling style of the match ostensibly allowed Michaels to compete without the big bumps that had been his trademark. But, once the ring rust was shaken off, Michaels managed to come back better than ever.

Michaels defeated Triple H to win the world title for the fourth time. It proved to be his last world title run, lasting one month until he lost the belt back to Triple H. From 2003 through 2010, Michaels largely moved out of the world title picture and firmly established himself as the company's best pure worker. His string of PWI Matches of the Year included a triple-threat against Triple H and Chris Benoit (2004), Kurt Angle (2005), Vince McMahon (proving Michaels could carry a non-wrestler to a tremendous match, 2006), John Cena (2007), Ric Flair (2008), and the Undertaker (2009 and 2010).

Having found God and beaten his issues with drugs and alcohol, Michaels set out to repair his legacy. He made amends with Hart and worked to help put over younger talent, including Chris Jericho, Cena, Batista, and many others.

"Shawn Michaels is someone who lives, eats, and breathes wrestling," said Derek Graham-Couch, who wrestled alongside Michaels in WWE as one-half of the tag team the Highlanders. "He has charisma, and charisma is what you need in professional wrestling. I don't mean to be mean, but you can take a lot of guys and make them pro wrestlers, but they just don't have the charisma and the showmanship to really make it. Shawn had it. That's what set him apart."

Michaels wrestled his retirement match against the Undertaker at *WrestleMania* XXVI in 2010. He made a one-night return in 2018, teaming with Triple H to face the Undertaker and Kane in Saudi Arabia.

That year, he was also honored by the Cauliflower Alley Club, which presented him with its top distinction, the Lou Thesz/Art Abrams Lifetime Achievement Award. "I've never seen someone more talented from bell to bell than this cat," said banquet emcee Jim Ross in presenting the award. Michaels accepted the award alongside Kliq buddies Hall, Nash, and Sean Waltman.

"The CAC is an organization steeped in tradition. There's a lot of people rolling over in their graves right now," he cracked. "Everything that I love about this business is the relationships with the people you run into along the way. I wouldn't have it any other way."

KEIJI MUTO

Picture it: Japan, 1984. New Japan Pro-Wrestling was reeling after an exodus of top stars. Akira Maeda, Tiger Mask (Satoru Sayama), Yoshiaki Fujiwara, and seven other wrestlers had left for the new Universal Wrestling Federation. Eighteen others — headed by Riki Choshu and Animal Hamaguchi — had left to start the renegade Japan Pro Wrestling organization. New Japan was left with a skeleton crew. Its future looked bleak.

Antonio Inoki looked at the students in the New Japan dojo, looking to see who could step up to fill the void. Fortunately for Inoki and New Japan, that dojo was packed with talented young lions. "In the 1984 New Japan dojo, you have Masahiro Chono, Masakatsu Funaki, Jushin Liger, Naoki Sano, Akira Nogami," said wrestling historian and journalist Fumi Saito, co-host of the *Pacific Rim Podcast*. "All those guys are trainees at the dojo, in serous competition. That was the best class. And Keiji Muto was the best in the class. He was Inoki's first pick to make a new star. Inoki looked him over and said, 'This guy's going to be something special.'"

Keiji Muto stood an impressive six-foot-two, had a black belt in judo, and had taken third place in a national judo championship tournament. He showed a natural aptitude for wrestling. And he had already developed a signature finishing move that would become one of the most emulated and popular moves in the business, a backwards somersault splash he had perfected horsing around on the playground in high school. It would come to be known as the moonsault.

Muto's first match was on October 5, 1984, against fellow trainee Chono. He was 22 years old. "He was a natural," Saito said. "He was

Though he's known for his face paint and flashy aerial attacks, Keiji Muto is also a superior grappler.

not raised to be the shooter type or the kicker type or not a submission wrestler. He wanted to do the dropkick. He was a high-flyer."

He also exuded a type of confidence not usually seen in rookies. He treated Inoki as an equal, rather deferring to him as most others would. "He was straightforward. He told Akira Maeda, 'Nobody's digging your shit,'" Saito said. "Maeda was doing stiff kicks — middle kicks, low kicks, submissions and suplexes where he just kills somebody, but it wasn't getting over. He told Maeda, 'You are doing things people don't understand.' You need knowledge to be able to understand that kind of style, and most fans didn't have that in the 1980s. The wrestlers in the dojo understood, but it didn't translate to the fans and Muto recognized that."

To gain some international experience and seasoning, Muto was sent for a run in the United States, where he worked in the Florida territory as "The White Ninja." Veteran Kendo Nagasaki served as a de facto babysitter, translator, and big brother. In May 1986, the White Ninja defeated Kendall Windham to win the Florida heavyweight title, though the belt was returned to Windham three years later, when it was ruled that Ninja used "illegal karate" to score the win.

Muto returned to New Japan in 1986 as the "Space Lone Wolf" and fit in right away. "Put two-year-experienced rookie Muto in the ring with Maeda and Takada and Fujiwara (those wrestlers all having returned to New Japan from the UWF) in 1985 and 1986, he was able to do it right away and make it look easy," Saito said. "He had the physical ability and talent and gymnastic ability, but as an overall worker, he could adjust to any opponent, whether it was New Japan style or American style."

In March 1987, Muto teamed with Shiro Koshinaka to win the IWGP tag team title, though that reign — his first major championship in New Japan — would only last six days. In 1988, he returned to the Western Hemisphere for a run in the World Wrestling Council in Puerto Rico (where he lost his hair to Miguel Pérez Jr. in a hair-versus-hair match) before settling in Dallas to work for Fritz Von Erich's World Class Championship Wrestling.

"It was evident, right off, that Muto was a special athlete," said WCCW referee James Beard. "He had size but could move like a junior heavyweight, and he was incredibly inventive. Personally, I believe he may be the most special athlete to come out of Japan. I recently had the opportunity to work with him again and, while he has changed his style and his look to account for aging, he could still show those unbelievably crisp attack moves that made him so fun to watch. He was a one-of-a-kind wrestler."

In March 1989, Muto moved up to World Class Championship, the former Jim Crockett Promotions, which had been bought by Ted Turner. Gary Hart, the former booker of World Class, was working in WCW as a manager and he had been impressed with what he saw of Muto on television.

"One day, (booker) George Scott pulled me aside and asked if I could develop another Great Kabuki," Hart wrote in his wonderful autobiography *My Life in Wrestling*, referring to Akihisa Mera, whose exotic gimmick Hart crafted. "I told him that while I couldn't recreate The Great Kabuki, I could make something similar. What I actually ended up creating was the 'son of The Great Kabuki.' However, I wanted to present him in a less scary manner than I had with his 'father.' I wanted to present this new character like he was a superhero that happened to be managed by a very bad guy, much like I did with The Spoiler and The Dingo Warrior."

Hart contacted Hiro Matsuda, who brokered the deal to get Muto into WCW. Given mysterious face paint and Kabuki's devastating green-and-red mist, Muto became the Great Muta. He received a major push and was slotted into a feud with fellow face-painted warrior Sting. In September 1989, Muta beat Sting for the WCW TV title. High-profile matches against Sting, Lex Luger, and Ric Flair followed. Though he was a heel, Muta's explosive handspring back elbow to the corner, jumping thrust kicks, and — of course — moonsault earned him a sizeable fan base.

In October 1989, Muta and Terry Funk teamed up to headline WCW's Halloween Havoc pay-per-view, facing Flair and Sting in a "Thunderdome" steel cage match refereed by Bruno Sammartino in Philadelphia. Over the following weeks, Muta had several world title matches against Flair, losing most by disqualification. After dropping the TV title to Arn Anderson, Muta returned to New Japan as a bona fide superstar.

On August 16, 1992, Muto (wrestling under this Great Muta gimmick) defeated Riki Choshu to win the IWGP heavyweight title for the first time. On January 4, 1993, he won the NWA world title by beating Chono in a match in which both the NWA and IWGP titles were at stake (though the NWA world title had been reduced to a secondary title in WCW, WCW having established its own "world title" and maintaining a tenuous connection to the NWA members). Nonetheless, it was a historic win, especially in Japan, where the NWA world title was still highly valued.

Muto would hold the IWGP title four times during his career. In 2002, he defected to the rival All Japan Pro Wrestling, where he would hold the AJPW Triple Crown title on three occasions and served as the president of the company. Throughout the years, he has made appearances throughout promotions in Japan and the U.S. for dream matches. When years of hitting moonsaults took their toll on his knees, he innovated the Shining Wizard knee strike as a secondary finishing move, a move that soon after was used by wrestlers worldwide. He has managed to navigate the political minefields of wrestling, has remained fresh with his gimmick, and has had one of the most storied careers in modern wrestling history.

"Among wrestlers, even Americans, a lot of the workers believe Muto was the best ever in the ring," Saito said. "For instance, when I spoke to Goldberg, Goldberg said he thought Keiji Muto was the best ever. Sting thought he was the best. Overall the best worker in the boys' eyes. I've heard it so many times."

Canadian wrestler Jake O'Reilly (real name Bill Matthews) idolized the Great Muta growing up. In 2011, when he made a tour for All Japan, Muto was his boss. O'Reilly was nervous.

"I met Muto at my second event for All Japan," O'Reilly said. "He seemed nice but didn't say much to me. My opponent that night was (fellow Canadian wrestler) Shawn Spears. We were up second and wanted to impress the boss. We went all out, and I ended up with a black eye. When I got to the back, Muto was sitting in a chair watching a monitor. I asked if he had any advice for me, and he looked sternly at me and said, 'More wrestling.' Needless to say, we didn't impress the Great Muta with our flashy style that night.

"Muto was everything you'd want your hero to be," O'Reilly continued. "Mystic, yet approachable. Respectful to the young talent. The kind of guy who leads by example. In 2011, after the tsunami, a group of us were stranded on a bus for 36 hours. Muto hadn't made that trip with us, but when we finally arrived back to the dojo, Muto and his wife had a feast of Japanese curry waiting for us. If that doesn't tell you what a great man he is, I don't know what will."

LOU THESZ

Lou Thesz's influence on professional wrestling is still evident 90 years after he first set foot in a wrestling ring.

The Thesz Press flying tackle? He invented it. The powerbomb? Thesz invented that too. The STF (stepover toehold/facelock)? Another Thesz innovation. The German suplex? Well, that's a bit more complicated; the suplex had its roots in Greco-Roman wrestling and judo and the German suplex earned that name in honor of Karl Gotch, but Thesz was using the tight-waist, overhead bridging suplex before Gotch was out of grade school, so let's credit Thesz with that one too.

Even today, you would be hard-pressed to find a match, let alone an entire card, in which one of those moves wasn't executed.

But Thesz's influence goes much deeper than the moves alone. He was the model world champion that every other titleholder who succeeded him tried to be. Articulate, well-dressed, and professional, a perfect ambassador for a business that struggled to achieve legitimacy and credibility. And Thesz was credible. Many of the sportswriters of the 1930s, 1940s, and 1950s turned up their noses at professional wrestling. They "knew" it wasn't on the up-and-up. But Thesz was virtually beyond reproach. Maybe some of those other matches were fixed, but Thesz had the aura and charisma of a true athlete and sportsman.

The world title didn't give Thesz credibility. Lou Thesz gave the world title credibility.

"It was different in my day, when our product was presented as an authentic, competitive sport," Thesz wrote in his autobiography, *Hooker*, which deserves a prominent place on the bookshelf of any serious wrestling fan or student. "We protected it because we believed it would collapse if we ever so much as implied publicly that it was something other than what it appeared to be. . . . 'Protecting the business' in the face of criticism and skepticism was the first and most important rule a pro wrestler learned. No matter how aggressive or informed the questioner, you never admitted the industry was anything but a competitive sport."

Thesz took pride in being a "hooker" — "the boys who had elevated their wrestling to the highest form and added a bagful of old carnival 'hooks' to their repertoire," in Thesz's own words. "Hooking requires high levels of wrestling knowledge, ability, and strength, and the few who were skilled enough to reach that level could do serious damage to an opponent, even a highly skilled shooter, with very little effort."

Thesz was a gentleman, but he wasn't a man you'd want to cross. He was the man who famously stepped up to Buddy Rogers and said, "We can do this the easy way . . . or the hard way." Rogers, fully aware that Thesz could bend him into positions the human body wasn't designed to bend into, wisely chose the "easy way" and went along with the planned finish, resulting in Thesz regaining the NWA world title.

Born April 24, 1916, in Banat, Michigan, Aloysius Thesz grew up in St. Louis. He started Greco-Roman wrestling at age eight and free-style wrestling at 14, after he had dropped out of high school. Wrestling proved to be an important outlet for Thesz, a shy, left-handed boy with a lisp, for whom English was a second language. "Years later, though, I learned that everyone in the family was seriously concerned that I had become a 'sissy,'" Thesz wrote. "I was shy, I had no friends to speak of, and my only real playmates were my sisters. Maybe that's what Pop really had in mind when he introduced me to Greco-Roman wrestling."

Thesz excelled in wrestling and caught the attention of veteran wrestler John Zastrow, who began to train with the 15-year-old Thesz. Zastrow introduced Thesz to another former wrestler, Joe Sanderson, who suggested he try his hand at pro wrestling. Thesz was intrigued and, in 1932, wrestled is first pro match in East St. Louis, Illinois.

He began working the circuit for promoter Tom Packs, earning up to $5 per night. Packs put him in touch with former Olympic wrestler and notorious hooker George Tragos for additional training. Tragos taught Thesz the savage arts of wrestling — how to tear ligaments, tendons, and muscles with a simple double wristlock, or how to dislocate vertebrae with a cross-face scissor hold. Though Thesz found it unethical to intentionally injure an opponent, he learned how to do it, should the need ever appear. He continued his training under former world champion Ed "Strangler" Lewis, who became Thesz's true mentor in pro wrestling.

Thesz soaked up lessons from Tragos, Lewis, German shooter and judo practitioner Ad Santel, submission specialist Ray Steele, and others, becoming one of the most well-rounded and well-conditioned grapplers on the planet. Had mixed martial arts existed at the time, Thesz would likely have excelled in that style of combat sports.

The incomparable Lou Thesz.

PHOTO COURTESY *PRO WRESTLING ILLUSTRATED*

On December 29, 1937, Thesz defeated Everett Marshall to win the American Wrestling Association (the Boston version established by promoter Paul Bowser) to capture his first recognized world championship. Thesz was 21, standing six-foot-two and a lean, muscular 225 pounds. He was young, handsome, a technical marvel. He had all the attributes for a world champion that a wrestling promoter could desire.

In February 1939, he won the National Wrestling Association version of the world title.

Despite a wonky knee resulting from a fractured kneecap in a bout against Bronko Nagurski, Thesz was draft by the U.S. Army in 1945 and stationed in Fort Lewis in Washington State. He was out of wrestling until the summer of 1946, and when Tom Packs retired in 1948, Thesz bought into the lucrative St. Louis office. However, Packs's former assistant, Sam Muchnick, was orchestrating a new coalition of promoters throughout the Midwest under the banner the National Wrestling Alliance. Muchnick's NWA recognized Orville Brown as world champion, while promotions with ties to Thesz continued to recognize him as champion.

Within a year, both Thesz and Muchnick realized they were better off as partners than rivals, and the fractured St. Louis office was restored. A title unification match was set between Thesz and Brown, but when Brown suffered a career-ending injury in a car crash, the NWA board unanimously voted to make Thesz the world champion on November 27, 1949.

Thesz would be the NWA's go-to world champion for the next 14 years. His first reign lasted nearly five and a half years (Leo Nomellini was briefly recognized by the California Athletic Commission in 1955, following a contested match where one fall was a disqualification, but Thesz "regained" the title four months later) until he dropped the belt to "Whipper" Billy Watson in Toronto in March 1956. Thesz defended his championship in all NWA-affiliated territories as well as internationally. He was particularly popular in Japan, where he put over Rikidozan for the NWA international heavyweight championship in 1958.

"He wasn't a huge crowd favorite, but he easily set a high standard for a touring World champion," Tim Hornbaker wrote in his book *National Wrestling Alliance: The Untold Story of the Monopoly That Strangled Pro Wrestling*. "In a universe governed by gimmicks and scoundrels, Thesz was a principled man playing a dirty game. He faced them all on the mat and in the dressing room, exposed the weaknesses of those trying to test him, and protected the coveted championship internationally. He raised the NWA World heavyweight title onto a distinguished plateau and was admired by his peers, promoters, and fans."

Thesz regained the title from Watson in November 1956 in his home territory of St. Louis. A year later, when Thesz had decided he needed a break from the rigors of being world champion, he dropped the belt to Dick Hutton in November 1957.

He continued to wrestle through the late 1950s and early 1960s, completing multiple tours of Japan and Europe, as well as throughout the United States. But retirement had no interest for Thesz, even as he approached his mid-40s. "I get bored," Thesz told the *Los Angeles Times* in 1960. "I try to keep busy waterskiing in Mexico, skindiving, sailing, swimming, skiing from Mammoth to St. Moritz and I was even an AKC judge for Doberman pinschers. But it isn't like being active. So, I've worked out a happy medium where I'm on the road only 175 days a year."

But, in 1963, the NWA came asking for help, and Thesz was happy to assist. World champion Buddy Rogers was working primarily for promoter Vince McMahon Sr. in the Northwest and threatened the stability of the alliance itself. Muchnick went to Thesz and asked him to take the title and restore the power balance within the NWA. Thesz was no fan of Rogers's gimmick-heavy style of wrestling and, at the age of 46, agreed to face "The Nature Boy" for the title. With Rogers putting up a fuss over dropping the belt, Thesz made him the offer he couldn't refuse: The easy way. Or the hard way.

Thesz's final reign as world champion lasted for three years until he put over Gene Kiniski for the title in January 1966 in St. Louis. He continued to wrestle until 1970 before "retiring" only to come back and continue to compete periodically throughout the 1970s, including a full-time return for promoter Nick Gulas in 1978. That year, he also won the inaugural Universal Wrestling Alliance heavyweight title in Mexico. He continued to work as a referee and trainer, particularly in Japan, where he was held in high esteem by fans and wrestlers alike.

Scott Casey told historian Scott Teal about one memorable interaction he had with Thesz.

"He was in his late 50s or early 60s. He was watching the matches through a crack in the curtain one night," Casey said. "I walked up behind him and said, 'Lou! What are you doing?' He said, 'I'm watching the matches, kid.' I said, 'You're the World champion. You've been the champion seven times. Why would you want to watch a match?' He said,

'Because everything I do out there, someone did it before me. I learned to imitate those people and I learned my craft from them.' After that night, I watched the matches all the time."

Thesz wrestled his final match in December 1990, facing his protégé Masahiro Chono in an exhibition match in Japan. Chono won the match with Thesz's STF submission lock. With that match, Thesz could say he had wrestled in seven different decades.

After his retirement, Thesz became president of the Cauliflower Alley Club, serving from 1992 through 2000. "Lou had the rare quality to make the people he was working with or talking to feel and know he really cared just how important you were to him," said Karl Lauer, who succeeded Thesz as president of the CAC.

In 1999, his name was added to the George Tragos/Lou Thesz Professional Wrestling Hall of Fame in Waterloo, Iowa. One of wrestling's most respected halls of fame literally bears the name of Lou Thesz — that's how vital Thesz was to the sport of wrestling.

He died on April 28, 2002, days after his 86th birthday.

"Lou Thesz was probably the greatest of all professional world champions, and for one reason: he conducted himself professionally inside the ring, in the gym, outside the ring, in the business world, and with the gentry (royal families) around the world," Billy Robinson wrote. "Everybody respected professional wrestling because of Lou Thesz. He may not have been the best competitive catch wrestler, but he certainly was the best world champion for the pro wrestling business."

SOURCES

The following books, websites, and magazines were valuable references during the creation of *The Wrestlers' Wrestlers*:

Hatton, C. Nathan. *Thrashing Seasons: Sporting Culture in Manitoba and the Genesis of Prairie Wrestling.* University of Manitoba Press, 2016.

Hornbaker, Tim. *National Wrestling Alliance: The Untold Story of the Monopoly That Strangled Pro Wrestling.* ECW Press, 2007.

Hornbaker, Tim. *Death of the Territories: Expansion, Betrayal, and the War that Changed Pro Wrestling Forever.* ECW Press, 2018.

Jares, Joe. *Whatever Happened to Gorgeous George? The Blood and Ballyhoo of Professional Wrestling.* Crowbar Press, 2015.

Laprade, Pat, and Dan Murphy. *Sisterhood of the Squared Circle: The History and Rise of Women's Wrestling.* ECW Press, 2017.

Matysik, Larry. *The 50 Greatest Professional Wrestlers of All Time: The Definitive Shoot.* ECW Press, 2013.

Oliver, Greg. *The Pro Wrestling Hall of Fame: The Canadians.* ECW Press, 2003.

Oliver, Greg, and Steven Johnson. *The Pro Wrestling Hall of Fame: Heroes & Icons.* ECW Press, 2012.

Oliver, Greg, and Steven Johnson. *The Pro Wrestling Hall of Fame: The Heels.* ECW Press, 2007.

Oliver, Greg, and Steven Johnson. *The Pro Wrestling Hall of Fame: The Tag Teams.* ECW Press, 2005.

Robinson, Billy, and Jake Shannon. *Physical Chess: My Life in Catch-as-Catch-Can Wrestling.* ECW Press, 2012.

Street, Adrian. *Violence is Golden*. Adrian Street, 2015.

Thesz, Lou, and Kit Bauman. *Hooker: An Authentic Wrestler's Adventures Inside the Bizarre World of Professional Wrestling*. Lou Thesz, 1995. (Crowbar Press, 2011.)

Pro Wrestling Illustrated

SLAM! Wrestling (www.slam.canoe.com)

The Wrestling Observer newsletter

Cagematch.net

In addition, the following wrestlers and historians were either interviewed or provided quotes for this book: Shayna Baszler, James Beard, Brian Blair, Sinn Bodhi, Colt Cabana, Buddy Colt, Bob Cook, Allison Danger, Barry Darsow, Joel Deaton, Tyson Dux, Bob Evans, Ron Fuller, Terry Funk, Barry Hardy, Luke Harper/Brodie Lee, Bruce Hart, Ron Hutchison, Chris Jericho, Steve Johnson, Kyle Klingman, Jimmy Korderas, Karl Lauer, Brandi Mankiewicz, Johnny Mantell, Bill Matthews, Robbie McAllister, Nigel McGuinness, Dave Meltzer, Vance Nevada, Paul Orndorff, Lanny Poffo, Mike Quackenbush, Bob Roop, Jim Ross, Fumi Saito, Stu Saks, Al Snow, Jonard Solie, Kevin Sullivan, Rob Van Dam, Baron Von Raschke, Koko B. Ware, Luke Williams, and Larry Zbyszko.

Thank you to everyone who took the time to share their thoughts with us.

AUTHORS' NOTES

DAN MURPHY

There's an intrinsic beauty in fine craftsmanship. You recognize it when you find it.

You don't have to be an architect to appreciate the beauty of a majestic cathedral. You don't need to know how to play a musical instrument to feel how a certain arrangement pulls you in and evokes some sort of feeling or emotion. You don't need a perfect palate to appreciate a delicious meal.

Professional wrestling, in itself, is not particularly complex. It's good-versus-bad played out, cooperatively, in a ring. But a truly exceptional wrestler can pull you into the match and make you suspend disbelief, if only for a moment. And the more you learn about how a wrestling match is designed, the more you can appreciate the little nuances that separate the masters from the rest of the pack.

My goal with this book was to shine some of the spotlight on the workhorses of professional wrestling — the guys I still enjoy watching. Competitors like Nigel McGuinness, Brad Armstrong, Rip Rogers, Jerry Lynn, and Mercedes Martinez will never headline *WrestleMania*, but they have made a lasting impression on the wrestling industry, their peers, and countless fans.

The Hulk Hogans, John Cenas, and the Rocks of this world have plenty of books written about them. This book is about the guys who made those guys look good.

And to any aspiring wrestlers reading this book, I encourage you to sit down and watch the matches of the wrestlers included in this book. Study them. I promise, they will help you become a better wrestler yourself.

For me, the genesis of this book was a man named Dick Beyer. Most wrestling fans know him as the Destroyer, or sometimes Dr. X. Beyer had a career that spanned four decades and was a star here in the United States, but even more so in his adopted home of Japan. But to me, Dick Beyer was a local legend. Beyer was born in my hometown of Buffalo, New York, and lived in the area most of his life. He was a Western New York fixture, often appearing at charity events or on local television during my childhood. Dick Beyer was a world champion, but he was our world champ. Sadly, on March 7, 2019, the Destroyer passed away at the age of 88. I read the news and was reminded of all the appearances I had seen over the years, and how he was always so kind and giving of his time.

A day or two after Beyer's passing, I called my friend Dan Murphy just to talk about Beyer and share some memories. Dan has been in the world of professional wrestling his whole life, first as a fan, and then as a writer and ambassador for the business, spending over 20 years writing for *Pro Wrestling Illustrated*. I knew Dan had known Dick personally, and I guess I just wanted to talk about him, maybe hear a story or two. I must confess that I am an outsider to the wrestling business. I was a fan when I was younger, especially the late 1970s through the mid-1980s, but I hadn't really kept up with pro wrestling. As Dan and I talked about Mr. Beyer, all I was thinking was, it's too bad nobody sat down and got his take on the business and fellow performers, not just an interview, but something more detailed. Vince Evans had written the wonderful biography *Masked Decisions: The Triangular Life of Dick Beyer*, but with Dick's passing, so many wonderful stories had gone silent forever.

This thought stayed with me for several weeks, and I didn't know why I couldn't stop thinking about it. Finally I decided I had to call Dan again and give him an idea for his next book. Why not try and talk to as many old-timers as you can get, get them to talk about the business and use their quotes to do a history of wrestling book? Dan said he was intrigued but had to think about it. My part was done, or so I thought.

A week later, Dan called me and asked if I could meet him out for coffee and talk about my idea. I wasn't sure what else I could tell him, but it's always good to get together with an old friend. The coffee was poured and Dan said he had thought a lot about my suggestion, but said, why just talk to old-timers? Wrestling is still a living, breathing business. Why not talk to a mix of older and younger guys, and not only get them to tell us about the business, but more specifically, talk about the guys they all respected — the ones that really had an impact on them as performers; not necessarily the biggest stars, but the ones that could be described as "Wrestlers' Wrestlers"?

I loved this idea and said that it sounded great and he should run with it. Then Dan floored me when he said he was glad I liked it because he wanted me to write it with him. I told him I was flattered, but I'm not a wrestling guy. I am a total outsider, what could I bring to such a project? And I'll never forget what Dan told me. "Brian, you're a historian. You're a writer. And you obviously care about the project." He also went on to explain that being an outsider could actually be a benefit, as I wasn't jaded and I would bring a different perspective to the subject. For this, I will be forever grateful, as this book has been among the most pleasurable projects I have ever been lucky enough to work on.

We set out on a quest to get in touch with as many people in the business as possible. Dan's background and the respect he has earned in wrestling was invaluable. Soon, word got around as to what we were trying to do and more and more doors opened — or should I say more telephones were answered. We would sincerely like to thank all those who were so unbelievably generous with their time and their insight. It was not only a pleasure but an honor talking to each and every one of you!

This book is meant to be not only a history text but also a love letter to the business of professional wrestling. One thing that became so clear during this journey was how dedicated everyone involved in pro wrestling has to be. It isn't just a job, it's a lifestyle, a lifestyle few people can even imagine. It's a difficult life, often times not even very rewarding, especially financially, yet all these people give so much of themselves for our entertainment. They put their bodies on the line, they give up the ability to have a "normal family life." And, amazingly, most when asked say if they had to do it over again, they wouldn't change a damn thing. Wrestlers are a special breed of athlete and performer and I, for one, gained a newfound respect for not just the boys, but for the industry as a whole.

My love for wrestling has been rekindled and for that I am so thankful. Hopefully this book will be both entertaining and informative. We hope it brings back wonderful memories to older fans; and for younger fans, we hope to give a glimpse of the past they may not be aware of.

So let me finish by saying thank you to Dick Beyer for being the inspiration for this project. You, sir, like all the people in this book, are a legend. And as Babe Ruth once said: "Heroes get remembered, but legends never die."

ACKNOWLEDGMENTS

DAN WOULD LIKE TO THANK:

Most sincerely, all the wrestlers, writers, referees, and historians who took the time to speak with us for this project. Thank you to Greg Oliver for the incredible job you have done with SLAM! Wrestling, which remains a go-to resource, as well as your tremendous books. Thank you to the photographers who shared their work with us, Michael Holmes and the team at ECW Press for making our vision a reality, and to Nathan Hatton for your suggestions, edits, and feedback for this project.

Tara — thank you for your love and support, Blackbird.

I would also like to thank the Cauliflower Alley Club. With its mission statement of "financially assisting those in the wrestling industry that have fallen on difficult financial times," it is a commendable organization, one that I am happy to have joined in 2010. I encourage anyone reading this book to consider joining the CAC or making a one-time donation to support those wrestlers who have given us so many magical memories through the years. For more information, please visit caulifloweralleyclub.org.

BRIAN WOULD LIKE TO THANK:

My father, Barry, for letting me "waste" all that time as a kid watching wrestling. My brother David, who showed me how "real" wrestling was by putting me in a figure-four leg lock when I was eight. My brother Kevin, who shares a brain and sense of humor with me. And especially my mother, Rosemary, for being the funniest, most understanding, and supportive parent anyone could ever hope for.

I would also like to thank Sarah Smigielski for putting up with the hours and hours of my research.

Also, Bob, Maria, Danny, Doug, Andy, and Justin, my June Family.

Bob, Barry, Mike, Jay, Angelo, Dave, Carl, and all the folks at Virgil Ave. Tobacco, my home away from home.

Michael Hawley, David Lundy, Lauren Davies, Daniel Mooney, Geoff Gorton, Paul Begg, Kurt Konecny, Anna Mayton, Jamie Wilday, Jake Grzybowski, Wes Slawiak, Chris Badura, Kevin Campbell, Kevin Szafranski, Tom Trotta, George French, Agnes Johnson, Julian Leggett, and all my co-workers and teammates, especially Jen Salciccioli, the best boss anyone could have!

Dan Murphy for co-writing this and making it become a reality.

ECW Press and all associated.

And Janis Perrin, my oldest and dearest friend.

And a very special thanks to all the men and women who have worked so hard in the wrestling business for our entertainment. This book is for all of you!

Purchase the print edition and receive the eBook free!
Just send an email to ebook@ecwpress.com and include:

- the book title
- the name of the store where you purchased it
- your receipt number
- your preference of file type: PDF or ePub

A real person will respond to your email with your eBook attached.
And thanks for supporting an independently owned Canadian publisher
with your purchase!